BEHIND DIPLOMATIC LINES

BEHIND DIPLOMATIC LINES

RELATIONS WITH MINISTERS

*An edited version of diaries recording the life
of a Foreign Office Permanent Under-Secretary
from 1986 to 1991.*

PATRICK R. H. WRIGHT

Biteback Publishing

First published in Great Britain in 2018 by
Biteback Publishing Ltd
Westminster Tower
3 Albert Embankment
London SE1 7SP
Copyright © Patrick R. H. Wright 2018

ISBN 978-1-78590-338-0

10 9 8 7 6 5 4 3 2 1

A CIP catalogue record for this book is available from the British Library.

Set in Minion Pro by Adrian McLaughlin

Printed and bound in Great Britain by
CPI Group (UK) Ltd, Croydon CR0 4YY

MIX
Paper from
responsible sources
FSC® C020471
FSC
www.fsc.org

CONTENTS

1986...1

1987...41

1988...85

1989...121

1990...203

1991...281

Index..331

1986

One week before taking over as Permanent Under-Secretary (PUS) from Sir Antony Acland, we were both invited to lunch with Mrs Thatcher. She opened the conversation by thrusting a newspaper cutting about Oliver Tambo in front of us, saying that it proved that we should not be talking to him (having agreed that morning that Lynda Chalker, a Minister of State in the Foreign Office, could meet him). She continued, both before and at lunch, to express her views about a return to pre-1910 South Africa, with a white mini-state partitioned from their neighbouring black states. When I argued that this would be seen as an extension of apartheid and homelands policy, she barked: 'Do you have no concern for our strategic interests?' I replied: 'Of course, Prime Minister; but I don't think this is the way to protect them.'

Otherwise, this was a very agreeable occasion, with the Prime Minister occasionally reverting to the topic of South Africa. She paid very warm tributes to Antony Acland, with the snide comment that his imagination and initiative were constantly being eroded by the unimaginative approach of the Foreign Office. She was also very complimentary about Charles Powell [now Lord Powell of Bayswater], whom she described as the best

1

private secretary she had ever had (a compliment I had personally heard her pay to his two predecessors). One of them, Sir John Coles, later told me that, at his farewell dinner at No. 10, Margaret Thatcher had gone over the top in her compliments, glaring at his successor and saying: 'Mr Powell is going to have an extremely difficult job succeeding you.' Her devotion to her private secretaries was to cause me endless problems during the next five years, not unlike the problems that my predecessors had encountered during Sir Philip de Zulueta's time as private secretary to Harold Macmillan. This prime ministerial reliance on their private secretaries ultimately made it impossible for de Zulueta, as it did for Charles Powell, to return to the diplomatic service.

On leaving No. 10, Antony and I bumped into the Foreign Secretary, Geoffrey Howe, who looked slightly put out that I had lunched with the Prime Minister before my first formal call on him. I therefore arranged to bring forward my call, the office having deliberately delayed it until I took over on 30 June.

24 JUNE 1986

I paid my first call on Geoffrey Howe, with only Tony Galsworthy (his private secretary) present. I talked about my impressions of the service, after an extensive tour of posts in Africa and the Far East, pointing out the financial strains on members of the service, particularly those abroad who, unlike their home civil service married colleagues, were unable, in those days, to benefit from double salaries. Geoffrey talked about his own impressions of the office, and his worries about staffing on Falkland Islands and other dependent territories questions. He also worried about one of his junior ministers, who he thought was much too ready to accept official advice without questioning it. No talk about the Prime Minister, though he was already having a very difficult time with her, particularly on South Africa, where their views were poles apart.

25 JUNE 1986

At a lunch with Robert Armstrong and Tom Brimelow (reminiscent of a lunch twelve years earlier, at which they had 'vetted' me for my job as Harold Wilson's private secretary), Robert Armstrong described relations between the Prime Minister and the Foreign Office as worse than he could ever remember with any Prime Minister. When discussing her views about another Foreign Office official [whom Antony thought – as it turned out, wrongly – was a likely successor to myself], Robert replied: 'All right, until 11 a.m.,' explaining that the Prime Minister had emerged from Cabinet to see this official talking to the Foreign Secretary. In present circumstances, this was apparently enough to damn anyone.

Margaret Thatcher's contemptuous opinions of the diplomatic service contrasted strongly with her complimentary views on almost every individual diplomat she met [sadly, not many, in view of the way in which the doors of No. 10 were fiercely guarded by her private secretary]. After almost every foreign trip she made, she appeared to be impressed by the head of mission (particularly if he was tall and good-looking), often complaining to me that so-and-so was 'far too good for X; why is he not in Paris or Washington?'

Curiously, one of her reservations was beards. When a bearded colleague of mine started a Foreign Office job which was likely to involve close contact with No. 10, I warned him [would this be acceptable nowadays?] that it might be better, given Mrs Thatcher's known prejudices, if he shaved it off. He replied that this put him in a dilemma between a Prime Minister who disliked beards, and a wife that liked them. But he shaved it off! Moustaches were also a problem. Of one moustached colleague, Margaret Thatcher is reported to have claimed: 'The trouble is, he looks like a hairdresser.'

Sherard Cowper-Coles, the private secretary I was to inherit from Antony Acland, told me that he had heard from Tony Galsworthy that my initial talk with Geoffrey Howe had gone very well. [I did not record, at

3

the time, an earlier talk I'd had with Geoffrey Howe soon after my return from Saudi Arabia.] Geoffrey said that there would, of course, be many things we would need to discuss, but he had one request to make. 'We must', he said, 'try to slow the merry-go-round, and leave heads of mission longer in post.' I replied that this was music to my ears. But I reminded him of two things: first, that he had pulled me out of Saudi Arabia after eighteen months to become his PUS; and second, that his request was pretty ripe, coming as it did from a member of a Cabinet that had had twelve secretaries of state for Trade and Industry in thirteen years.

27 JUNE 1986

Today I went through the Green Safe, skimming the files, including several dating back to my days as private secretary to Sir Paul Gore-Booth in the mid-1960s. One of these concerned an Iraqi Prince, Prince Sami, who claimed a payment from the secret fund, on the grounds that he had been deprived of his inheritance by the Iraq Petroleum Company. He had once turned up at the Foreign Office with his entire family and threatened my predecessor, Nicholas Gordon Lennox, that he would camp on the premises until he was paid. My own earlier contact with Prince Sami had been in Washington where, as private secretary to the ambassador, I was instructed by Douglas Hurd [then private secretary to the PUS] to deliver a message to Prince Sami in a particularly expensive Washington hotel, telling him that he would receive no more payments.

The lead story in the *Evening Standard* today was of a serious split between Geoffrey Howe and Margaret Thatcher, including an alleged (and accurate) quote of her saying in Cabinet, on the topic of his mission to Africa: 'If you feel like that, perhaps you had better stay at home.' I was told last night that Geoffrey, in fact, minds these attacks much more than he shows. I discussed with Antony and Sherard last night whether, like Antony, I was going to be faced with a Foreign Secretary resigning in my first week as PUS (Lord Carrington having resigned over the Falklands on Michael Palliser's last day before Antony succeeded him as PUS). Sherard thought that Geoffrey loved the job (and Chevening) much too much. Antony commented that you wouldn't know it, and he thought that the office would be astonished to be told it.

I called on Janet Young, the FCO minister in the House of Lords, who became a good friend, but who sadly did not enjoy Geoffrey's confidence (as he made abundantly clear during a large office meeting on the Turks and Caicos Islands). The trouble is that Geoffrey tends to reflect his own uncertainty over taking decisions by looking for faults in others.

2 JULY 1986

I called on Lynda Chalker, who confessed to having had a crisis of confidence. She obviously regards herself as a non-intellectual, surrounded by brilliant officials who all quote Latin at her. I reminded her that by far the most popular and most successful Foreign Secretary since the war had been Ernie Bevin, who had commented on a marginal reference to the phrase 'mutatis mutandis': 'Please do not write in Greek; I have never learned it.'

3 JULY 1986

This morning was the first of many presentations of credentials, for which I wore full diplomatic uniform. [There is a picture of me, accompanying the credentials ceremony for the United States ambassador, Ray Seitz, in 1991 on the back of his book *Over Here*, with the comment, in the text itself, that I was 'immaculate in [my] dark-blue diplomatic uniform and cradling a great plumed hat across [my] front like a pet ostrich'. Simon McDonald later sent me a Christmas card showing himself in diplomatic uniform, with a picture on the back of me in an identical pose.]

On this occasion, the talk with the Queen was mainly about whether the German von Weizsäcker had used the English words 'common sense' in his speech at the German state banquet on the previous evening out of politeness, or because there was no German word for it. Von Weizsäcker's speech-writer had told me that the Germans normally used the English words, and he did not think there was a German equivalent. This recalls Harold Nicolson's claim, which I was frequently to quote in my talks on diplomacy, that common sense was perhaps the most important qualification for a diplomat.

At the later banquet, [my wife] Virginia and I talked to Lord Hailsham, who denied that he kept a diary. He claimed that Barbara Castle had dictated her diaries immediately after the event, with subsequent re-editing two weeks later. Tony Benn's fairly blatant keeping of diaries during Cabinet meetings once provoked Denis Healey into cutting short a presentation to Cabinet with the words: 'Tony, am I speaking too fast for you?'

I attended a meeting with Geoffrey Howe this afternoon on South Africa, in the face of indications that P. W. Botha may not see him on his first visit, which would look very bad. Geoffrey realises what a viper's nest he is walking into.

5 & 6 JULY 1986

Virginia and I were invited to spend the weekend with the Howes at Chevening [which they adored, and which caused them more regrets than almost anything else when Geoffrey was kicked upstairs to be Deputy Prime Minister]. Other guests included the opera singer Geraint Evans and his wife Brenda. After dinner on the Saturday evening, there was a sing-song, for which I was invited to play the piano. Geraint, who had apparently sworn that, in retirement, he would never sing again, retreated to the window looking out over the garden. But the sound of a succession of songs from *The Scout's Song Book* through to *Irish Ballads* and *The Messiah* was too much for him. [Happily, I still have a photograph of me accompanying Geraint, with Geoffrey Howe almost sitting on my lap, and with everyone else ranged around the piano.]

Next morning, Geoffrey and I retired to work on his box. The omens for his South African visit were not looking good, and he was coming to the conclusion that we might have to change our policy on sanctions. The Prime Minister would be very difficult indeed, and he was facing his next bilateral with her tomorrow.

The *Sunday Telegraph* carried headline stories today – so far as I could see, without any justification – that Geoffrey might be considering resignation. He discussed with me the idea of holding a meeting this evening, but decided against it. The trouble is that, for domestic political reasons, the government has felt bound to present a more optimistic picture of the prospects of moving P. W. Botha than is remotely justified.

8 JULY 1986

An early start today, with an 8 a.m. meeting on Southern Africa. Geoffrey Howe decided that he should go ahead with his planned visits to Zambia and Zimbabwe, in the face of P. W. Botha's refusal to see him until later in the month. I wrote him a personal letter to thank him for the Chevening weekend, and expressing the hope and confidence that the story in the *Sunday Telegraph* about his resignation was completely unfounded.

At 11 a.m., I attended a meeting in Lady Young's office to discuss her parliamentary questions in the Lords, with all parliamentary private secretaries (PPSs) present. It is quite a challenge for Lords ministers to face a wide variety of questions, and I once heard a former Secretary of State claim that he found questions in the Lords much more demanding than those he had faced in the Commons, because questions in the Lords usually came from peers who had deep knowledge and experience of the subject.

On the other hand, there is the probably apocryphal story that Lord

Goronwy-Roberts, when the Lords minister, received a brief which ended with the words: 'This is not a very good reply, but it should do for the House of Lords' – and he read it out.

8 JULY 1986

I called this morning on Tim Eggar, the parliamentary under-secretary described in the parliamentary guide as 'very right wing, and a Labour basher' – a rather macho character, who obviously feels, like most junior ministers, excluded from decision-making. [He later developed a strong interest in diplomatic car parking and non-payment of parking fines, adopting it as almost a personal crusade.]

At dinner this evening, Lord Chalfont was quoted as comparing the Foreign & Commonwealth Office's (FCO) relationship with its junior ministers to that of an oyster and a piece of sand: a source of constant irritation, and only likely in the rarest instances to produce a pearl.

[My memory of leak procedures during my time as deputy under-secretary (DUS), when Lord Chalfont was a Foreign Office minister, having previously been the defence correspondent on *The Times*, was that the inquiry nearly always ended with the conclusion that Chalfont himself was almost certainly the source, but never proceeded with. I once told him this many years later, when we were colleagues on the cross benches of the House of Lords.]

9 JULY 1986

Ghana today pulled out of the Commonwealth Games, with an offensive démarche in Accra, followed by Nigeria. I spoke to Sonny Ramphal, and asked him to do what he could to stop the rot. I attended a large office meeting with Lynda Chalker to agree instructions to Commonwealth posts.

I had a meeting with Robert Armstrong to discuss office buildings.

The Prime Minister has revealed a clear, and predictable, prejudice against the FCO and Overseas Development Administration (ODA), and is trying to block the ODA's agreed move to Richmond Yard, to which everyone thought she had agreed a long time ago, but which she now denies. Her prejudice against the FCO building in Downing Street is alleged once to have provoked her complaint that the FCO blocked all the sunshine from No. 10.

I dined at the American embassy to meet Bill Casey of the CIA, after a cock-up which implied that the dinner was at Grosvenor Square. After I had dismissed the car, I had to take a taxi to Winfield House. Casey seemed a bit more intelligible than usual; on a previous call on Geoffrey Howe, during my time as DUS for Defence and Intelligence, we had to ask the American embassy to tell us what he had said; they agreed to an exchange of draft records, if only because they had found the usual difficulty of hearing Geoffrey Howe. It was said of Casey that he had for so long been involved in intelligence that he had learned to speak in cipher. I thought it an interesting, and sad, reflection on the UK–USA intelligence relationship that two of Casey's aides cut the dinner for a German function; and that Casey himself described his visit here as 'en route to Bonn'.

10 JULY 1986

Robert Armstrong called on me this afternoon – a rare occasion nowadays for the Cabinet Secretary to call on the Foreign Office – to discuss the problem of ministers calling in foreign diplomats without telling the FCO, as Tom King had just done. I had been involved in a slightly different problem during the Falklands War, when the Air Force in the Ministry of Defence had made covert contacts with the air attaché in the Chilean embassy, without informing us. I later received an apologetic visit from the head of Defence Intelligence, Lieutenant General Sir Maurice Johnston (an Old Wellingtonian who had been in my father's house, and who later turned up as a fellow officer with me in the 40th Field Artillery in Dortmund, before defecting from the Gunners to a smarter regiment, the Queen's Bays).

As for Cabinet Secretary calls, I recall that during my time as private secretary to Paul Gore-Booth, he and Sir Burke Trend regularly exchanged calls – one of which must have provoked Trend's private secretary, William Reid, to initiate a practice of exchanging doggerel with me – Reid and Wright – a practice which has continued in our retirement. [A recent exchange referred to my exclusion from the *Times*'s birthday list on my eighty-fourth birthday.] Simon McDonald (who was private secretary to both David Gillmore and John Coles) has confirmed to me that the then Cabinet Secretary never called on the PUS – though my last private secretary, Tim Simmons, apparently insisted on the PUS being put through on the telephone at the same time as Robin Butler, on the grounds that while one was head of the civil service, the PUS was his equivalent as head of the diplomatic service.

A group of Conservative MPs visited the office today for a presentation on the diplomatic service over a sandwich lunch, one of a very successful series which has done something to improve the office's relationship with Parliament.

11 JULY 1986

Charles Powell confirmed to me today that the Prime Minister is still adamantly opposed to Geoffrey Howe's ideas on the Falklands. There is now a complicated scenario with the Ministry of Defence, which is very keen to get ministers to decide on force levels, and the need to impose a fisheries programme which Geoffrey is, rightly, reluctant to institute without a parallel diplomatic conciliatory move.

I lunched with John Fieldhouse, and later stayed for a private talk covering the Falklands and Conventional Disarmament, on which the chiefs of staff have been outraged by Geoffrey Howe minuting George Younger on the latter without prior consultation at working level. I left for Ditchley at 4 p.m., having hurriedly minuted Geoffrey on the Falklands.

14 JULY 1986

An early drive to Chevening, for a session of talks between Geoffrey Howe and Eduard Shevardnadze, who arrived by helicopter at 9.15 a.m. Talks round the table in Geoffrey's study upstairs were mainly on bilateral relations; chemical weapons; Southern Africa; and the Middle East. The time available was halved by interpretation, but it was quite a good dialogue, and Shevardnadze has a ready Georgian wit. Although not recorded at the time, I vividly remember that, in the midst of a discussion on disarmament, a white dove flew through the open window – it was a very hot day – circled the room, and flew out again. I think the Russians must have thought it was some devilish British trick!

In the afternoon, I drove back to London for a brief spell on my in-tray before going to the rehearsal of the St Michael and St George service in St Paul's. The rehearsal was unnecessarily long, and could have been done in twenty minutes, if properly organised. As secretary (ex officio) of the order, I had to parade directly in front of the chancellor's page and banner (tickling my head, with the chancellor himself – Peter Carrington – muttering in a Carringtonian way about 'all this ridiculous ceremonial').

Geoffrey Howe telephoned me last night to say he had decided not to push his Falklands ideas at the moment, but described the Prime Minister's attitude to this question as 'little short of manic'. There was a good profile in this week's *Observer*, assuming (as most people do) that Geoffrey is, for the present at least, her potential successor, if she was to fall under the proverbial bus (on which *The Observer* quoted Peter Carrington's remark: 'No bus would dare').

15 JULY 1986

I am told that Geoffrey really did come very close to resignation last night, presumably on the grounds that the Prime Minister was so far apart from him in her approach to South Africa. The press are becoming increasingly interested in (or inventing) a supposed constitutional crisis between the Prime Minister and the Queen.

16 JULY 1986

An early meeting on South Africa, on which Geoffrey is determined to try to produce a more conciliatory formula, and to get the Prime Minister to accept that we shall almost certainly – I think certainly – have to accept some measures against South Africa at the Commonwealth meeting in August. The Prime Minister is still holding out for no move, or hint of a move, before the Howe mission is over in three months' time.

Following the meeting, Geoffrey had quite a good session with the Prime Minister, which enabled him to make a positive statement in the House this afternoon. The important thing will be to ensure that the PM does not go back on it at *Question Time* tomorrow.

Another case today of a senior diplomatic posting leaking, with David Goodall being congratulated by the Chief of General Staff on his posting to India before he knew about it himself – an echo of Norman Reddaway's experience in the Beirut souk in the 1950s, when he was allegedly congratulated by some Lebanese on his posting as ambassador to Warsaw before the personnel department had notified him.

Robert Armstrong called on me to air his worries about the Commonwealth meeting and a possible constitutional crisis, on which there had been some press speculation, though my impression was that the Palace was fairly relaxed on the subject, attributing worries in No. 10 more to Nigel Wicks than to the Prime Minister herself. Robert suggested that

Christopher Mallaby (then on secondment to the Cabinet Office) should do some very private contingency planning with someone (perhaps Tony Reeve) in the FCO.

In the evening, I dined at Lancaster House with the Exports Credits Guarantee Department (ECGD) Advisory Council, sitting next to my host, Alan Clark, the Minister of State for Trade. When I told Geoffrey Howe, who I was dining with, he advised a long spoon. Clark told me that he had always been 'infatuated' with the Foreign Office, but that it had been a 'frustrated love affair'. When he claimed that relations were bound to be bad between the two departments, and were deteriorating, I replied firmly that I had only recently agreed with Permanent Under-Secretary Bryan Hayes (who was present) that relations had never been better.

[Many years later, Virginia asked me what I wanted for my birthday. When I said that I would like Alan Clark's diaries, she replied that she was prepared to give me anything I wanted, but not them. We had both been extremely angry about Clark's account of members of the diplomatic service, including his outrageous comment that one of his ambassadorial hostesses (admittedly anonymous, but nevertheless easily identified) proved that people with muscular dystrophy were always the most boring (or words to that effect).

After I had joined the board of BP, I discussed Alan Clark's diaries with John Baring (Lord Ashburton, the then chairman). John told me he had shared rooms with Alan Clark at Oxford, so knew him well. He commented that, from reading the diaries, you would think the Clarks were a rather grand family. 'Actually,' he added, 'they were merely traders – like the Barings.']

17 JULY 1986

The Commonwealth Games seem to be crumbling, with nine participants having fallen out so far. My attempt to get the PM to use some positive wording in the House of Commons today (and which could be used to encourage a positive decision from the Frontline States meeting in Harare tomorrow) failed, since Charles Powell took it on himself not to show Geoffrey Howe's advice to the PM 'on grounds of tact'.

21 JULY 1986

A call from Ramsay Melhuish (Harare) who is nervous, as a lot of high commissioners should be, that some Commonwealth governments may decide to break diplomatic relations with us over sanctions for South Africa. The walkout from the Commonwealth Games has now reached twenty-four countries.

A meeting this afternoon in Robert Armstrong's office on intelligence estimates, at which Peter Middleton (Treasury) infuriated us all by looking rather self-satisfied. In fact, he had little reason for self-satisfaction, since the Treasury's attempts to cut back intelligence expenditure were invariably reversed by Margaret Thatcher, who was a strong defender of all three services [none of which, incidentally, was at this stage avowed].

23 JULY 1986

Geoffrey Howe told me today that he wanted me to be the 'third man' at the Commonwealth review meeting on South Africa in August. When I discussed this with Charles Powell, he said firmly that the PM had 'decided' that Robert Armstrong should do it (even though she is alleged to have said, after the Nassau meeting, that she did not want him to do it again).

24 JULY 1986

A brief (and rare) call from Jacques Viot, the French ambassador, asking to present a request for *agrement* for Luc de Nanteuil as his successor.

A pity that Viot is going; he has gone down well in London. But French ambassadors in London have never, in my experience, regarded it as part of their duty to cultivate the FCO. I remember that when Michael Palliser was PUS, he once asked all the under-secretaries, at his morning meeting, which of them had received the French ambassador or even a senior official from the French embassy; virtually none of them had. This neglect was not, of course, helped by the general impression that Margaret Thatcher gave to all and sundry that the FCO was an object of contempt. Luc de Nanteuil (le vicomte) turned out to be an even less frequent visitor than his predecessors.

25 JULY 1986

Charles Powell told me today that (allegedly unknown to him and to Bernard Ingham) the Prime Minister had given a private interview to the *Sunday Telegraph*, who were insisting – in spite of appeals both to the editor and the proprietors – on publishing the South African bits of the interview this Sunday. Charles claimed to be appalled; when I saw the text later, I agreed that it would be thoroughly unhelpful – and more worryingly, could be seen by Geoffrey Howe as another deliberate attempt to undermine him.

28 JULY 1986

I called on Timothy Raison at the ODA, who seems to be very conscious of morale problems in the FCO/ODA relationship. He asked me to try to get Geoffrey Howe to pay the ODA more attention. He also pointed out that the honours list regularly contains a long list of FCO awards, but very seldom any from the ODA.

John Fawcett (Sofia designate) called today. He was later to end his mission with a highly eccentric valedictory despatch, calling for total disarmament. When Geoffrey Howe heard (from Fawcett on his farewell call) that the department had recommended against printing the despatch, he immediately suspected a bureaucratic cover-up, and asked to see the file copy. Having read it, he expressed total agreement with the decision not to print it.

29 JULY 1986

I held an early meeting to coordinate briefing for next week's Commonwealth review meeting. The main brief will depend on Geoffrey Howe's talk with the PM on his return from Southern Africa, and on Thursday's Cabinet. As far as I can tell, most of the Cabinet accept that we have got to adopt, or at least to undertake to adopt, further measures against South Africa. The departmental ministers, such as Transport, are predictably opposed to measures which hurt their interests; but both the PM and Norman Tebbit are still fairly adamant against putting on any extra pressure.

I attended the first half of Tim Renton's meeting on Arab/Israel with Middle East heads of mission. Having for years thought we should upgrade our contacts with the PLO, I found myself arguing rather strongly that this would be a quite inappropriate and irrelevant time to do so. It would also cause great trouble with King Hussein and President Mubarak.

Robert Armstrong tells me that the PM is not going to accept the move of the ODA to Richmond Terrace, and asked if Geoffrey Howe would drop the idea. I said that I thought it was an outrageous situation, and that the PM should be made to record her decision, the reasons for it, and the specific authorisation for the extra money involved from the Contingency Fund. The Public Accounts Committee could well have something to say about it.

Geoffrey Howe had a bad meeting with the PM today. Ewen Fergusson told me it was quite clear that the prospect of meeting her had overshadowed the entire Africa visit. It has also become government by bully!

In a letter, dated 30 July, to the service, I put it like this:

The Prime Minister's approach to the whole question of further sanctions or measures against South Africa has throughout been clear and consistent. She believes that sanctions are wrong and ineffective, and that they will serve only to damage our own interests as well as those of the blacks within South Africa and of South Africa's neighbours. Her argumentation is flawless, but although the words of her pronouncements on this subject may in logic be right, the music has often been open to misinterpretation. The truth is that her statements, like those of President Reagan, have all too readily been seen in Africa and elsewhere as support for President Botha and apartheid. Her own conviction that she is right has made it all the more difficult for the Secretary of State to persuade her that we may have to be ready to move very quickly to some further measures if the pressures become too great. Failure to do so could result in real damage to our interests both in black Africa and more widely.

31 JULY 1986

After a Cabinet meeting which reached unanimous, if unsatisfactory, conclusions on further measures against South Africa, Bernard Ingham appears to have briefed the lobby that Geoffrey Howe had been isolated, and was considering resignation. Geoffrey told me this afternoon that he believed that Bernard was speaking without the PM's authority.

David Thomas called today to say goodbye on leaving the service. He is leaving early because his wife Susan (a Liberal candidate who later became a Liberal peer as Baroness Thomas of Walliswood) does not want to go abroad again. David himself told me he found the world such a disturbing place that he virtually wanted to 'get off'. He also wondered whether the PM knew [I didn't!] that the Assistant Under-Secretary dealing with Latin America for the past three years had been an Argentine subject, as well as the husband of a Liberal candidate. He said that when he had been in Moscow, there were more Argentines in the British embassy than in the Argentine embassy – an extraordinary illustration of the size and diaspora of the Anglo-Argentine community.

1 AUGUST 1986

The lead story in *The Scotsman* today – Mrs Thatcher is in Edinburgh – quotes a senior FCO source as denying that No. 10 had deliberately misled the press yesterday with the story of Geoffrey Howe's resignation. Mrs Thatcher rang Charles Powell at 6 a.m., and was said to be 'incandescent'. Tony Galsworthy told me that Geoffrey had been on the point of writing to the PM to say that either he or Bernard Ingham must go. He did eventually write two personal letters this evening: one, expressing his extreme displeasure over press handling; the other, urging the PM to adopt an emollient stance in her bilateral meetings and at the Commonwealth review meeting this weekend. Charles Powell later assured me that the PM was determined to adopt a calm and conciliatory approach 'unless provoked', at least in her bilateral meetings. Unfortunately, the PM is clearly looking forward to a row, and interprets recent opinion polls as showing that the electorate support a tough attitude towards sanctions and Southern Africa. She is probably right!

2 AUGUST 1986

Lunch at Wargrave Manor with Sultan Qaboos, for the PM and Denis Thatcher. Robert Alston (ambassador in Muscat), Tim Landon, the Omani ambassador and Charles Powell were also there.

I had earlier considered with Tim Renton whether the PM should be briefed on the signals we were getting that the Sultan wanted to recover the embassy building in Muscat – in my experience, one of the most beautiful ambassadorial residences in the diplomatic estate – for his own purposes.

I decided (mistakenly) not to brief her, on the grounds that the Sultan was most unlikely to raise the subject, and that Margaret Thatcher would be furious if she discovered that Geoffrey Howe had offered to hand it back (in exchange for a prime site on the coast, looking out over the Arabian Sea).

As it was, in the middle of lunch, the PM fixed Robert Alston with one of her glares and said: 'I hope Mr Alston is looking after that beautiful residence. We want to keep it for a long time.' She turned her glare on me, and said: 'Permanent Under-Secretary, you know my views about residences.' I was extremely embarrassed, as I knew that the Sultan was under the impression that Geoffrey Howe had accepted the idea of an exchange. Robert Alston cleverly retrieved the immediate situation by assuring the Prime Minister that he was looking after the site, and that about eighty workmen had been working on it when he had left Muscat a few days earlier.

3 AUGUST 1986

After dictating several records from the Wargrave lunch, I went to Robert Armstrong's office to hear Charles Powell's description of the PM's bilaterals with Mulroney, Gandhi and Kaunda. The first two had been surprisingly calm and good-tempered; the last was described as 'fairly disagreeable'.

At the review meeting itself, I spent most of the day waiting around at Marlborough House and doing a certain amount on my box. I arranged with my old Indian colleague from Damascus, Venkateswaran, to lunch with him tomorrow, since Gandhi had hinted fairly strongly to Tim Renton that our bilateral problems were better discussed without the involvement of their Foreign Minister. I suggested to Venkat that our lunch should be à deux, since his deputy, Daulat Singh, is virulently anti-British, and probably a major cause of our current difficulties.

The review meeting broke up soon after 6 p.m., and I was asked to join a wash-up meeting in the PM's study at No. 10. A standard performance by the PM of either glaring at or ignoring Geoffrey Howe, whose patience must be wearing pretty thin. At one point, when she was being particularly rude to him, he simply picked up his red box and started doing signatures. This threw her for a moment; but then she quickly turned her fire on me!

Alan Watkins in today's *Observer* described Geoffrey as 'Mrs Thatcher's Challenger', which won't have helped him. She again started talking about partition as a solution to South Africa. I just hope she does not try this out as an idea at the review meeting. All her (and Denis's) instincts are in favour of the South African Whites. She described today's meeting as 'worse than Nassau'.

4 AUGUST 1986

Much of today was spent hanging about in Marlborough House, waiting for reports on the meeting from Robert Armstrong and Geoffrey Howe. In spite of an apparent determination to play it cool, the PM started disastrously with an abrasive statement, saying that Britain was an independent state, and would not give aid to help the military struggle (though no one had suggested that we should).

I gave lunch to Venkat, in view of Gandhi's hint about avoiding ministerial discussion, though it has since occurred to me that it may have been designed to bypass Tim Eggar as much as the Indian Foreign Minister, Shiv Shankar, since Tim had an extremely rough meeting with the Indian High Commissioner two weeks ago. Venkat was very critical, both of Eggar and of our High Commissioner, Robert Wade-Gery, but agreed that Daulat Singh was not helpful, and claimed to have just blocked a long letter which Singh wanted to send.

5 AUGUST 1986

The Commonwealth review meeting having ended at midnight, I had left a free morning in my diary. Geoffrey Howe held a meeting at 11 a.m.

to discuss what work was needed, including messages to all and sundry explaining the outcome. There was a general consensus that the meeting could have gone worse, but that we are not out of the woods, particularly on air links, where British Airways may well find their over-flying rights in Africa removed from them. But the immediate prospect of breaks in diplomatic relations seems to have receded.

Ramsay Melhuish later gave us a vivid description of the non-aligned rally in Harare, where Mugabe was giving a spirited call for sanctions against South African flights, when his voice was completely drowned out by the roar of a South African Airways flight taking off from Harare airport for Pretoria! If British Airways divert round the bulge of the African continent (which they will soon be able to do with their new aircraft) there is a strong risk of retaliation against their flights elsewhere, including India and Malaysia.

6 AUGUST 1986

Percy Cradock called, and opened the subject of the PM's attitude to the office, which, as he put it, loses nothing in the way in which her comments are passed on by Charles Powell. I doubt whether Charles expends much effort on the sort of literary contortions that I went to at No. 10 in translating brusque, and sometimes obscene, comments on papers into phrases like: 'The Prime Minister has expressed some reservations…' [Bill Harding, who had been one of the deputy under-secretaries, later told me that, on his farewell call on the Prime Minister, she kept him for a quarter of an hour without any comment on the service, other than remarks about the need to find good posts for young people 'like Charles Powell' (who was present throughout).]

7 AUGUST 1986

I called on Lady Young before going on leave. She is clearly nervous about being left in charge of the office, particularly with the South African problems, on which she once made an unwise speech, for which she was rebuked by Geoffrey Howe.

David Goodall reported to me that Robert Armstrong had told him that Geoffrey Howe had passed him a note during the Commonwealth review meeting, while the PM was speaking, saying: 'I suppose there may be more unhelpful ways of presenting our case, but I can't think of them.'

1 SEPTEMBER 1986

I returned from holiday in Salcombe today, during which I read the memoirs of two predecessors, Lord Hardinge and Sir Alexander Cadogan. (The latter was the subject of one of the more remarkable coincidences I can remember. When visiting Hatchards, I had asked the shop assistant whether Cadogan had written his memoirs. A lady standing next to me said: 'Yes, indeed he did. I am his widow.') I was struck by the extent to which Hardinge (who was appointed Viceroy of India during the First World War, and then returned to a second stint as PUS) was treated as a courtier, accompanying King Edward VII on numerous trips abroad, in place of ministers; and by the amount of drafting that Cadogan did for both the Foreign Secretary and Prime Minister on the basis of telephoned instructions, and with apparently very little back-up from the office.

Geoffrey Howe held an office meeting today to prepare for a ministerial meeting on visa regimes for Bangladesh, India, Pakistan, Ghana and Nigeria, under pressure from the Home Office, following bad congestion at the airports here. Christopher Mallaby later reported to me that Geoffrey Howe had been totally isolated at the ministerial meeting (widely trailed by press leaks), and had to give way to a decision to impose regimes 'at an early date'. When I saw Geoffrey later, he was gloomy about it, and rather predictably casting around with criticisms of the office. But he commented that the PM seemed to be taking a harder and harder line on racial questions. The opposition have already attacked the measures as 'racist'.

Charles Powell looked in at 11, with a very disapproving message from the PM about a *Daily Telegraph* story alleging direct quotations from FCO officials on the visa regimes. I said that I thought it most unlikely that any diplomatic service officer had spoken as alleged, but pointed out that the story was only the culmination of three days of extremely unhelpful, and anti-FCO, press briefing. Charles said that the PM was aware of this, and suspected the Home Office (Bernard Ingham is away at present).

Geoffrey Howe spoke to me again today about the alleged anti-feminine bias in the administration (having spent part of his summer holidays with Pauline Neville-Jones). He also raised several instances in which Robert Armstrong had minuted to the PM on foreign affairs questions without adequately consulting him.

3 SEPTEMBER 1986

There was a ridiculous editorial in today's *Sun* about visa regimes, referring to pin-striped FO officials worrying about their tiffin and cocktails. Christopher Meyer put up a robust draft letter, in *Sun*-style, for Geoffrey Howe to send to the editor.

The German ambassador called at 4 p.m., presumably to discuss my visit to Bonn and the forthcoming summit. It turned out that he did not know about the first, and his instructions were five days out of date on the second. Not very impressive; he was visibly embarrassed.

7 SEPTEMBER 1986

Lunch with the Callaghans at Ringmer. Jim has delivered his memoirs to his publisher for launching next April, commenting that I might have to vet them officially. He thought there might be a difficulty over his account of Guadeloupe; but added that Helmut Schmidt and others had already produced their accounts, and that Schmidt had, in his view, given a very inaccurate account of the meeting.

8 SEPTEMBER 1986

I lunched with Ray Seitz (then the no. 2 in the American embassy), who gave an interesting account of the problems facing the US Foreign Service, in which over 50 per cent of ambassadorial appointments are now political. [An interview in the *Financial Times* on 7 November 2015 with Bill Burns claims that he had retired from the United States government after a 33-year career 'as only the second career diplomat in US history to have made it that high in the Department'. Since much of these diary extracts must appear very critical of Margaret Thatcher, I should mention, in her favour, that there were no political appointments to embassies or high commissions during her time as Prime Minister; and the plethora of political advisers was only to blossom when Tony Blair arrived in No. 10.]

9 SEPTEMBER 1986

Robert Armstrong told me today that the PM has given way (with extreme ill grace) on the move of the ODA to Richmond Terrace, in the face of a warning minute from Robert that the Public Accounts Committee might wish to delve into the reasons for extra expenditure of £3–4 million. He thinks she will only give up after a 'bloodbath meeting' at which Geoffrey Howe will be exposed to maximum flak (and attacks on alleged FCO misuse of the old Home Office building). Robert again commented that the tone of the PM's anti-Foreign Office feeling was very strident, and not exactly countered by Charles Powell.

Virginia and I dined at ICI, for their annual dinner for permanent secretaries, with Denys Henderson as host. I am not sure if it was at this dinner, or a subsequent occasion, when Denys, or his successor, walked me down the corridor, along which were portraits of all previous chairmen, and told me that when Margaret Thatcher had similarly come to dinner, she had ticked off each portrait with the words: 'He wasn't bad,' 'He was dreadful,' and so on.

12 SEPTEMBER 1986

An awkward situation has arisen today over sanctions. Hans-Dietrich Genscher telephoned Geoffrey Howe to say that Helmut Kohl was adamantly against sanctions on coal. This puts the whole package of Hague measures into confusion, just at the moment when the US Congress has reached agreement on a stronger package. It will tempt Margaret Thatcher to unravel the whole thing, particularly when the Frontline States themselves are backsliding fast on sanctions. Geoffrey himself thinks the situation is manageable, since dropping coal will certainly lead some community colleagues to press for sanctions on vegetables and fruit, which the PM is adamantly determined to block.

17 SEPTEMBER 1986

I had an hour's meeting with Geoffrey Howe to prepare him for his public expenditure bilateral with the Chief Secretary on 19 September. We may have some difficulty stiffening him, since he let the office down badly two years ago. There may be some psychological problem of the Chancellor poacher having turned Foreign Secretary-gamekeeper – just as I later faced problems with Douglas Hurd, as a diplomatic-service-officer poacher having turned ministerial-gamekeeper.

When John Major was (to his surprise) moved by Margaret Thatcher from being Chief Secretary to Foreign Secretary, I asked him whether he knew what the Treasury brief was for the diplomatic service and he claimed that the only brief he had looked at was the Transport brief, since he had been convinced that if he was moving anywhere it would be to Transport.

Television last night showed the PM in Bonn, gratuitously drawing attention to her opposition to sanctions, and ridiculing the idea of 'signals' to South Africa at precisely the moment when Geoffrey Howe had put together a reduced package in Brussels and was telling the press that it would be a clear 'signal' – having successfully left the onus on the Germans and the Portuguese. [A foretaste of Margaret Thatcher's later undermining of John Major at the Commonwealth heads of government conference in Kuala Lumpur three years later.]

18 SEPTEMBER 1986

Geoffrey Howe rang me at 1.30 a.m., with a complicated request for advice on a Soviet swap. I first of all did not realise who Geoffrey was; and then found it very difficult to understand what the question was. No doubt it will be clear tomorrow. [It did, indeed, transpire that it was an American proposal to include Oleg Gordievsky's family in a deal with the Russians.] Geoffrey asked me whether it was a capital offence to telephone PUSs in the middle of the night, and said that when he had done the same to the Chief Secretary, and apologised the next day, the Chief Secretary had totally forgotten that he had telephoned, or why!

[Geoffrey's habit of telephoning people at unsocial hours led to an amusing incident which Nick Browne recounted at his farewell party from Middle East Department for Tehran in early 1997. His young son had come into his bedroom at 6.30 a.m. one morning on April Fool's Day to say that Sir Geoffrey Howe was on the telephone and wanted to speak to him. Nick – assuming this to be an April Fool – said: 'Tell him to bugger off.' The son returned a few minutes later, saying: 'I told him to bugger off; but he says that he still wishes to speak to you.']

20 SEPTEMBER 1986

Virginia and I drive to Chequers for the Prime Minister's lunch for King Hussein and Queen Noor. One rather tiresome guest (an American wife) told me loudly that she 'didn't think people should marry wogs' – obviously taking pride in shocking people. This reminded me of a call I received, as head of Middle East Department in the early 1970s, from the Saudi ambassador, Abdulrahman Al-Helaissi, to ask if I would be offended if someone called me a wog. I told him that I would be even more offended if he had been (as he clearly had), but that the origin of the expression was said to be an abbreviation for Westernised Oriental Gentleman, and therefore not intrinsically offensive.

There was a brief discussion after lunch about the strategic importance of the Gulf and the Cape route, on which Peter Carrington was splendidly direct in telling the PM that the latter depended on which war you were fighting. As NATO had only fourteen days of ammunition to fight a war, he thought that the sea route via the Cape for any strategic materials was going to be a bit slow.

Elspeth Howe asked me if I could arrange for Geoffrey to visit Jordan, to which I replied: 'How much is it worth?' In reply, she promised not to raise the position of women in the service for a whole week.

23 SEPTEMBER 1986

I gave lunch to Nigel Wicks, who thought that the PM was even more anti-FCO since her holiday than before. He commented on Geoffrey Howe's poor showing in Cabinet, but thought that the PM's antipathy was primarily a difference of philosophy from his, and resentment of the FCO's attachment to compromise and consensus (although he made the familiar comment that she has little quarrel with such individual members of the service that she meets).

26 SEPTEMBER 1986

I called on Janet Young for a round-up, mainly on staffing questions, including morale and recruitment, on which she is very keen to help and has the right ideas. The sad fact is that she has little clout with Geoffrey Howe, and even less with other ministers.

A flood of weekend papers tonight. My ration could just be squeezed into one box. Geoffrey Howe had four – and loves it! (I later reported that he had returned from New York, having demolished six boxes.)

29 SEPTEMBER 1986

Geoffrey Howe held a meeting on Hong Kong, on which he is likely to find the Chancellor of the Exchequer and the Governor of the Bank of England in opposition to him. He is also fighting a lone battle (with Tom King) on the question of three-man courts in Ireland. But he seems to thrive on it all.

A launch party this evening at George Weidenfeld's for Paul Wright's book *A Brittle Glory*, at which Lord Chalfont told the story of the beaver at the foot of Beaver Dam telling a friend that someone else had built it, but it was based on his idea.

7 OCTOBER 1986

In a discussion with Geoffrey Howe about James Craig's leaked valedictory despatches (it having emerged that several newspapers, including the *Financial Times* and *The Independent*, had copies), Geoffrey, rather characteristically, tended to be critical of James's rudeness about the Arabs, and the unwisdom of being that frank in government documents. He even tried to get me to warn heads of mission to be more careful in their drafting. I refused, on the grounds that it would be quite wrong to curb any member of the public service from giving frank advice, however unwelcome.

8 OCTOBER 1986

An injunction on the Craig despatches was granted this morning. I received a telephone call at 1.30 a.m. from the resident clerk [who identified himself many years later as Charles Crawford, after Matthew Parris's parting shots had included one of the despatches in 2011] to say that the *Glasgow Herald* was printing both despatches and was about to release them. After I had contacted John Bailey, the Treasury solicitor, a judge was found in Edinburgh prepared to issue the Scottish equivalent of an injunction, which had to be driven – in a coach and four? – to Glasgow at 4.30 a.m. By that time, of course, hundreds of copies of the *Glasgow Herald* were already on the streets.

I agreed with Robert Armstrong this evening that the police should be called in to investigate the leak. Anthony Loehnis telephoned me from the Bank of England to say that one of the journalists who interviewed James Craig (called Forbes) was an ex-Bank of England man; and that the bank had discovered (very efficiently) that Forbes's signature was on the official receipt of the despatches.

Two days later, I was asked to call on the Attorney General, Sir Michael Havers, at the law courts. As I had a credentials appointment at Buckingham Palace later that morning, I had to go in diplomatic uniform, telling Sir Michael that I was merely trying to uphold the dignity of the FCO – which the *Daily Mirror* claimed this morning was the reason for all this fuss about a leaked despatch. I also had a further conversation with John Bailey, who told me that *The Observer* was now claiming that the full text of the offending despatch was not only available to the Saudi embassy; it was also being carried extensively both on agency tapes and on Israeli radio.

I commented: 'The press have behaved unspeakably this week. It is not as if there is any particular principle they are trying to defend.'

13 OCTOBER 1986

My morning meeting of under-secretaries was largely taken up with the Reykjavík summit, and the implications of Reagan's stated hopes for the abolition of all nuclear weapons within ten years. This will cause considerable alarm, both in the Quai d'Orsay and in No. 10.

21 OCTOBER 1986

The PM chaired a meeting today to discuss the Hindawi trial, and decided, with only Tim Renton putting up a contrary argument, that we should break relations with Syria. I met a rather disconsolate Tim afterwards, who said that he had received no support from other ministers. I imagine that the expulsion of Haider might well have led to a break anyway; but this is bad news, and we are already thinning out our embassy in Beirut (a fact that unfortunately leaked in the press today).

22 OCTOBER 1986

Geoffrey Howe returned from Hong Kong this morning and held two office meetings – one on arms control and one on Syria, on which he is dismayed by the ministerial decision, but has concluded that there is no hope of changing minds – an appalling case of decision by intimidation. A verdict on Hindawi is now expected tomorrow, and it is not excluded that he may be acquitted. Geoffrey (as an ex-lawyer) commented this morning that it was a case that he would have enjoyed defending.

A meeting at 6 p.m. with Robert Armstrong and others to consider his draft brief for the PM's meeting tomorrow on Richmond Yard; but the meeting was interrupted by a dramatic intervention from Nigel Wicks, who arrived to tell us that the PM had agreed after all that the ODA move should go ahead, and that her meeting had therefore been called off. The PM has however demanded an assessment of the FCO's use of the main office buildings, on which she clearly has a vision (or has heard reports) of extravagant and wasteful use of them. But at least one piece of bloodshed has been saved.

23 OCTOBER 1986

The Hindawi jury failed to reach a decision today, but will presumably do so tomorrow. Geoffrey Howe was recorded in a letter from No. 10 as having 'agreed totally' with the decision to break relations, which is strange; but presumably he decided that if he was not going to try to reverse the decision, he had no other option.

24 OCTOBER 1986

Sherard interrupted my talks with the Austrians by passing me a note at noon, to say that Hindawi had been found guilty, and sentenced to forty-five years. The Syrian ambassador would be in the office at 12.50 p.m. When the time came, I saw Haider, with Patrick Nixon, in the waiting room, and virtually read out a speaking note, ordering him and his staff out of the country by 7 November. Haider responded by saying that he had expected this, but assured me that he was totally innocent of any involvement. A very frosty and unpleasant interview, and I left it to Patrick Nixon to see the ambassador out. I learned later that Haider had made some pretty offensive personal comments about me to the press [recorded by Sherard Cowper-Coles in his 2012 book, *Ever the Diplomat*].

Charles Powell called, mainly to discuss the PM's Washington visit, because of which she has overturned Geoffrey Howe's advice that we should vote for the Nicaraguan Resolution at the United Nations.

29 OCTOBER 1986

On my way to lunch with Greville Janner at Veeraswamy, I bumped into Michael Heseltine. Assuming that I was still in Saudi Arabia, he asked how the Tornado deal (which he had signed) was going. When I told him that I was now PUS, he exclaimed: 'Good God! You'd better not be seen talking to me, then,' – a reference to his walkout of Margaret Thatcher's Cabinet over the Westland affair. When I told Greville Janner this, he commented that it would surely do my career much more harm to be seen lunching with him!

30 OCTOBER 1986

I pulled Geoffrey Howe's leg about a letter from the *Financial Times*, revealing to me that Geoffrey had given them a copy of a despatch from Belgrade, and suggesting that there should be a Howe award for the best official document of the year. In the light of the Craig despatch row, I told Geoffrey I would keep the letter, and use it in evidence against him, but wouldn't put it in the hands of the Director of Public Prosecutions for the moment.

1 NOVEMBER 1986

My relations with Tim Eggar are slightly strained, since I had to draw his attention to the undesirability of including officials in party political discussions about electoral registration.

4 NOVEMBER 1986

Charles Denman reported to the office today on a fascinating talk with Zaki Yamani (who was sacked as Saudi oil minister last week), and who told Charles that two ministers had wished to issue a statement of solidarity with Syria over the Hindawi affair, but had been shouted down by their colleagues. Yamani himself said that he was 200 per cent in favour of what HMG had done, and congratulated us on having the guts that his own government lacked.

6 NOVEMBER 1986

Credentials for the new Romanian ambassador (under a changed name), who turns out to be the one Romanian at Harold Wilson's lunch in Bucharest in 1975 who took his coat off in the summer heat, explaining to Ken Stowe that this was because he was the only Romanian at the table who was not carrying a gun.

This afternoon, I attended a wreath-laying ceremony by Geoffrey Howe at the diplomatic service memorial in the main entrance hall. It is a sad coincidence that two of the three members of the service who were murdered by the IRA – Christopher Ewart-Biggs and Richard Sykes – were both pupils of my father at Wellington College. Both their names appear on a similar memorial in Wellington Chapel.

10 NOVEMBER 1986

Lynda Chalker called on me this afternoon to ask about Robin Renwick (whose help in European Community (EC) matters she is obviously terrified of losing) and about Pauline Neville-Jones.

11 NOVEMBER 1986

An early meeting with Geoffrey Howe, at which he complained about alleged inactivity by the office over Chirac's extraordinary intervention in the *Washington Times* about Syria and hostages, accusing British Intelligence reporting of being garbage, and discussed Robert McFarlane's arms deal with Iran. I defended the quality of reporting on both subjects from Paris and Washington, but agreed that more thought should be given to what we should say to both the Americans and the French.

Geoffrey also complained about the briefing provided for the ministerial meeting on AIDS, pointing out that it urged ministers to reach early decisions, but gave no guidance on what those decisions should be. A fair point, though Geoffrey tends to whinge when he is uneasy about things. [I had already noted that the Department of Health and Social Security (DHSS), now under my former No. 10 colleague Ken Stowe, had made a surprisingly poor showing at Robert Armstrong's preliminary briefing meeting.]

12–16 NOVEMBER 1986

My visit to Washington, which coincided, from 14 November, with the Prime Minister's visit. Both visits were conducted against a backdrop of the arms for Iran scandal. At lunch with Mitch and Mary Ellen Reese on 15 November, Mary Ellen commented to me that the whole arms for Iran scandal could have come out of one of her own spy novels. When I called on Bob Gates at the CIA, I told him that I had hoped to call on Rear Admiral Poindexter, but that the meeting had been cancelled. Gates told me I was in good company, since both he and Bill Casey had been similarly put off.

At a private dinner that evening in the embassy, Margaret Thatcher was in a good mood (except for one point, when she was reminded of the FCO building, on which she is slightly mad). She talked about her succession to the leadership, claiming (rather implausibly) that it was all a matter of chance, and that Keith Joseph would have had the leadership if he had wanted it.

17 NOVEMBER 1986

On my return, I called on Geoffrey Howe this evening to find him agonising over whether to try to insert himself into the PM's visit to Moscow, I think he should; but quite understand that he does not want to court a rebuff. He is also worried about our relations with the Northern Ireland Office, and has asked me to try to get closer to Robert Andrew. I told him that I had so far been reluctant to add Northern Ireland to my 'action portfolio', but that I knew Robert Andrew well – we had been at Merton together – and would try. The problem is Tom King, who is absurdly sensitive about FCO responsibility for the Republic of Ireland. A day or so later, I discussed this with Nick Fenn, who is designated for the embassy in Dublin. We agreed that Tom King's neurosis will not be improved by David Goodall's responsibility for our relations with Ireland, given his history of master-minding the Anglo-Irish Agreement from the Cabinet Office.

20 NOVEMBER 1986

Gordon Manzie, the Chief Executive of the property services agency, and I discussed Margaret Thatcher's hang-ups about the FCO and the ODA. He told me that he had attended a meeting at which Margaret Thatcher, with real hatred in her eyes, had virtually instructed him to charge the FCO to the hilt for our accommodation.

The Prime Minister had been rather put out by a recent meeting with President Museveni of Uganda, who had reacted in a very off-hand way to her offer of a £10 million grant; she once commented that she liked to be thanked for our aid, and once firmly told Chris Patten and myself, when we called on her to discuss the aid programme, that on no account should we reduce aid for Kenya: 'One thing about President Moi: he does know how to say thank you!'

I lunched with David Watt, a leading political journalist, who was very critical of our decision to break relations with Syria. He contested my claim that it had been politically necessary, arguing (perhaps correctly) that it was just a question of what the Prime Minister wanted.

21 NOVEMBER 1986

I called on Tim Eggar to discuss the FCO's relations with Parliament, on which he has a lot of ideas, some of which certainly breach the rules for civil servants; others will tread heavily on the toes of his ministerial colleagues. But several are quite sensible, and worth pursuing. But the rules are tightly drawn, and are personally endorsed by the Prime Minister.

Michael Jenkins (minister in Washington) came to my morning meeting and described the Prime Minister's talks at Camp David and the political situation over the arms for hostages deal with Iran, on which President Reagan lurches from bad to worse, though he has made it difficult to sack Poindexter by taking on full responsibility himself.

Nicky Gordon Lennox (Madrid) told me today that the Spaniards are being increasingly difficult again about Gibraltar, partly because of obtuse and unimaginative officials in the Foreign Ministry. The Spanish ambassador in London has told Nicky that he now corresponds with his Foreign Minister via his home address.

I called briefly on Bryan Hayes to discuss Alan Clark's performance in Baghdad, where he failed to read his briefs, and spoke badly out of line about our arms policy towards Iran and Iraq. Bryan Hayes described him as a 'curate's egg', and doubted whether it was necessary to send specific warnings to other heads of mission.

But Clark is obviously an unguided missile – something that became abundantly clear during the Scott Inquiry, and after the publication of his diaries. As Minister for Trade, the DTI (Department of Trade and Industry) have been trying for a long time to get him to meet members of the British Overseas Trade Board. Having finally arranged it (by getting him to join one of their meetings), Bryan told me he kept them waiting for five minutes, and simply abandoned the meeting. He also, on his own initiative, kept the Moroccan Foreign Minister waiting 'to teach him a lesson for King Hassan's rudeness to the Queen'.

[In a private exchange with William Waldegrave about his memoirs in 2015, I mentioned both Alan Clark and Ted Rowlands – the latter in the context of my instructions to rebuke Rowlands for leaking in Parliament our interception of Argentine naval codes during the Falklands War. William commented that Rowlands 'was not really a bad man; Clark was'.]

24 NOVEMBER 1986

A call today by the French ambassador to lobby for the British vote on New Caledonia – singularly embarrassed, since the French are clearly going to vote against us on the Falklands Resolution this week. I enjoyed myself by pointing out that we were being lobbied to vote the other way by our friends in the South Pacific, who had supported us on the Falklands. I also saw the record of the Prime Minister's talks in Paris, at which she had lambasted Chirac over the Falklands, saying that the French were prepared to throw other people's Christians to the lions.

25 NOVEMBER 1986

Geoffrey Howe kept me back after a meeting on the *Spycatcher* case, to express some general worries about intelligence work, for which he is hankering after a ministerial group that would not include the Prime Minister; and his concern about Robert Armstrong's excessive area of responsibility. He is also worried about the whole complex of American activities over arms sales to Iran (on which Poindexter resigned, and Oliver North was sacked, today). He has asked me, in a very Geoffrey Howe-like way, to arrange for a general review – though it is not quite clear of what!

In a letter to the service dated 1 December, I included the following:

> Although, for understandable reasons, the Prime Minister in Washington
> affirmed her support for the President in ringing terms, the number

of questions raised by the NSC's foray into unconventional diplomacy, and by the President's defence of it, is, if anything, growing. The whole incident has only increased the Secretary of State's anxieties about the difficulties of formulating a consistent Western policy towards countries such as Iran, Libya, Syria and Nicaragua, where stated American policies do not always coincide with their covert intentions and activities. (It will also have reinforced his belief (not shared by the Prime Minister) that we may have, as he puts it, to leap from the American to the European trapeze sooner than we think.)

I went to St Margaret's Westminster for a service and reception of the World Council of Churches. As I was representing Geoffrey Howe, my enquiries about the seating arrangements obviously caused a flurry (and no doubt some acid comments about my self-importance); as a result, I was rather ostentatiously greeted at the service and at the later reception – courtesies made all the more embarrassing since the lesson was all about humility.

26 NOVEMBER 1986

Percy Cradock told me today that the Prime Minister had twice referred to the Peter Wright case in Australia as the 'Patrick Wright case'. Charles Powell told me later that she had once thrown her entire private office into confusion by asking, as she left her office for Prime Minister's Questions: 'Is there anything new I should know about Patrick Wright?' I also discussed with Percy – as chairman of the Joint Intelligence Committee – the supervision of intelligence, and Geoffrey Howe's ideas for a ministerial group.

28 NOVEMBER 1986

A ministerial group has been formed, consisting of Geoffrey Howe, Douglas

Hurd and the Attorney General (Michael Havers) to handle the *Spycatcher* case; but Geoffrey feels strongly that the Attorney General won't be up to it. It now emerges that, contrary to Robert Armstrong's evidence, the Attorney General was never even consulted about Chapman Pincher's book, and could well resign as a result.

18 DECEMBER 1986

After a gap, which included my attendance at the Commonwealth officials' meeting in Bangladesh, I paid my first call on Chris Patten at the ODA, to be told on arrival by Crispin Tickell that John Caines's appointment as his successor would be announced tomorrow. We had a very relaxed talk, during which Chris Patten commented on the very high standard of people in the diplomatic wing (and, to a lesser extent, in the aid wing) compared with elsewhere in the civil service. This applied particularly to the standard of briefing.

19 DECEMBER 1986

My last bilateral meeting with Geoffrey Howe before Christmas, at which I presented him with a sixtieth-birthday present – a copy of *Victorian Ballads*. I had also written him a personal note congratulating him on behalf of the whole diplomatic service. Sherard hinted strongly to me that not everyone in the office shared my enthusiasm for Geoffrey Howe, and was even doubtful whether I should send my note at all. It is, I'm afraid, true that Geoffrey is widely regarded as unnecessarily nit-picking and work-creating.

Many years later, when we were both in the House of Lords, Geoffrey continued to send me occasional letters and articles, asking for my comments – as if I was still his PUS.

1987

I lunched at the Oxford and Cambridge Club, and walked back with Brian
Cubbon, who is convinced that there will be a May or June election and
that if, as everyone assumes, the government is returned, Geoffrey Howe
will become Lord Chancellor and Douglas Hurd Foreign Secretary. He
was not very complimentary about Douglas as Home Secretary, joking
with me that, as a former diplomat, he did not seem to be committed to
any principles. But I think he would be quite a good Foreign Secretary,
though his influence with Margaret Thatcher would probably be as slender
as Geoffrey Howe's.

Charles Powell tells me today that the PM is virtually certain to choose
David Wilson for Hong Kong, and later confirms this in writing. When
I told David, he was flabbergasted and overawed, but obviously very
flattered. I consulted Tim Renton on which, if either, of us should go to
Hong Kong to present the decision to EXCO (the Executive Council). Tim
is obviously very nervous about the idea, which he thinks could turn into
an embarrassing and public wrangle, with some trying to change ministers'
minds. David's own preference is for me to do it, since in his view Tim
Renton is not wholly popular with EXCO. I sent a telegram to Geoffrey

Howe in Mexico, and have drafted a provisional telegram to consult David Akers-Jones on the best way to proceed.

6 JANUARY 1987

Tony Galsworthy telephoned me from Bermuda to say that Geoffrey had discussed the idea of a visit to Hong Kong with David Gillmore, and they were not in favour of the idea. David Akers-Jones later confirmed that he was also not in favour of it.

7 JANUARY 1987

I had a one-hour meeting with Gordievsky, which I found a fascinating experience, having been involved as DUS – one of the very few officials to be briefed on his case – when he was still in the Soviet embassy in London. Indeed, I had the extremely awkward duty of trying to persuade Robert Flower – then deputy head of PUSD (the Permanent Under-Secretary's Department) with special responsibility for the Security Service, but unbriefed – that Gordievsky's boss should be expelled (on pretty fragile grounds), so that Gordievsky could move up in the embassy hierarchy.

[Geoffrey Howe explains in his memoirs that this was one of the few subjects on which he was briefed (by me) without his private secretary (Brian Fall) being present. Brian took a lot of persuading that I could talk to the Secretary of State without him being there to take a note, no doubt deeply suspicious that I wanted to talk about his own future.]

I recall one meeting at 10 Downing Street when I was DUS for Defence and Intelligence. Margaret Thatcher – in a very rare breach of security – had referred to one of the Gordievsky reports, which no one else would have seen. I intervened to say that I was pretty certain that she was referring to a recent article in the *New York Times*; she took the hint!

8 JANUARY 1987

I discussed with Geoffrey Howe the PM's forthcoming visit to Moscow, on which he told me to take a very firm line about his own attendance and participation, saying (quite reasonably) that he insisted on being there, at least when Shevardnadze is.

Michael Weir (ex-Cairo) called today, and advised me to try to go to the lunchtime concerts at St John's Smith Square [I never did!], for the music, but also for the excellent impression it would make in the service – echoes of Douglas Hurd's later reply to my question about which former PUS he would like me to emulate: Harold Caccia or Derek Hoyer Millar (to both of whom Douglas had been private secretary)? Douglas's reply was firmly in favour of Hoyer Millar [later Lord Inchyra], since he had always left London for Scotland at midday on Friday, and did not return until Monday midday – in marked contrast to Harold Caccia's very hands-on style.

Once, when I was Caccia's private secretary in Washington, he had handed me a letter about Cuba, and had asked me to draft a reply for him. Having walked down the corridor to Gill Brown's office (she looked after Latin American affairs in the Chancery), I handed her the letter and asked her to draft a reply. A few minutes later, Caccia asked me if I had yet drafted a reply, so I told him what I had done. He immediately walked down the corridor to discuss a draft reply with Gill!

9 JANUARY 1987

I pressed Charles Powell today on Geoffrey's attendance at Moscow. He thinks that a compromise is workable, but strongly advised that Geoffrey should not talk to the PM about it, or 'there would be blood on the floor'.

10 JANUARY 1987

Antony Acland called and described Geoffrey Howe's meeting with Shultz in Bermuda, at which Antony thought Geoffrey was too tired after his Colombia visit to have focussed properly on the detail of his briefs. I commented that it was too easy to assume from Geoffrey's physical and intellectual energy that he is not capable of exhaustion. I once commented, rather cheekily, during a bilateral meeting with him, that I knew that he, like Margaret Thatcher, had a reputation for needing very little sleep; so far as I could tell, the only occasions on which he slept properly were when I was talking to him.

In a letter to the service, dated 12 January, I wrote:

> Sadly, my visit to Southeast Asia was interrupted by a detour to Hong
> Kong for Teddy Youde's funeral, which Tim Renton and I attended. We
> both found it a deeply moving occasion, both because of the excep-
> tional level of official recognition of Teddy's services to Hong Kong
> and because of the very obvious affection and respect which the people
> of Hong Kong of all races had for the late governor. The funeral itself
> had been preceded by a quite remarkable display of grief in normally
> undemonstrative Hong Kong. 80,000 people signed condolence books
> in government offices all over the territory, and some 11,000 paid their
> last respects during the lying-in-state at Government House.

I reflected many of these comments when I was later asked, by Pam Youde, to give the tribute at Teddy Youde's memorial service in Westminster Abbey on 17 February – a service rather dauntingly attended by at least three Prime Ministers.

18 JANUARY 1987

I attended Geoffrey Howe's meeting to discuss the latest Argentine approach on Falkland fisheries, which may be a trap but appears to open the way for bilateral talks without discussing sovereignty. It is important to appear positive; but it will cause difficulties with No. 10.

I face a very embarrassing and difficult row with Buckingham Palace, having asked Roger Hervey to raise with Princess Margaret's private secretary the size and cost of her entourage when visiting China. Lord Napier was extremely resistant and thought that Princess Margaret at least would strongly object to being asked to contribute to the cost. Geoffrey Howe (to whom I had earlier reported on the problem) thinks I am not asking the Palace for enough. I am likely to end up on the anvil, if not in the Tower.

20 JANUARY 1987

Roger Hervey spoke to Lord Napier today about her China visit, and I later spoke on similar lines to Bill Heseltine, who reacted robustly, describing the proposal that the government should pay for Princess Margaret's children as 'quite monstrous', and said he would talk to the Queen.

21 JANUARY 1987

Today was my first appearance before the Public Accounts Committee, after nearly two hours of rehearsal with Sherard, who took great delight in giving me a very hard time! But the practice was invaluable, and the meeting went quite well. I was well supported by officials, both from the FCO and from the auditor general's office.

22 JANUARY 1987

An extraordinary day in which ministers spent most of the time trying unsuccessfully to stop dissemination of Duncan Campbell's film and article on the Zircon Project [which was treated as so secret when I was a DUS in 1982/83 that I was not allowed to keep any papers on it in my office]. In spite of injunctions yesterday, the *New Statesman* carries full details today, and MPs managed to see the film, notwithstanding unprecedented injunctions against them. There was also a tussle about ministerial responsibility for Government Communications Headquarters (GCHQ), ending with a prime ministerial ruling that the FCO should be responsible for the news handling of this. I commented that it looked as though there would have to be a revision of the Official Secrets Act; but attempts in the recent past to do so have always come to nothing, and Duncan Campbell himself was unsuccessfully prosecuted in the famous ABC case.

Not only was GCHQ still unavowed at this date. I had an early meeting today on the avowal of Secret Intelligence Service (SIS), which reached no conclusions. My diary describes this as 'a typical Howe meeting, consisting largely of philosophising. Presumably Geoffrey himself ends these meetings a bit clearer in his own mind, even if no one else does.'

25 JANUARY 1987

The resident clerk telephoned at 2 a.m. (Sunday) to say that the White House had contacted the embassy in Washington following the capture of three or four more hostages in Beirut, and had asked for contingency permission to preposition a force of approximately 500 at Akrotiri, in preparation for a 'rescue mission'. Geoffrey Howe had already been told, and was worried about the continued incarceration of Terry Waite. I suggested we should ask some further questions about the nature and planning of the mission, and set up a 9 a.m. meeting. By that time, Charles Powell had drafted a first reply, which my meeting amended to point out more strongly the virtual impossibility of rescue missions without intelligence on the whereabouts of the hostages; the grave risks for other hostages and communities in Lebanon if the prepositioning became known [as it certainly would]. I telephoned Geoffrey Howe in Leicester to give him a guarded account of the line taken, which he endorsed. We have also pointed out to the Americans that the Islamic conference starts in Kuwait tomorrow. I was later telephoned to say that the Americans had decided to put off any troop movements for the moment. So far, so good.

26 JANUARY 1987

I attended a meeting in Robert Armstrong's office to discuss what should be said to the PAC about accounting for GCHQ's finances. We agreed on a formula stating that there had been no changes in the arrangements or procedures which had been followed by successive administrations. But like avowal of SIS, the arguments are illogical, and often consist of not admitting what everyone knows to be true. But we are rapidly slipping down the American slope, particularly in relation to Parliament, and ministers could be faced with demands for an intelligence select committee (though the PM will resist it strongly). By 2015, there was, of course, a joint parliamentary intelligence and security committee, chaired, for a time, by Malcolm Rifkind.

27 JANUARY 1987

I held a meeting on Terry Waite, hostages etc. to prepare for the PM's meeting with Geoffrey Howe and George Younger. Still no firm news of Terry Waite, but reports from Washington suggest that the idea of a rescue mission has died, at least temporarily.

I chaired a lunchtime meeting at Chatham House, at which Dr Alex Pravda launched a five-year study programme on Soviet foreign policy. It would be interesting to look at the product of this programme, which must have coincided with the aftermath of the collapse of the Soviet Union.

30 JANUARY 1987

The new Dutch ambassador, Hans Jonkman, called. When I asked him whether he already knew any of his diplomatic colleagues in London, he said that he had been in New York with Luc de Nanteuil. Having asked me how well I knew him (and clearly ready to be indiscreet, which I encouraged), he said that, having worked closely with de Nanteuil for about six months, he had said to him: 'We have now worked together for quite a time. Would you call me Hans; and may I call you Luc?' To which de Nanteuil had replied: '*Pourquoi?*'

2 FEBRUARY 1987

I lunched at the Mansion House for the annual ECGD gathering, hosted by Paul Channon, looking rather battered after his daughter's death and the Guinness affair. He had been a delightful guest when we were in Riyadh, and wrote me a wonderful spoof thank-you letter, based on the *Yes, Minister* film about a reception in an Arab capital, thanking us for the opportunity to meet General Gordon's grandson, though he had been a bit surprised, since he had always understood that General Gordon never married. I also taught him, during the visit, how to count from one to ten in Arabic. On my first appearance in his office at the DTI, the gathering group of DTI officials were astonished to hear their minister faithfully repeating the numbers to me as I entered the room.

Geoffrey Howe attended a disastrous meeting of the new Government Accommodation Committee, at which he received no support for the long-standing decision that the FCO should occupy the capital's old public offices. Both the DES (Department of Education and Science) and the DHSS (Department of Health and Social Security) want space in it, and the PM has evidently seen her chance of getting her pound of flesh, having capitulated on the ODA's move to Richmond Terrace. She really can be very vindictive at times – in which context we have now received a rather gloomy acceptance of

Robin McLaren's new job. This relates to reports that Robin had made some disloyal comments on the Falklands War during his time in Hong Kong.

3 FEBRUARY 1987

My bilateral with Geoffrey Howe this afternoon was entirely taken up with a long, and rather bad-tempered, argument about Whitehall accommodation, on which Geoffrey found himself isolated yesterday. He clearly thinks that he will have to give up part of Richmond Terrace or the main old public offices, for at least a team from the DES and DHSS. I argued fiercely that it was inefficient and extravagant to change long-laid plans.

Later this evening, I went briefly to a delayed New Year party given by the special advisers (John Houston and Adam Fergusson), at which Geoffrey Howe asked me if I had recovered from my bad temper. I said that it was the first grumpy meeting we had had, and was sure it would be the last. When I later told Geoffrey that Virginia had given me a trampoline for Christmas, he said that it should be good for shaking down my bad temper.

4 FEBRUARY 1987

Gordon Manzie and Crispin Tickell called at 9.30 a.m. to discuss tactics on accommodation, on which Gordon was extremely critical of his Secretary of State, Nicholas Ridley, who he said did not understand the subject, and was simply pandering to the PM's prejudice against the FCO.

A later meeting was interrupted by a long and angry telephone call from Tim Renton about my questioning (with Geoffrey Howe's support) his air ticket to return from Prague for a constituency dinner.

5 FEBRUARY 1987

I was told that Sir David Nicholas had paid a very warm tribute to the

FCO at a launch party held by ITN, at which Norman Tebbit was heard to say loudly that he was glad to hear that the Foreign Office had done something useful for once. Gordon Manzie told me that any solution to the accommodation problems which appeared to make the FCO suffer would be very popular in Whitehall.

6 FEBRUARY 1987

I discussed with Charles Powell today the very different attitudes of the PM and Geoffrey Howe towards the Strategic Defence Initiative (SDI), on which Margaret Thatcher predictably takes a much more bullish view in the face of recent indications that the Americans may be ready to break away from the narrow interpretation of the ABM Treaty. I have advised strongly that Geoffrey should reveal his hand to the PM, even at the risk of a difference of opinion.

9 FEBRUARY 1987

I went to Brooks's this evening for a dinner for permanent secretaries and their wives. Sad that Ken Stowe, who has now worked for Norman Fowler for five and a half years at the DHSS, enjoys his job so little.

17 FEBRUARY 1987

Today I gave the memorial address for Teddy Youde in Westminster Abbey. Some very complimentary remarks afterwards, including from Margaret Thatcher, who greeted me at the end. Alec Home (who had given the address at Macmillan's memorial service a week ago) told me that he thought composing and giving addresses of this sort added years to one's life. Jim Callaghan (who was in his element, surrounded by Cardiff constituents) later telephoned me in glowing terms, and asked for six copies of my text.

20 FEBRUARY 1987

I lunched today with Robert Andrew, following up Geoffrey Howe's request to interest myself in Irish affairs, given his nervousness about the implications of David Goodall's departure – David having taken on Ireland in his DUS portfolio (unlike his predecessors, including myself). Robert confirmed to me that Tom King is the most difficult of the three secretaries of state he has worked for, and is neurotic about the FCO – and particularly about FCO attendance at meetings.

23 FEBRUARY 1987

Robin McLaren called, having started today on his Hong Kong duties. When I told him that the Prime Minister had had strong reservations about his appointment, he volunteered that he knew there had been a Security Service investigation; that he much resented the long gap before he was first given the opportunity to comment on the allegations; but that the PM, to his surprise, had come up to him in Peking and had said: 'You don't need to worry about all those stories; I think you are doing a first-rate job.'

24 FEBRUARY 1987

Lynda Chalker called today to moan about her relationship with Tim Eggar, who is obviously irritating all his colleagues by interfering in their business.

I accompanied Geoffrey Howe and others this evening to an IPU (Inter-Parliamentary Union) dinner in the House of Commons, sitting between David Crouch and Peter Temple-Morris – a dinner arranged to thank Geoffrey for his, and the office's, support. I was invited to say a few words, and expressed appreciation for Geoffrey's encouragement of closer links between officials and Members of Parliament.

25 FEBRUARY 1987

The administration produced today a list of potential successors to myself, to which I added the name of David Gillmore (rather surprisingly omitted by the department).

Paul Nitze and Richard Perle called on the PM this morning as part of their consultations on SDI. Geoffrey Howe had persuaded the PM that he should be present, but Percy Cradock later told me that there had been quite a sharp exchange between Geoffrey and the PM during the meeting (which will get straight back to Washington – unhelpfully). The trouble is that the PM believes that only she understands the subject, or knows how to play it.

Charles Powell later told me that the last half hour of the call had been virtually devoted to this sharp exchange. Geoffrey had later reverted to the subject at Cabinet, and had been rudely slapped down by the PM. Charles commented that I would not recognise Cabinet from my days in the mid-1970s, since no one now dares to speak up to, or contradict, Margaret Thatcher. The trouble is that eight years of experience in No. 10 merely increases her self-confidence and autocracy.

26 FEBRUARY 1987

I held a meeting with heads of department this morning, at which there were some fairly sharp comments about the lack of improvement in terms of service, and a clear feeling that ministers were interfering too much, but not achieving any real improvements. A fairly draining session. Sherard asked me afterwards if he could get me either a whisky or a Mars bar!

27 FEBRUARY 1987

I had left my programme free today in case (surprise, surprise!) I was after all invited to join the PM's Soviet seminar; needless to say, I wasn't.

I had to deal with a sudden crisis which has blown up involving a Mexican diplomat who had presented himself to the police as a material witness to the murder of a prostitute, following its coverage on *Crimewatch*. We had some difficulty restraining Tim Eggar from giving public assurances that in similar circumstances we would waive diplomatic immunity. Apparently, he said this to the Mexican chargé, but the latter did not write it down!

2 MARCH 1987

Brian Fall, the Secretary of State's private secretary, called at 10.15 a.m. to discuss the handling of a very full record which the Americans have given Michael Pakenham, in strict confidence, of the PM's talks with Nitze and Perle – revealing the full extent of the PM's argument with Geoffrey Howe. I am havering whether to show it to Geoffrey Howe, but will probably not; he must himself know what happened at the meeting, and will probably only fret if he knows that a full record exists. There is nothing of substance in it which posts do not already know, but it is fairly humiliating that the PM should treat him this way.

6 MARCH 1987

In an attempt to take a more strategic approach to foreign policy objectives and priorities, planning staff drew up a 100-page paper two years ago, which was never used. It did not take into account the increasing tendency to give high priority to questions that have been blown up by the media, or by parliamentary sensationalism (like the misbehaviour of diplomats in London).

[David Owen was asked, after he had finished being Foreign Secretary, what foreign policy issue had taken up most of his time and energy during his time in the Foreign Office, and he had replied that it was the case of Timothy Davey, the young drug-smuggler in Turkey, whose story was later dramatised in the film *Midnight Express*.]

9 MARCH 1987

I telephoned the Archbishop of Canterbury this afternoon after Robert Runcie had told Geoffrey Howe that he wanted senior-level contacts in the FCO to discuss Terry Waite. Runcie is obviously worried by the emerging stories of Waite's contacts with Oliver North, quite apart from the continuing lack of information about Waite's whereabouts. I told Runcie that David Miers would be ready to contact him whenever he wanted.

There have also been increasing stories over the weekend about British assistance to the Contras; as far as the FCO knows, there has been no offic- ial assistance at all. I wondered this morning whether Sir Alfred Sherman (who used to be a policy adviser to the PM) might be behind some of these allegations.

10 MARCH 1987

I called on Lady Young at the House of Lords today for a general talk. Neither of us could remember quite why the call had been arranged in the first place. We talked mainly about recruitment, allowances and morale. She showed some resentment at the extent to which her colleagues are encroaching on her responsibilities for management and the administrative side of the office.

11 MARCH 1987

Lynda Chalker telephoned me from Strasbourg today to lobby me to vote for Ted Heath as Chancellor of Oxford University. I told her that I had already told Ted that I could not be there, but undertook to instruct Sherard to vote!

12 MARCH 1987

A lunchtime seminar with Labour MPs, including Bernard Donoughue. As usual, extraordinary ignorance was revealed about the diplomatic service. Patrick Nixon told me afterwards that one of them was astonished to discover that heads of department ever served abroad (as, indeed, they usually didn't before the 1943 reforms). I put in a plug for boarding schools, claiming that most members of the service would be very happy to send their children to local schools, but that career mobility made it quite impracticable.

23 MARCH 1987

I discussed with Geoffrey Howe a proposal that he should break the news of Arthur Watts's appointment as legal adviser to Henry Darwin (who, as John Freeland's deputy, probably expects to get the job). Geoffrey did not like the idea, pointing out that it was an administrative decision for me to handle. He told me that the only time he had ever spoken to anyone about their appointment was to Ewen Fergusson, when I had been appointed PUS (in favour of Ewen and Crispin Tickell). But how ironic that I should find myself in the position of giving disappointing news to the man who was a god-like head boy at Marlborough when I was a junior boy. Indeed, one of my early, maturing experiences was when – sitting in the choir as a junior alto – I noticed that Henry's hands were shaking with nerves while he stood at the lectern to read the lesson.

[The above reference to my appointment as PUS is being typed – by an astonishing coincidence – on 25 July 2015, the day after our son-in-law Simon McDonald telephoned us from Berlin to tell us that he had been appointed PUS to succeed Sir Simon Fraser.]

I discussed with Geoffrey Howe today the PM's continuing resistance to taking FCO officials with her to Moscow, on which he is becoming increasingly irritated; he says that he will raise it again this week.

24 MARCH 1987

Geoffrey Howe held one of his worst meetings ever this afternoon on overseas students, with Chris Patten and a large team from the ODA, and Nicholas Barrington and others on the FCO side. There was only limited time, and Geoffrey had given an untypically inadequate study of his brief, which produced some incomprehensible requests for a paper to be produced in a different format. No conclusions were reached at all. I think he must have the election and politics very much on his mind.

1 APRIL 1987

I chaired a DUSs' meeting for one and a half hours on AIDS; and on the scope for British initiatives in the Security Council, and our chances of remaining permanent members. [My diary comments – in 1997 – on how many of us would have thought we would still be there ten years later; but in 2017 we still are.]

Crispin Tickell was there, probably for his last meeting before his departure for New York. I shall need to watch relations with the ODA when he goes; there have been two signs recently of Chris Patten becoming irritated by wire-crossing.

2 APRIL 1987

At my morning meeting, Michael Forsyth (Geoffrey Howe's PPS) suggested that ways should be found to give the FCO some credit for the success of the PM's visit to Moscow, and reported that MPs were already saying that it had only gone well because No. 10 had organised it. Geoffrey Howe did a lot of background briefing today, which may help.

I saw Geoffrey Howe after lunch, who revealed his opposition to the length of the FCO honours list, claiming that his own knighthood was ex officio. Tony Galsworthy pointed out that many of the FCO honours were also ex officio, and that they were, in any case, a cheap compensation for inadequate pay (good for him!).

3 APRIL 1987

David Owen told me that a recent opinion poll had shown that the PM had gained 25 per cent from her trip to Moscow; Neil Kinnock had gained 7 per cent from his trip to Washington; and the [SDP] Alliance had gained 17 per cent from not travelling at all! David is now reported to be forecasting a 7 May election, which will cause me some awkward decisions over travel.

14 APRIL 1987

One of the events during our absence in Israel and Turkey was Mugabe's arms deal with the Soviet Union, on which the PM is taking a hawkish view and threatening to cut off aid. Geoffrey Howe later told me he thought it important that we should collect information on those states which have been pushed into the arms of the USSR, like Cuba, and others, like Jordan, with whom we have maintained amicable relations.

15 APRIL 1987

I attend the Zeebrugge ferry disaster memorial service at Canterbury, sitting immediately behind Geoffrey and Elspeth Howe and one other. Geoffrey later told me he had no idea who the latter was, and that when he asked Margaret Thatcher she didn't know either, saying he was either a whip or a junior minister. He is, in fact, John Moore, Secretary of State for Transport.

I had a meeting this afternoon to brief Geoffrey Howe on my visits to Israel and Turkey. He was shocked by my account of Israeli impediments to Palestinian family reunification, and has asked for further details, so that he can brief the PM 'to steer her away from Finchley'. After I had criticised several aspects of Israeli life, Geoffrey laughed and said: 'I see you have maintained your admirable objectivity about the Middle East.'

Peter Wallis called to warn me that the Oldfield story about the Kincora Boys' Home may surface in a book by Barrie Penrose. I discovered that Christopher Mallaby had already warned Geoffrey Howe, who had been previously unbriefed – presumably during my absence. But signs of increasing Cabinet Office involvement?

22 APRIL 1987

Following revelations in the *Mail on Sunday* of Maurice Oldfield's homosexuality, I attended a meeting at No. 10 this morning to discuss the text of a parliamentary written reply, revealing that Maurice had finally admitted his homosexuality after his appointment to Northern Ireland (having given false replies on previous occasions, and having had his positive vetting withdrawn). When the Prime Minister and Home Secretary, plus others, entered the Cabinet Room, the PM was evidently discussing the latest bomb outrage in Colombo, and said to the Home Secretary: 'We must send all the Tamils back; they are all bombers!' When discussing the Oldfield case, the PM initially questioned whether he had to admit his homosexuality at all. But everyone pointed out the risk that knowledge of the 1980 inquiry, and police reports at that time, would leak out subsequently. She was obviously enraged by Chapman Pincher's disloyalty to his friend, describing him twice as Judas, and was particularly (and characteristically) concerned about the effect on Maurice Oldfield's family.

I later gave Sherard an imitation of the PM's behaviour during the Oldfield meeting, when the No. 10 servants were handing round coffee. She brought proceedings to a close, staring frenetically round the room and turning over her papers (with the particular look on her face when she is discussing security). Sherard told me it was a great pity I was not keeping a diary, saying that he was quite certain that Antony Acland had done so.

23 APRIL 1987

I caused hilarity at my morning meeting today by reading out to Michael Forsyth the *Times* diary piece describing his conversion from a 'madcap right-winger' to 'an intelligent and balanced MP, tipped for ministerial promotion'.

24 APRIL 1987

I discussed with Philip Wetton, the new head of the Energy, Science and Space Department, the problem of Peter Walker, whose failure to consult others in Whitehall is becoming even worse than usual. His department has just concluded an agreement with the Russians without consulting either the FCO or the legal advisers. I told Philip about the problems I had had over Peter Walker's contacts with Yamani.

An amusing incident yesterday over Alan Clark, the Minister of Trade, who was due to leave last night for a visit to Venezuela and (in spite of FCO dissuasion) Chile. He had earlier this week received a rocket from the PM, who complained that ministers were travelling too much. At the airport, after three accompanying businessmen were already on board the aircraft, Clark developed toothache, and said he wouldn't go. Three furious businessmen took off a few minutes later.

29 APRIL 1987

I told Geoffrey Howe today that when Margaret Thatcher had received Crispin Tickell before Crispin's departure for New York, she had unfairly criticised John Thomson, our permanent representative at the United

Nations, for his inactivity. I had sent No. 10 John's valedictory despatch as a corrective, which displeased Geoffrey – nervous, as ever, of the PM seeing FCO papers before himself.

I also discussed with him the PM's reaction to Mugabe's possible arms deal with the Soviet Union with words like: 'Teach Mugabe a lesson.' Geoffrey will have a hard task keeping her from damaging our position in Southern Africa; her relations with Mugabe are already tense, and Ramsay Melhuish has several times recommended that messages to Mugabe should not be signed by her.

1 MAY 1987

There were some interesting signs this week of the PM's ambivalent attitude to the FCO. She told Crispin Tickell that it was a pity that an FCO candidate had not succeeded him at the ODA; she also questioned Janet Young this week about what she thought of the office (on which Janet claims that she described us as impressive, but inadequately rewarded). Charles Powell advised David Miers, when discussing the PM's criticism of our performance on Iran/Iraq, and the production of a paper for No. 10, to be ready to admit that we had not got it right – 'since the one thing the PM can't stand about the FCO is their assumption that they are always right'.

I pointed out to George Younger today that if, as is likely, the local election results are bad for the government, a decision not to call a June election will make them look even worse than they otherwise would, since the government will seem as if they are scared of fighting another election so quickly. George Younger nevertheless thinks that a September election is not to be excluded, since it would successfully disrupt the SDP conference.

5 MAY 1987

Continuing speculation in the press about Geoffrey Howe's future, including renewed gossip (which Lynda Chalker told me today she thought was well founded) that Nigel Lawson might become Foreign Secretary if Geoffrey becomes Lord Chancellor. Lynda herself expects to return to the FCO, possibly in the Lords (having told me in strict confidence that her name would appear in the birthday honours list, though she did not explain how). Tony Galsworthy told me today that Geoffrey is determined to stay on at the FCO, if at all possible. I nevertheless wrote Geoffrey a private letter this evening, expressing the hope that he would.

6 MAY 1987

DUSs had a discussion this afternoon on DOFFCO – the acronym used for 'image' to describe the whole process of disseminating the truth about the service. Robert Rhodes James commented to me again last night on how ignorant most of his parliamentary colleagues are about the FCO. At a dinner in No. 10 this evening for President Chissano of Mozambique, I learned that Margaret Thatcher had asked him a question about sanctions this afternoon, on which his reply was so staunchly negative that she immediately promised him £15 million of aid – having earlier expressed doubts about aid for Mozambique (doubts which were no doubt refuelled when Geoffrey Howe was photographed in Mozambique, apparently giving the communist salute!).

7 MAY 1987

Anthony Kershaw congratulated me today on my recent appearance before the Foreign Affairs Committee. I told him that I had told Geoffrey Howe that he had been a very considerate and helpful chairman, having blocked three of the questions put to me on the grounds that they should be addressed to ministers. Tony told me that he had got into trouble for it afterwards!

13 MAY 1987

Janet Young asked to see me this morning to tell me in confidence that she has told the Prime Minister that she intends to retire from public life after the election. She spoke very warmly about the office and the service, comparing it very favourably with the three civil service departments in which she has served. She is worried about pay and about some of the poor management – both justifiably, in my opinion. I thanked her for the interest and concern that she has shown for the service, which had been widely recognised and appreciated.

Michael Palliser called today to solicit FCO funds of an IISS (International Institute for Strategic Studies) seminar – the second ex-PUS I have received in a week, though not as remarkable a coincidence as Antony Acland's experience, whose engagements blackboard in the outer office once showed calls from the Duke of Marlborough and the Duke of Wellington on the same day!

19 MAY 1987

I went to the Hilton for the vast annual CBI (Confederation of British Industry) dinner, at which Nigel Lawson spoke. I sat between Alan Clark and Sir Michael Clapham, an ex-President of the CBI. I noticed that, for once, I was seated above the Chief of Naval Staff (who commented on it afterwards!).

28 MAY 1987

Dreadful news today from Tehran, where Edward Chaplin has been hijacked. I agreed that Alan Munro should summon the Iranian chargé, who appeared to know nothing about it, though there is at least a suspicion that it might be in retaliation for yesterday's arrest of the Iranian vice-consul in Manchester on shoplifting charges. There will be pressure from ministers to react very toughly, but there is little we can do other than break relations even further. The Prime Minister would probably be happy to do this, since she is very sceptical of the FCO's balancing act between Iraq and Iran. I am uncomfortably aware that Jimmy Carter lost the presidential election because of the American hostage-taking in Tehran. We have to remember that Iran is our third largest trading country in the world.

Meanwhile, Neil Kinnock has done his best today to lose the election, by promising (very foolishly) to decommission Polaris within two weeks of forming a government.

29 MAY 1987

Edward Chaplin was released today, or rather dumped and left to walk the last mile home.

2 JUNE 1987

The Prime Minister is said to be becoming very agitated about the Chaplin case, and inclined (as she has been before) to go straight for a total break. This was by no means the only occasion on which the FCO had to resist Margaret Thatcher's instincts that we should not maintain diplomatic relations, or renew them when broken, with 'nasties'. Geoffrey Howe is arguing for the expulsion of the vice-consul first, but almost any reasonable solution will look like a deal. Christopher MacRae reported today that Velayati is said to have returned to Tehran, furious at the mess that Khomeini's people have got them into.

4 JUNE 1987

I attended a lunchtime talk by Tim Eggar on the service – a packed audience and a thoughtful and provocative speech, with some sensible criticism of FCO methods, arguing that the bureaucratic method prevented radical thinking about choices, to which ministers should be exposed. When he claimed that decisions should be taken at a lower level, I pointed out that this was not easy with a Prime Minister who took such a close interest in foreign affairs.

5 JUNE 1987

At a Sunningdale weekend, I had a spirited discussion with Arthur Walsh of STC (Standard Telephones and Cables), who complained about the alleged failure of posts to support commerce. It emerged that he was in fact complaining about the failure of embassies to support one British company when another was in competition. I pointed out to him that he needed to get ministers to change their policy on this, to which he replied dismissively that ministers were run by their civil servants. After quite a row, we ended the weekend walking round Sunningdale Park together.

An interesting article in *The Economist* this week on Margaret Thatcher, claiming – depressingly, but probably correctly – that her greatest contempt is reserved for the Foreign Office, and that she had been influenced by the fact that she had had to fight to win the budget row with the European Community. I discussed this with Michael Franklin (who had played a major part in the negotiations), and he claimed that allegations of lack of FCO support were totally unfair, and that the office had backed up the PM superbly.

9 JUNE 1987

I gave lunch to Michael Checkland, the new director-general of the BBC, who thought that the BBC had weathered the election period without too much controversy (although Denis Healey lashed out at a BBC interviewer this morning, calling her 'a shit' for raising Edna's treatment on a discussion about the national health). Nigel Lawson yesterday accused Roy Hattersley of telling lies; tempers are getting increasingly frayed as the election approaches.

11 JUNE 1987

Election day. Charles Powell called briefly to confirm that Geoffrey Howe will stay on as Foreign Secretary. He could not give much of a forecast otherwise, though he hinted that Cecil Parkinson will definitely return to the government, and that John Patten is a likely Minister of State for the FCO (an interesting mis-forecast, since Patten is said to be a close friend of Charles).

I asked about Lynda Chalker (since her retention, though welcome, would involve some minor reshuffling of private secretaries). Charles said that the Prime Minister likes her, and in any case wanted to keep women ministers at that level. It was, of course, a great sadness for Lynda that she never reached Cabinet rank, and for Janet Young that she was demoted from Cabinet rank to be a Minister of State again.

On news department's advice, I telephoned George Thomson at the IBA this evening to point out that any lampooning of Ayatollah Khomeini by *Spitting Image* in their live election show at 10 p.m. could make an already difficult and dangerous situation in Iran explosive. He reacted well, and telephoned later to say that they had intended to include something on Iran, but had dropped it.

12 JUNE 1987

Geoffrey Howe appeared in the office this afternoon for a long and difficult meeting on how to respond to the latest Iranian expulsions. The sad conclusion was for a total pull-out, but not to be described as a break of relations. It is a sad comment that, having never before broken relations, except on declaration of war, we have now broken off five times since 1960 – with Argentina, Uganda, Libya, Syria and now Iran. And only in the case of Uganda did we leave no one behind.

15 JUNE 1987

The new FCO ministerial team emerged today, with David Mellor from the Home Office succeeding Tim Renton, and Lord Glenarthur succeeding Janet Young from the Scottish Office.

Malcolm Rifkind told me this evening that Simon Glenarthur is very nice and easy to work with (Eton and the Hussars). Mellor on the other hand is rather different (Conservative Member for Putney). Lynda Chalker, who was made a privy counsellor in Saturday's honours list, becomes no. 2, and I spent most of today working on possible combinations of ministerial duties.

I called on Lynda Chalker this evening, and discussed her role as the ministerial member of my no. 1 board – the only case, I believe, in all Whitehall where a minister sits as a member of an official committee. [Many years after my retirement, the PUSs' board included a non-executive director.]

16 JUNE 1987

I called on Lord Glenarthur and David Mellor this morning. Both seemed rather daunted by their respective empire, but were friendly and ready to listen to advice on their initial briefing. Both also seemed to like their first look at their private secretaries, so at least we shall not have to switch them. I also called on Tim Eggar, to welcome him back in his new office (the first of the ministers' to be refurbished, having given up the former Home Secretary's office for Geoffrey Howe to move into this autumn). Tim is pleased at getting Latin America, and seemed genuinely surprised to be back in the FCO, though presumably disappointed by his non-promotion.

17 JUNE 1987

I arrived in the office to discover that the Prime Minister had refused to agree to last night's proposal to accept a variation of the Iranian compromise on staffing, and had insisted on going ahead with a mutual withdrawal. Geoffrey Howe had argued for an hour, but unsuccessfully. I immediately rang Charles Powell to see if there was any chance of changing the PM's mind, but it was already too late, and instructions had gone to Tehran. The Iranians reacted to our second démarche today by begging that there should be no publicity, since a senior meeting was to be held this afternoon.

This morning's meeting of PUSs produced some interesting reactions to the new ministerial team. Richard Lloyd-Jones (Welsh Office) said that he had to be told three times of Peter Walker's appointment as Welsh Secretary before he would believe it. In a discussion on why the Tories did so badly in Scotland, Clive Whitmore quoted George Younger as saying that there were three crimes in Scotland: 1) to be English; 2) to be a woman; and 3) to be bossy; and Margaret Thatcher had committed all three. The last two crimes listed by Clive Whitmore ring oddly, given the later ascendancy of Nicola Sturgeon.] Kerr Fraser, Permanent Under-Secretary at the Scottish Office, denied that her sex was relevant, and thought it was her condescension rather than her bossiness that put off the Scots. But Andrew Neil of the *Sunday Times*, to whom I gave lunch today, also thought it was personal dislike of Thatcher in Scotland that had done it.

The Foreign Secretary's diplomatic banquet this evening. We sat with the Danes, the Russians, the Nigerians and the David Orrs. I also managed to introduce a lot of ambassadors to Simon Glenarthur and to the new Chief Secretary, John Major.

18 JUNE 1987

Geoffrey Howe had a letter today from Simon Jenkins about diplomatic service reform; some fearful nonsense, which we shall have to deal with carefully, since Geoffrey and Simon are close friends. But interesting that Geoffrey should have invited him to send it.

19 JUNE 1987

Both the Americans and our community partners are putting heavy pressure on us to renew high-level contact with Syria, given some quite clear indications that Abu Nidal's offices in Damascus really have been closed. The next step is to exchange assessments with the Americans, but Charles Powell tells me that the PM is not adamantly opposed to a gradual relaxation. It will be a nice change to resume relations for once, rather than break them off. But it always tends to be a more difficult process.

Charles confirms that David Mellor is very much a favoured high-flier, who might have got a Cabinet job this time round; the Prime Minister, on the other hand, does not know Simon Glenarthur at all.

26 JUNE 1987

I lunched with Robert Andrew (Northern Ireland Office) who is worried that the government will now start to make concessions to the unionists, and hoped that Geoffrey Howe would keep up his breakfast meetings with Tom King, who may need a restraining hand. He speculated on the reason for John Stanley's transfer from Defence to the Northern Ireland Office, wondering whether he was being groomed to be Secretary of State. (Charles Powell told me that it was he who had suggested the move!)

29 JUNE 1987

I was told today of an incident at a recent European Council meeting when Geoffrey Howe had put forward a proposal and sought views round the table, getting unanimous approval, until it reached Margaret Thatcher (sitting next to him), who rejected it out of hand!

2 JULY 1987

Virginia Bottomley attended my morning meeting today and spoke (very well) about Parliament this week, including the Prime Minister's statement on the European Council, South Africa etc. She commented that the new intake of MPs seem even less aware of Foreign Affairs than usual – as did Robert Rhodes James, whom I saw at lunch.

Geoffrey Howe held a drinks party at noon for staff returning from Tehran, including Christopher and Mette MacRae. Of the half dozen I asked, only one said that she would not want to go back. Most of the others would, with enthusiasm.

The PM this morning approved all the No. 10 board proposals, except for Charles Powell's posting to Berne, whom she now says she cannot spare with Robert Armstrong leaving. It is not yet clear whether this definitely scuppers Berne, or whether it is Charles's own doing; nor whether it is related to Cyril Townsend's remark in the foreign affairs debate 'that any fool can be ambassador to Switzerland' – a remark unfortunately made in contrast to the high qualities needed for the ambassador to Syria!

I attended the last session of the East/West heads of mission conference, addressed by David Mellor – very fluent and self-assured, but a bit embarrassing in his tendency to preach to experts (after two weeks' experience in the office).

3 JULY 1987

On the following day, I met the Prime Minister, talking to Ken Stowe at the latter's retirement party, and she referred interestingly to Townsend's remarks, having told me that Berne was not nearly good enough for Charles, and asking whether Madrid would be available for him in two years' time. I replied that Berne was a good job for Charles, with plenty of commercial content; that Charles is not a Spanish speaker; that I hoped that she was not going to let some daft remarks by Cyril Townsend influence her; and that, while I hesitated to make this point to her, another year and a half would put a heavy strain on both Charles and Carla. The PM glared at me, and after answering most of my points, started on about the Europeans and their wet performance at the European Council. She was otherwise perfectly amiable towards me, but made it quite clear that Charles must have any job he wanted.

Charles Powell told me this evening that the PM is prepared to consider gradual moves to resume relations with Iran, but not yet with Syria, by whom she feels personally offended to a much greater extent.

Problems are beginning to emerge between ministers. Apparently, Lynda Chalker chaired her first meeting as Geoffrey Howe's deputy, and crossed swords with David Mellor, who told her, apparently very rudely, that he did not need her advice on how to answer parliamentary questions. She is said to have omitted to consult him about the No. 10 board, and is consulting Tim Renton instead – quite sensible in practice, but not very tactful!

7 JULY 1987

I lunch with Tony Fanshawe at Brooks's. He agrees with me that there is likely to be a reshuffle in about a year, and thinks that Cecil Parkinson is then likely to get the Foreign Office. He thinks that Parkinson would do it well.

9 JULY 1987

An early meeting with Geoffrey Howe and all other FCO ministers on export work. David Mellor put on a strong performance, arguing that diplomatic service officers should be judged and rewarded by the Trade figures in their posts – a suggestion that would have ludicrous implications, and which would have made me a millionaire in Riyadh, as against the permanent representative to NATO, who would presumably have lost his job!

I had both Virginia Bottomley and John Houston to my morning meeting this morning for the first time. Virginia is excellent, and gave a very clear account of what is going on in Parliament. Indeed, her subsequent performances at my morning meetings were so frank that I had to remind under-secretaries that not a word she said was to be repeated outside.

13 JULY 1987

Lynda Chalker asked to see me this morning, mainly to discuss Charles Powell and her worries about relations with No. 10, and to ask if there was anything she could do to help. I doubt if she can; even though the policy advisers at No. 10 are worried about the degree of Charles's influence over the Prime Minister. Lynda also told me that the PM had been heard to refer publicly to Geoffrey Howe as 'that old bumbler'. The *Daily Telegraph* produced an article today claiming that the Prime Minister had decided to run Europe herself, and to take it away from the FCO. (The writer of this article, Norman Kirkham, was at my drinks party last week, but had said nothing that could conceivably account for this nonsense.)

16 JULY 1987

Moroccan state visit this week, at which King Hassan had apparently made a surprisingly good impression (though not on the press).

King Hassan had opened his call on the Prime Minister by saying that he had heard so much about her, including from President Giscard, who had told him she was utterly impossible! George Younger told me that this reminded him of his constituency chairman, who had welcomed Ted Heath to his constituency, saying that everyone had told him what a difficult, impolite and boorish man he was, but how charming he had found him.

King Simeon of Bulgaria told us at the Buckingham Palace dinner for the Moroccans that he had been invited to Buckingham Palace for lunch, but had fainted just as they were going in. The Queen had earlier asked him what his crest was, and he had said 'Saxe-Coburg' – i.e. the same as hers. He had come round lying flat on the floor, and opened his eyes to see the Saxe-Coburg crest on the ceiling. He thought he must have died and gone to heaven!

22 JULY 1987

A visit to the Royal Fine Arts Commission, at which John Wakeham talked very frankly to me about his difficulties in managing the House of Commons, given Neil Kinnock's inexperience and unreadiness to take advice from his more experienced colleagues like Peter Shore and Roy Hattersley.

29 JULY 1987

I paid a pre-leave call on David Mellor, who claimed that Douglas Hurd had told him, on leaving the Home Office, that he would find life a holiday in the FCO, with lots of agreeable travel, and that he had been surprised to discover how hard everyone, including himself, had to work. He is already making a useful contribution to policy, and Geoffrey Howe appears to trust him (though he is worried about his discretion). On a later occasion, when Douglas Hurd was Foreign Secretary, I made some sort of apology for the amount of paper we were giving him, to which he replied, rather squashingly, that it was nothing compared with the boxes he'd had to deal with as Home Secretary.

30 JULY 1987

I paid a pre-leave call on Simon Glenarthur. He is anxious to involve himself helpfully, but, like Lynda Chalker, he is nervous at the prospect of being in charge for half of August.

31 AUGUST 1987

A quiet and undisturbed August, during which David Mellor took charge in Geoffrey Howe's absence, achieving maximum media exposure, including profiles in three of the heavy Sundays in two weeks. His ministerial colleagues must be livid with envy. I found that Geoffrey Howe himself had been put out by this, and was openly looking, on his return, for TV spots for himself.

August has also seen David Owen's apparent eclipse as a politician, following his humiliating defeat in the SDP for his preference against a merger with the Liberals. He looked sad and old on television last night.

2 SEPTEMBER 1987

I told Robert Armstrong today about the John Newhouse profile of Margaret Thatcher in the *New Yorker*, in which Newhouse says that the one organisation for which the PM reserves her greatest contempt is the diplomatic service. After I had moved to my new offices in Downing Street (east) to allow for the refurbishment of Downing Street (west), Percy Cradock tried to call on me in my old office. Finding it laid waste, he told me he had assumed that Margaret Thatcher had finally achieved her aims!

7 SEPTEMBER 1987

This morning I attended Chris Patten's fortnightly meeting with his under-secretaries at the ODA – quite interesting, but useful symbolically as a step towards improving relations between the two wings. Chris is obviously taking a much closer grip on the department than Tim Raison ever did. But relations between the diplomatic and aid wings are difficult, and I am holding a meeting later this week to consider what else should be done.

8 SEPTEMBER 1987

I lunched with Michael Partridge (DHSS), who gave me some background on David Mellor from his Home Office days. Michael agreed that Mellor is bright and very ambitious, though too ready to reach firm conclusions on inadequate evidence.

Michael's responsibilities (with seventy-two under-secretaries) sound formidable, but he seems to work a much gentler week than I do, with virtually no boxes to take home.

11 SEPTEMBER 1987

I lunched today with Rupert Pennant-Rea and others at *The Economist*, and told them my story about Ian Winchester, who was the desk officer for the Buraimi Dispute, and therefore responsible for the red, green, yellow and blue lines on the map demarcating the oasis between Saudi Arabia and Abu Dhabi. It was only later that he was discovered to be colour-blind!

18 SEPTEMBER 1987

A long bilateral with Geoffrey Howe today, during which he aired his worries about not being sufficiently involved in domestic policy, partly because of the Prime Minister's attitude to Cabinet committees. Her response to a recent proposal that OD should meet to discuss the Gulf War was typical – i.e. that it was better discussed among small groups of ministers and officials, as it was in the summer. She does not like those Cabinet committees which she does not chair herself. I undertook to have a word with Robin Butler about the Cabinet committee system.

Although Geoffrey complained to me that his colleagues, e.g. Douglas Hurd, did not speak up in front of the Prime Minister, he is certainly at fault himself.

Charles Powell discussed with me today the Prime Minister's reaction to the FCO bid for improved conditions of service, on which she has helpfully weighed in with the Chancellor of the Exchequer in support, though with a typical sideswipe at FCO 'extravagancies', with a rather obscure reference to the ballroom in the Washington residence. I commented that I thought that ballrooms in residences were exactly what Margaret Thatcher liked? Charles thought it must be a reference to a double redecoration within a few years.

21 SEPTEMBER 1987

Slight embarrassment at my morning meeting when I referred to some proposals by Tom King to 'suspend' the Anglo-Irish Agreement while talks continue with the unionists. Christopher Mallaby reminded me quickly that this was extremely secret, and I had to shut up – conscious that I was blushing furiously. Much amusement among the under-secretaries; Rodric Braithwaite told me afterwards that everyone was relieved and delighted to see Homer nodding for once!

I spoke today to John Acland (Antony's ex-General brother) to follow up reports of improper arms dealing with South Africa. I had told Geoffrey Howe last week that I was slightly nervous of being sued for slander, in spite of the legal adviser's view that this was not possible. When Geoffrey said that he agreed with that advice, I told him it was a comfort to have reassurances from my resident QC.

22 SEPTEMBER 1987

After talks with, and a lunch for, Gilbert Pérol, Secretary General at the Quai d'Orsay, I took him to call on Lynda Chalker. Lynda talked to him for an hour, mainly on community subjects.

25 SEPTEMBER 1987

A minor row blew up this morning over the arrangements made by the embassy in Paris for a Home Office minister, John Patten, which led him to comment that the FCO only gave proper treatment to their own ministers, and to write (according to his private secretary) an offensive letter, saying that if the embassy were not prepared to make proper arrangements for him, they could lend him a car, book him into a hotel, and leave him to himself – pretty ungracious, considering that Ewen Fergusson had offered him the residence and a meal.

29 SEPTEMBER 1987

I gave lunch to Robin Butler, who told me of some extraordinary behaviour by the Lord Chancellor (Michael Havers) at the bicentennial celebrations in Philadelphia this month, at which Havers publicly complained that he had been treated 'like a ghost'. David Wilson later sent a telegram from Hong Kong, saying that Havers had behaved badly there, also showing that he was incapable of mastering a brief or maintaining his attention for more than a minute or two. I am very worried that this could bring forward Geoffrey Howe's transfer. [A few days later, I told Geoffrey Howe about Havers's misbehaviour in Hong Kong and Washington. Geoffrey assured me that there was no question of him becoming Lord Chancellor. It sounds as if another candidate, Lord Mackay of Clashfern, is likely to replace Havers soon. Many years later, we were on the same Swan Hellenic Cruise with the Mackays. I told him that Swan Hellenic was having difficulty fitting Lord Wright of Richmond on their computers. James Mackay replied: 'That's nothing! They call me Lord Mackay of Clash F'.]

30 SEPTEMBER 1987

Discussion at perm secs (the weekly meeting chaired by the Cabinet Secretary) this morning on the new taxation rules, at which the chairman of the Inland Revenue, Anthony Battishill, told an astonished meeting that all gifts were taxable, whether they were passed on elsewhere or not. I pointed out that this presumably made me liable to be taxed on a £4,000 watch offered by King Fahd, and which I had passed on for disposal by Customs and Excise. Battishill looked fairly shaken, and admitted that this was technically correct. He agreed that the rules would have to be looked at again. I also talked to Brian Unwin, who has just taken over at Customs and Excise, and said I would like to discuss with him the whole question of the disposal of gifts. [Geoffrey Howe later pulled a remarkable coup by getting the sale of gifts repayable to the FCO budget to be put towards the purchase of gifts for VIP visitors.]

2 OCTOBER 1987

Other ministerial misbehaviour came to light today, with accounts of a meeting between Lord Trefgarne and the Australian High Commissioner, Doug McClelland, about Australian naval personnel in the Gulf, whom the Australians want to withdraw. Trefgarne apparently implied that Anglo-Australian relations would be severely affected. McClelland is said to be bitterly offended, but efforts are in hand to smooth things down and apologise.

Charles Powell told me it had been a bad week for the PM's relations with Geoffrey Howe, who had irritated her enormously by insisting on arguing that we should keep our minds open on the question of United Nations activity in the Gulf (on which the PM had expressed her views with ludicrous firmness in Berlin).

5 OCTOBER 1987

I started the day with a bilateral with Geoffrey Howe, whose view of one of my colleagues seems to have softened slightly following David Mellor's appreciative comments. Geoffrey said he was prepared to move him from *bête noire* to *bête grise*! His main worry, as he put it, is that a meeting between the Prime Minister and the official in question would be like two trains moving towards each other on the same track.

There is a widespread feeling in the service that if the government really thinks that the economic situation in Britain, and Britain's status, have so improved, we should be prepared to put more resources into abroad. The paradox is that the PM thinks that our status has improved precisely because she has reduced public expenditure. Perhaps she is right?

19 OCTOBER 1987

After my absence in Vancouver for the Commonwealth Heads of Government Meeting (CHOGM), John Caines gave a description of the proceedings at my morning meeting today. Tony Reeve is bitter that all the strategy carefully worked out for CHOGM was totally ignored. The Prime Minister was rather naively affected by what she described as African ingratitude for our aid – quite unjustifiably, since the Mozambicans are constantly telling everyone how helpful she has been to them.

20 OCTOBER 1987

My honours meeting this afternoon broke up after Alan Munro had told an improbable story about a Nigerian chieftain called the Bum of Tum, who was invited to join a Durbar for the Queen, and to give a loyal address. Unable to attend, he sent a telegram saying: 'My Loyal Address is PO Box 1, Tum; signed BUM.'

21 OCTOBER 1987

I had a long bilateral with Geoffrey Howe, much of it on the subject of the PM's isolation and unwillingness to accept advice. Geoffrey discussed the possibility of himself or others, e.g. Whitelaw or Hurd, talking to the PM about it, but they won't. Tony Galsworthy commented that this was nearly a plot discussion. Geoffrey mentioned the possibility of even threatening resignation again, as he did last summer.

He also gave me an account of a private minute that John Houston had given him, recording a talk with Ray Pendleton of the US embassy who, very unprofessionally, had told him that the Americans did not bother at all with the FCO, and concentrated all their attention on No. 10 'which, as we know, tells the FCO what to do'.

Geoffrey also discussed with me how we could keep our position open vis-à-vis the ANC, after the PM's extraordinary outburst at Vancouver, where she publicly called it a terrorist organisation, and claimed that Geoffrey had only met Oliver Tambo in his capacity as President of the European Community. We think there is an FCO spokesman's comment which directly contradicts this and which some clever MP is going to dig up. Geoffrey dealt quite skilfully with the question in Luxembourg yesterday.

23 OCTOBER 1987

A call by our ambassador to Sweden reminded me of the ambassador who called on George Brown as Foreign Secretary. After some discussion on the Swedish economy, George Brown said: 'I hope you won't mind my saying this, but I don't think I have ever met anyone who speaks English as well as you do' – to which his caller replied: 'Secretary of State, you do realise, don't you, that I am the retiring British ambassador to Sweden.'

10 NOVEMBER 1987

I called on David Mellor to discuss Romania in advance of Geoffrey Howe's meeting with Foreign Minister Totu next week. He is turning the heat on the Yugoslavs over the Zagreb air crash claims, and has turned down an invitation from Fitzroy Maclean (already accepted) as a mark of displeasure. I rather doubt whether this is sensible.

12 NOVEMBER 1987

A lunchtime meeting in the office with new Labour MPs – a pretty unimpressive lot, except for Diane Abbott, who infuriated her colleagues by talking too much, but who met her match in Catherine Pestell after a snide remark about the FCO all coming from Oxford and Cambridge. Tim Eggar pointed out that she herself had been at Newnham; but most of them seemed very ignorant and full of prejudices.

16 NOVEMBER 1987

Virginia and I went to the Lord Mayor's banquet, sitting opposite John Wakeham, the Lord Privy Seal, and his wife (an ex-secretary at 12 Downing Street, whom he married after his first wife was killed in the Brighton bombing). She complained that the size of three Conservative election victories had resulted in an undisciplined and inexperienced opposition, who were no longer susceptible to deals 'through the usual channels'. Parliament has been becoming increasingly rowdy, with an expulsion last week.

John Wakeham also told me that the new Lord Chancellor, Lord Mackay, is (apart from Geoffrey Howe) the first Lord Chancellor in living memory (did he mean senior politician?) to have the total support and respect of both politicians and lawyers. Michael Havers is still hanging on to his Admiralty House flat (supposedly on security grounds) immediately below the Wakehams, who either have to pass through the Havers flat or climb ninety-one steps!

18 NOVEMBER 1987

Geoffrey Howe held the third of his priorities and resources meetings today. I introduced the meeting by describing the steady decline in FCO finances, due largely to the high proportion of our expenditure which goes on pay and allowances, inadequately refinanced by the Treasury. Chris Patten played a helpful role, while David Mellor and Tim Eggar vied with each other in claiming to represent the yuppies! Mellor also – with supreme tactlessness – pointed out that East–West relations had previously been given so little importance that they had been entrusted to a parliamentary under-secretary! He is not loved by his colleagues – particularly by Tim Eggar, who is, of course, a parliamentary under-secretary.

1 DECEMBER 1987

A bad day, with two rather unsatisfactory meetings with Geoffrey Howe. This morning's meeting was to look at visa policy in the light of a community threat to harmonise visas, on which Geoffrey was at his most Hovian – dithering and indecisive.

The second was a small meeting on finance, at which he was in a bad temper and grumbling about 'managerial incompetence' over the discovery of a shortfall in this year's budget. But he has had a hell of a programme recently, including unproductive and difficult visits to Madrid and Brussels in the past two days. [Somebody later told me that Geoffrey had been so struck by the look of gloom and despondency on my face at the end of this meeting that he was full of remorse, and wondering what he could do to make me happy! He apparently admitted that he had been quite unreasonable. Two days later, Geoffrey again reverted to his complaints about 'managerial incompetence'. Not much sign of remorse!]

I spent most of the morning and lunch with Jürgen Sudhoff, the newish German PUS (Meyer-Landrut having gone to Moscow). One problem is that Kohl and Thatcher so dislike each other. Sudhoff and I agreed that it would help if they occasionally telephoned each other. Sudhoff told me that Kohl had telephoned her after the Brighton bomb, and felt hurt that she had never called him back.

2 DECEMBER 1987

Alan Urwick called before leaving for Ottawa later this week. I told him that I had pulled Derek Day's leg at Vancouver, saying that he could be confident that he was leaving Canada when the relationship between our two heads of government (Thatcher and Mulroney) could never be worse!

Mrs Thatcher's relations with her European colleagues are not much better. Not only are the press, as usual, painting lurid pictures of Britain versus the rest; we are cross with the French about hostages; with the Germans about the Franco-German Treaty; with the Spaniards about Gibraltar airport; and with the Irish about the Extradition Treaty.

10 DECEMBER 1987

Geoffrey Howe spoke very well at a Near East and North Africa Department (NENAD) heads of mission conference, including a reference to the view of Britain as a 'has-been' – having today seen Julian Amery's account of his call on Sultan Qaboos, who had been told by King Hussein that Shultz had advised him to pay no attention to 'The two European has-beens', i.e. Britain and France. Pretty intolerable behaviour and very unwise; virtually everything said in the Middle East gets repeated sooner or later.

14 DECEMBER 1987

The news tonight reports that Willie Whitelaw [Lord President and Deputy Prime Minister, of whom Margaret Thatcher once famously claimed that every Prime Minister needs a Willie] had collapsed during a carol service – coincidentally, just after some press speculation that Geoffrey Howe might take his place. I am sure that Geoffrey would resist hard the idea of going to the Lords, particularly having just issued a rather magisterial letter to his constituency chairman about the public services.

15 DECEMBER 1987

I was nevertheless told that Geoffrey Howe had this morning been making some rather nervous enquiries of the Chief Whip about Whitelaw's illness and his own position.

17 DECEMBER 1987

The press are still speculating on who will succeed Willie Whitelaw, with a vicious attack on Geoffrey Howe in *The Sun* today suggesting that he is a useless and sleepy Foreign Secretary – 'the worst ever' – and that he might as well sleep in the House of Lords. There is also speculation that Humphrey Colnbrook might succeed; but he told Geoffrey today that he would like to be Governor of Bermuda.

23 DECEMBER 1987

I minuted yesterday on whether the foreign affairs committee should visit

Iran or not. The majority opinion in the office is against; but I endorsed Middle East Department's view that they should go if they want to. Geoffrey Howe was said this evening to be very doubtful, but 'reluctant to disagree with the views of his PUS'!

1988

4 JANUARY 1988

A letter today from Nicholas Barrington, reporting on Lord Glenarthur's visit to Islamabad. I shall have to have a word with Geoffrey Howe about it, particularly since he supervises Hong Kong Department.

Geoffrey is not yet back from his Christmas break, but has been firing off comments and questions throughout!

5 JANUARY 1988

The press today is full of David Mellor's remarks of disapproval ('an affront to civilised values') of Palestinian camps on the west Bank and Gaza – clearly a deliberate piece of publicity-making, though he may genuinely have been driven to go further than he meant to do by his emotional reaction to Israeli treatment of Palestinian children. He nevertheless rang up News Department last night, obviously worried that he might have gone too far. The Independent summed it up, rather unkindly, with a cartoon showing one Palestinian saying to another: 'You have just been visited by the Mellor Publicity Show.'

7 JANUARY 1988

I was told today by David Logan (head of Personnel Department) that the process of getting the present top jobs in place had been a very long tussle with No. 10, and that my own appointment as PUS had only been agreed by Margaret Thatcher as a 'trade-off' for Michael Alexander's posting to NATO. I am not sure if this means that she wanted Michael as PUS, or, indeed, if she was persuaded that he could wait for five years.

8 JANUARY 1988

The Prime Minister's visit to Nigeria shows that she could not resist saying at her press conference in Kano about sanctions: 'We have won the argument.' (Why does she have to spoil things by triumphalism of this sort? She did the same at Nassau, with her gesture to show how little Britain had moved on the sanctions argument.)

11 JANUARY 1988

The PM has clearly returned from Africa convinced that she has acquired a special relationship with Moi and Babangida, and that she really has won the argument over sanctions. It will now be even more difficult than before to persuade her that the rest of the Commonwealth have anything to say on South Africa. She is also apparently convinced that we should have more contact with Savimbi over Angola.

The press today has backlashed against David Mellor over the West Bank, including a particularly poisonous leader in the *Mail on Sunday* against FCO Arabists (and myself in particular), describing Mellor as 'the Boy Minister', sent by me to the West Bank to insult the Israelis. [Peter Jenkins later produced a staunch riposte in *The Independent*, arguing that the 'Rolls-Royce Diplomatic Service' was regularly treated as a scapegoat by ministers and public opinion; that the scapegoats have served us well; and that skilled diplomacy has 'continued to buy Britain an influence considerably greater than our true weight and status in the world'.]

Willie Whitelaw resigned over the weekend, but Geoffrey Howe has not been appointed to succeed him as Deputy Prime Minister. There was much telephoning yesterday, including contact with the Chancellor, about whether Geoffrey should in future chair the Star Chamber. It would be ironic if he decided he could not, after all, put in a public expenditure bid for the FCO because it conflicted with his Star Chamber duties.

12 JANUARY 1988

There is continuing press speculation that Geoffrey will go to the Lords this autumn. Douglas Hurd is today's favourite to succeed as Foreign Secretary, though Nigel Lawson is thought by some to be very keen to be Foreign Secretary.

13 JANUARY 1988

A very full day, starting with a discussion with Lord Glenarthur on how to produce the necessary cuts in our personnel vote this year. He enraged Mark Russell (who already feels that ministers are far too involved and interfering in management and the administration of the service) by saying that he would want to consult not only the Secretary of State but also his fellow junior ministers.

14 JANUARY 1988

Permanent secretaries' dinner at Brooks's this evening, to say goodbye to Robert Armstrong. He told a good story about his appointment as private secretary to Heath at No. 10, allegedly because his predecessor, who had worked for Wilson in his first administration, had prepared beer and sandwiches for Heath and Carrington after a long session in the Cabinet Room. He had announced 'grub up' while Heath and Carrington were discussing whether they should slope off to Lockett's for dinner.

15 JANUARY 1988

Geoffrey Howe told me today that the PM was fed up with David Mellor's performance, and has asked him to tell Mellor to keep quiet (though No. 10 has behaved scrupulously over the affair, declining either to endorse or to repudiate him). Charles Powell tells me that Mellor's promotion chances have taken a very sharp step backwards.

18 JANUARY 1988

David Gore-Booth produced a gem on Margaret Thatcher's attitude towards Europe. In reply to a question from the Foreign Press Association as to whether, after nine years as Prime Minister, she felt more or less European, she said: 'I feel exactly as I have always felt – totally British and ready to do a tremendous amount in this world.'

27 JANUARY 1988

The Foreign Affairs Committee called on Geoffrey Howe today for a general talk. They were then shown the Communications Centre and FOLIOS (the new system for sending enciphered telegrams, which was later shown not to work), before a meeting with Lynda Chalker in the India Office Council Chamber. Quite a helpful session, though Michael Jopling [ex-Minister of Agriculture who was later to serve, and to succeed me, on my European Sub-Committee in the Lords] revealed some hang-ups on the service. When he asked why we sent 'low-grade diplomats', rather than politicians, to important posts like Los Angeles and San Francisco, I denied that they were low-grade; but accepted that there might well be an argument for sending politicians there if they were prepared to spend their own money in maintaining the right 'style'. But the session went well, and Virginia Bottomley told me later that she had heard one of them describing me as 'a good egg'!

I later accompanied Geoffrey to the House of Commons for a formal FAC session on arms control and the Gulf. Very tame stuff and Geoffrey had no problems, though I had to prompt him occasionally on the Gulf.

[A later diary entry was written in February 1999, just after the FAC – now under Donald Anderson – had published its damning report on the Sierra Leone arms affair. They have lashed out at John Kerr, claiming that he has 'failed in his duty to ministers' – about as damning a comment as one can level at an official. John Kerr and the service have been staunchly defended by Tony Blair and Robin Cook – though unkind gossip says that they only did so having been threatened with revelations about the extent to which ministers had been kept informed at an early stage. John Kerr told me that his own, very visible, embarrassment at hearings before the FAC was due to his attempts to tell the truth, and to save ministerial reputations. But the service has been badly damaged – Donald Anderson has talked about the famous Rolls-Royce having turned out to be an old banger after all.]

There is a very damaging piece in *The Independent* today, revealing differences between No. 10 and the FCO on Europe. Both No. 10 and Geoffrey Howe are rightly furious, and there will be a witch-hunt, if not a formal leak inquiry, to discover who has been talking to Peter Jenkins.

An extraordinary letter today from Charles Powell about briefing for a visit by President Ortega of Nicaragua (which has since been cancelled). The letter says in effect that only the Americans know about Nicaragua, and that the PM would want to be briefed by them. David Gillmore is steaming!

29 JANUARY 1988

I saw Geoffrey Howe this morning to discuss the Peter Jenkins piece in *The Independent*, and agreed with him that I should send a personal telegram to Brian Fall in Washington. [Brian later replied, admitting that it was, indeed, he, and apologising for his naiveté in not realising that Jenkins would look for an opportunity to exploit the gap between the FCO and No. 10. Peter Jenkins later claimed to Paul Lever that his source had been No. 10 – perhaps to protect Brian Fall? When I saw Robin Butler today, he told me he had found it strange that No. 10 had not complained about the story – deep waters!]

I received a call from Lieutenant General Vernon Walters, the US permanent representative to the UN, who told me a story, which he attributed to himself, that Cuba is the largest country in the world: capital in Cuba; government in Moscow; army in Africa; and population in Florida. [Much later, I repeated this in a letter to *The Times*, in view of the resumption of full diplomatic relations between the US and Cuba in 2015.]

1 FEBRUARY 1988

Geoffrey Howe had a bad day today in Brussels. We seem, as usual, to have become isolated, and the Prime Minister's recent meeting with Mitterrand and Chirac was very bad-tempered, with the PM at one point telling Chirac not to threaten her.

5 FEBRUARY 1988

I went to Chevening today for Geoffrey Howe's lunch for Dick Murphy – the latter had just seen King Hussein in Paris this morning, and was going on to Damascus and elsewhere to pursue the new Reagan 'initiative' on the Middle East. David Miers and I questioned Dick Murphy so negatively that Geoffrey asked me later to telephone the ambassador, Charlie Price, to thank him for Dick Murphy's visit, and to welcome American readiness to contemplate a new move (which we have been urging on them for months). Charlie barely concealed his own scepticism, and one of Dick's (Jewish) aides made it quite clear that there was no question of Shultz putting any real pressure on Shamir.

John Stanley telephoned me today from home – presumably in a characteristic attempt to bypass his own private office – about a potential FCO recruit for Northern Ireland. After I had told him that the job description provided by Robert Andrew did not fit the official concerned, Stanley virtually said we should ignore anything told to us by officials; he was dealing with this subject. I told Geoffrey Howe later that John Stanley should be a significant contributor to close cooperation between the FCO and the NIO!

The Prime Minister has now cancelled three successive bilaterals with Geoffrey Howe; a string of subjects for discussion are being held up as a result. I wonder if she is deliberately trying to put Geoffrey down – the press is full of stories of enhanced status for Douglas Hurd, Cecil Parkinson and John Moore.

23 FEBRUARY 1988

A long meeting with Tim Eggar about MPs' correspondence on immigration, which he wants Migration and Visa Department to deal with, rather than his own office. I am worried, perhaps unnecessarily, that this goes against the principle of ministerial responsibility, though it apparently follows a Home Office precedent.

I also had a private talk with Lynda Chalker, who is in a depressed mood, having asked Geoffrey Howe about her chances of getting into the

Cabinet, and getting what she described as 'her worst school report ever'. Although she is upset by press rumours that she is going to the commission in Brussels, she left me with the impression that she would in fact like to go there, if she doesn't get a Cabinet job. She also thinks that Geoffrey is likely to be moved on later this year, though Len Appleyard told me that Geoffrey is determined to stay.

24 FEBRUARY 1988

There was a public row today about which department was dealing with Waldheim's war crimes files. An article in *The Times* carries quotes from two press officers (FCO and MOD) revealing an unseemly squabble, which has enraged Geoffrey Howe. The Prime Minister has ruled that the MOD is in charge; but the whole subject has also been a fair muddle, with the (probably false) impression given that important and damaging files have been destroyed.

Christopher Mallaby today hosted a DUSs lunch in the Cabinet Office, at which we had a general discussion about the PM's attitude to Cabinet committees. OD (the Foreign Affairs and Defence Committee) hardly ever meets nowadays – a potentially dangerous situation, as the Franks Committee on the Falklands pointed out [and as I was later to remind the House of Lords in my speech on Iraq on 7 September 2004].

2 MARCH 1988

I attended a meeting held by Lynda Chalker and Chris Patten to look at policy towards Ethiopia and Sudan – quite interesting, but once again I got the impression that it was largely staged to boost Lynda's image as the senior FCO minister.

Robert Alston (Muscat) told me today that David Mellor really has achieved a very good relationship with Yusuf bin Alawi of Oman; as Robert pointed out, this is just as well given the speed with which we change ministers of state!

4 MARCH 1988

An article in *The Independent* by Nicholas Budgen MP, arguing that Foreign Office officials 'can hardly be expected to understand the man in the Wolverhampton pub'. David Wright later wrote a strong minute (which I would dearly love to send to *The Independent*) pointing out that he was born in Wolverhampton, and went to Wolverhampton Grammar School. He thinks he understands people in Wolverhampton pubs better than an ex-Guards and Corpus Christi MP! (Echoes of George Brown, who was staggered to learn that Geoffrey Arthur had been educated at Swadlincote Grammar School, in his own constituency.)

8 MARCH 1988

I discussed with Geoffrey Howe a foreign policy meeting yesterday at Chatham House, on which he was pretty sceptical, agreeing that the experiment might be repeated 'every three permanent under-secretaries'. I suggested that we might settle for 'every three foreign secretaries, or whichever is the less'. [Ironically, if this timing had been followed, we would have been due for the next Foreign Office Day at Chatham House by the time I became chairman of Chatham House in 1995.]

21 MARCH 1988

Geoffrey Howe is very cross with Simon Glenarthur, who wants to spend eight days in Outer Mongolia. He is never happy about other ministers travelling; but he has put his foot down on this occasion.

22 MARCH 1988

David Mellor asked to see me this afternoon to question me about Yehuda Avner's remarks at his recent lunch with me (claiming that he had been working hard to undo the damage of television coverage of the West Bank, and that Jewish opinion is still very solidly behind Shamir). David also asked me about the BBC project to make a film on the diplomatic service, making it clear that he would like to play a major role. He claims, probably rightly, to have played a prominent part in getting the BBC film on Customs and Excise going.

23 MARCH 1988

A long meeting to consider our approach to the public expenditure round. Geoffrey Howe is in a difficult position, having today again been asked to chair the Star Chamber in succession to Willie Whitelaw. I am very nervous that, if he does, he will not be prepared (or able) to press for any extra bid for the diplomatic service or the ODA, let alone the Intelligence Services, if the Treasury have their way and make him defend their budgets with the Chief Secretary. [I later expressed my worries to Geoffrey, who reacted badly, and is obviously attracted by the idea on political grounds.]

Poor David Gillmore is in a state, having discovered that his valedictory despatch from Kuala Lumpur, which contained some very frank and unflattering remarks on Mahathir, has fallen into the latter's hands. There will have to be another leak inquiry.

28 MARCH 1988

I reported to my morning meeting, and later to Geoffrey Howe, on the Wilton Park seminar which I attended over the weekend involving FCO, Treasury, DTI, ECGD, MAFF (Agriculture, Fisheries and Food) and others. Peter Middleton was surprisingly flexible, possibly because he had come straight from a meeting with the Prime Minister on the exchange rate. Her last words to Peter, on leaving for Wilton Park, were: 'Don't listen to anything the FCO says.' He agreed with me that Margaret Thatcher has no idea how to cooperate with people, whether officials or foreigners – quite a comment from the Treasury!

30 MARCH 1988

Both John Caines and Geoffrey Howe are aghast at discovering today that Colin Chandler and George Younger have concluded a Tornado deal with Malaysia, involving an apparent promise of £200 million in aid for Malaysia – with not one word of prior consultation. It is outrageous behaviour, and will lead to a major row. [It did; and resulted in a very rare Permanent Secretary's minute to the Public Accounts Committee by John Caines's successor, Tim Lancaster.] Poor Geoffrey will have to sort it out before he visits Kuala Lumpur next week.

7 APRIL 1988

I went to Cambridge today for a Königswinter Conference, at which four groups were introduced by their chairmen. A member of one of the other groups told me that when Paddy Ashdown, the ex-Liberal Social Democrat MP, was asked to introduce himself, he called himself a Liberal by mistake, and then corrected himself, saying: 'I can never remember what my party is called nowadays.'

11 APRIL 1988

I held a briefing meeting for this week's appearance before the Foreign Affairs Committee, for which we have less idea than usual of the sort of questions they are going to ask. [In fact, I later received good warnings by the clerk, Robert Wilson; but many years later, in 1999, there was a row about the leaking of FAC reports in draft to Robin Cook, which are said to have improperly alerted him – exactly what the clerk did for me.]

20 APRIL 1988

With the release of both hijackers and hostages in Algiers, both Lynda Chalker and David Mellor were asked to appear on radio and television – the former outraged because the latter rang up to offer her advice. She later asked to see me, in a low state of morale, and worried both about relationships between junior ministers, and about Geoffrey Howe's attitude to herself. She is still very hurt by his response to her question about her own future (when he immediately started to praise David Mellor, and then went to sleep!).

But Lynda is also cross because Geoffrey won't let her travel while he is away. She also thinks he may be preparing to give up this autumn, and told me that he is deeply unhappy with several of his colleagues and their policies – particularly Nicholas Ridley and the poll tax. She is scared that Cecil Parkinson may be appointed Foreign Secretary (on the face of it, not unlikely if Geoffrey goes, since he will no doubt have reminded the Prime Minister that he was promised the job during the Falklands War).

A crucial meeting on our PESC [Public Expenditure Survey Committee] bid with Geoffrey Howe and all his ministers (minus Simon Glenarthur, who is in India). The other ministers intervened helpfully, though some of them got their heads bitten off for their pains.

21 APRIL 1988

This evening to the Albert Hall for the fortieth anniversary gala of Israel's independence, which I had accepted largely to correct the *Mail on Sunday*'s impression of anti-Zionists in the FCO. Some difficult moments (e.g. a reading which referred to the Jews returning to 'Empty Zion'); but otherwise a rather jolly evening of songs and readings. And the Chief Rabbi, Jacobovitz, thanked me warmly for my gesture in attending.

25 APRIL 1988

There was aggro over the weekend on Ireland, on which the Prime Minister has responded angrily to Geoffrey Howe's emollient speech, and with fury at Charles Haughey's speeches in the United States. [On the former, Percy Cradock later warned me about the Prime Minister's displeasure, and at Geoffrey's failure to consult her in advance. I did not tell him that this was entirely deliberate, and that Geoffrey had rejected advice that No. 10 should be alerted beforehand. The press was later predictably full of stories about a Thatcher/Howe rift.]

29 APRIL 1988

I went to Chevening for our annual meeting with the Ministry of Defence. I told Geoffrey Howe and George Younger about the Prime Minister's interview in the *Daily Mail* this morning (which neither had seen), in which she talks of the need to return to the manners of the 1930s, 'when there was gentleness and courtesy'. Geoffrey told me he had seen her yesterday, just after she had given the interview, and thought she was exceptionally mild!

3 MAY 1988

I lunched with Ray Seitz for Bob Gates – a very interesting lunchtime discussion, mainly about Soviet foreign policy and chemical weapons. David Mellor spoke frankly and well about the dangers of the President of the United States remaining unable, or unwilling, to pressure the Israelis.

6 MAY 1988

Much of today was spent on the forthcoming Gibraltar SAS/IRA inquest. A ministerial meeting yesterday revealed strong dissatisfaction at the failure of officials to ask the right questions, let alone provide the right answers. David Mellor was charged with the task of discussing with me the possible formation of a special task force. After discussing this with Mellor and Geoffrey Howe, I called on Robin Butler, John Weston and others this evening, and agreed a) that John Weston's official group should meet very regularly in the period up to late June (when the inquest will be held); and b) that Duncan Slater (on leave this week) will be put virtually full time in charge of the affair for the FCO.

I lunch with John Stanley in the House of Commons. The real purpose of his invitation was obscure, unless it was to persuade me that the Northern Ireland Office was 'far from the political backwater that some people assume' – perhaps a bid for a ministerial job in the FCO? He is an odd character: poor with his own civil servants, and obsessed by secrecy and intelligence. His fairly frequent visits to Dublin are cloaked in total secrecy, and often unknown to even his own PUS (now John Blelloch). I rang John this morning to let him know about the lunch engagement, and to say that if anything of interest emerged, I would send it to him in a triple-sealed envelope.

12 MAY 1988

Geoffrey Howe half ticked me off today, having seen the record of my talk with Neil van Heerden (the South African PUS) last week; he thought I had not been sufficiently brutal with him (with some justification). I pointed out that I had merely been running over rebukes which Robin Renwick had already delivered. Geoffrey argued that, with the PM as soft as she is on the South Africans, the rest of us should pull no punches.

14 MAY 1988

I collected Virginia on Saturday evening and drove to Salisbury to dine with Ted Heath at Arundells, his fabulous house in full view of Salisbury Cathedral, with the rivers Avon and Nadder joining at the end of a superb garden. As we arrived, a few guests were already dotted round the garden, drinking champagne, but no sign of our host. I was rather alarmed, when talking to a Swiss banker, to hear him say: 'Ah! Here comes the Prime Minister.' For an extraordinary moment, I thought Ted Heath had actually invited Margaret Thatcher! As it was, of course, it was the Continental habit of calling a Prime Minister (or an ambassador, for that matter) by that title for life.

16 MAY 1988

The press is again full of stories of splits between the PM, Lawson and Howe – with particular emphasis on Geoffrey's relations with Margaret Thatcher. We meanwhile received detailed comments on Geoffrey Howe's draft speech to the Royal Commonwealth Society – every proposed change predictably designed to soften criticism of South Africa, and to heighten criticism of the ANC etc. Since the PM's disagreement over exchange rates is with both Lawson and Howe, perhaps that at least diminishes the prospect of Lawson becoming Foreign Secretary! But the press have pointed out that Geoffrey has now been Foreign Secretary longer than anyone since the First World War.

17 MAY 1988

The PM today agreed a statement saying that she fully agreed with Geoffrey Howe's speech on Africa; she also made a firm statement in the house expressing her full agreement with Nigel Lawson. Geoffrey is still resentful of her style and rudeness in her remarks to the press (e.g. a claim that when told he was waiting during her interview with Sir David English of the *Daily Mail*, she replied: 'He can wait.')

18 MAY 1988

Press articles on Geoffrey Howe continued today, with a particularly bad one on the Powells in the *Evening Standard* last night. I sat next to Peter Jenkins at the Irish dinner tonight. It is generally thought that Bernard Ingham is not responsible for them. Peter Jenkins obviously suspects the Prime Minister's personal intervention; at least, he claimed that she could stop it at once if she wanted to, since most of the articles have come from well-known associates like Andrew Alexander and David English.

I later met Percy Cradock, who confirmed that the PM regards her argument with Nigel Lawson over the exchange rate as over; but she is still very angry about Geoffrey Howe's intervention on the subject last Friday in Scotland. One journalist referred to it as 'indiscretion of Heseltine proportions'.

19 MAY 1988

I talked to Tony Galsworthy about Geoffrey Howe, who is very resentful about the continuing press campaign. There was a sympathetic article by Hugo Young in *The Guardian* this morning, but again contrasting the respective influence on Margaret Thatcher of Geoffrey Howe and Charles Powell, and comparing Geoffrey with John Biffen, who cooked his goose with remarks about the need for 'balance' in government. Geoffrey Owen, the editor of the *Financial Times*, told me at lunch today that he (and, as far as he knew, his staff) had received no calls from No. 10, and he doubted, as I do, that Bernard Ingham is responsible. But it must have been a very rough week for Geoffrey.

20 MAY 1988

I wrote a brief note to Geoffrey Howe today, expressing my sympathy over the continuing press articles about his row with the Prime Minister. In reply, I received the following from him on 22 May.

> Dear Patrick,
>
> It is characteristically kind of you to write as you did – and a great comfort to us both.
>
> You're right, I think, to attribute most of it to the press' herd instinct – and I hope it will not long endure.
>
> The principal irritation is that it risks casting a shadow over our important mission to Hong Kong at the end of this week. All the more reason to be grateful for the support and loyalty of the service – which I greatly value, and yours particularly.
>
> With warmest thanks,
> As ever,
> Geoffrey.

Charles Powell told me today that he doubted if the PM herself was even aware of half the things the press were saying. Unlike some of her predecessors and successors, she pays very little attention to the press. It is said that Clement Attlee was so dismissive of the media that the only way in which the staff could persuade him to agree to have a Reuters ticker tape installed was to point out to him that he could get virtually immediate news of the cricket scores. Contrast my problems with Harold Wilson, when arrangements broke down to provide us with the British newspapers on his travels abroad.

6 JUNE 1988

First day back from my West African tour, with a flurry today about this week's talks with the Iranians on compensation for damage to their embassy premises. [By coincidence, this is being edited within a few days of the Foreign Secretary, Philip Hammond, visiting Tehran in August 2015, after the successful conclusion of negotiations to agree Iranian compensation for their damage to *our* premises.]

President Reagan's visit last week seems to have gone well. He put on a professional performance at the Guildhall, with very few people realising that he was using a prompt machine. He has lavished praise on Margaret Thatcher, virtually claiming that she will have to pick up the baton for the free world after his presidency.

Meanwhile, Geoffrey Howe went dangerously near to endorsing Bush's candidature for the presidency in a television interview yesterday, though the press have so far concentrated predictably on his remarks about continuing to serve under Margaret Thatcher.

Geoffrey is on good form, chuckling over the menu card for the diplomatic dinner in the Natural Science Museum, which contains caricatures in the shape of dinosaurs, two of which are clearly identifiable as Geoffrey and myself. But he is tired after his fairly demanding visit to the Philippines and Hong Kong, and sets off this evening for New York, returning tomorrow before visiting Madrid on Wednesday. Crazy.

8 JUNE 1988

I arrived at the office to find Lynda Chalker also arriving, and in a great stew about the Iranian premises talks. The Prime Minister had attacked her 'in a steaming fury' last night, though it was not clear if she was cross about the substance, or the fact that No. 10 had not been forewarned before the leak last week. Lynda herself was cross at being caught unawares, and talked to me about the difficulty of her position as Deputy Foreign Secretary.

Geoffrey Howe held a ministerial meeting, at which there was a lot of sniping about the handling of the Iran case, with Tim Eggar apparently claiming that it should have been his business, and that Middle East Department (by implication, David Mellor) had fouled it up. Mellor summoned me, and I went over the saga with him, pointing out that ministers and officials shared responsibility for not consulting No. 10 at an earlier stage, and that the leak was partly the fault of a young and inexperienced desk officer. I recalled that I had myself been similarly let down by the *Daily Mail* in Beirut, and hoped that there would not be a witch-hunt against the poor young man. David Mellor said that the atmosphere between ministers in the FCO was quite unlike that in the Home Office, and that he wished Geoffrey Howe would not discuss these problems in front of all the ministers and parliamentary private secretaries.

I attended a meeting with Geoffrey Howe at lunchtime to discuss the Sowan case (related to the murder of the Palestinian journalist Ali). He started by saying that he wished to complain 'in an unexplosive way' about being faced with such difficult decisions, with no prior warning. Having got that over, there was a good discussion; but ministers have concluded that at least one Palestinian and one Israeli are going to have to be chucked out. And the case is almost certain to end while Crown Prince Abdullah is here.

I went to credentials for Fiji, and saw for the first time the Fijian greeting of dropping to one knee and clapping three times. There is a story, possibly apocryphal, of a new and nervous head of mission questioning the marshal of the diplomatic corps about the correct procedure for introducing his staff at the Buckingham Palace diplomatic reception, and being told to follow what the neighbouring head of mission did. Unfortunately, this turned out to be the Fijian!

13 JUNE 1988

Geoffrey Howe had seven boxes of work this weekend. I have asked Tony Galsworthy to go through them carefully and identify which papers he need not have seen. Tony pointed out that papers of that sort are nearly always something Geoffrey has asked for, or was interested in.

Crown Prince Abdullah read his speech at the Mansion House this evening with hardly a hesitation, heaping praise on David Mellor for his remarks in the occupied territories, at which I passed a note to Stephen Egerton saying: 'With thanks like that…'

At a meeting in No. 10, Nigel Wicks told me there were rumours (which he says he does not believe) that Margaret Thatcher may be thinking of giving up next spring; it sounds most improbable, but then, so did Harold Wilson's resignation (which incidentally took Nigel Wicks – then the Treasury private secretary – completely by surprise, until Ken Stowe and I asked him to look up a quotation).

15 JUNE 1988

Percy Cradock called, having just come from a briefing for the Toronto summit, at which the PM had revealed all her old prejudices against the Japanese – 'in a repining mood', as Percy put it.

16 JUNE 1988

I wrote a private note to Geoffrey Howe this morning 'as one of those who contributed to the bucketfulls of cold water poured on his suggestion for last night's dinner' (see 6 June, above) and to congratulate him on its success, and on his speech. I suggested for next year either the Tower of London or the disused underground under Hampstead Heath.

21 JUNE 1988

I lunched with Stewart Steven of the *Mail on Sunday*, who told me that I obviously had a lot of friends, since his editorial about monkeys and organ-grinders (see p. 86, above) had provoked a number of protesting telephone calls, including one from David Owen. The conversation remained very civilised throughout.

We also discovered that both of us had been together on Michael Stewart's visit to Poland in 1965. He told an amusing story about Denis Greenhill trying to stop Stewart Steven from writing a story about the extent of drunkenness, including Michael Stewart, at Polish official dinners in Kraków. I told him that I had completely forgotten it myself – perhaps because I was also drunk! He said that Denis had made it clear that he would tell everyone (truthfully) that Stewart Steven had been as drunk as everyone else.

22 JUNE 1988

Sherard Cowper-Coles, now in Washington, called at 9 a.m., passing on Antony Acland's hope that the Foreign Secretary would accompany the Prime Minister to Washington in November, if only because he thinks the chemistry with Dukakis will be bad (on many subjects, not least South Africa), and that Geoffrey could help soften any confrontation. I am doubtful whether Geoffrey will be prepared to fight that battle, which he would almost certainly lose.

24 JUNE 1988

It later transpired that the PM's visit coincides with the Buckingham Palace diplomatic reception, and that Geoffrey had virtually been commanded to remain for it.

27 JUNE 1988

The Hanover European Council starts today, concentrating on monetary cooperation, on which the PM has already expressed forceful views about the impracticality of a Central European Bank. No doubt there will be more accusations from the French and Germans about our non-Europeanism.

The main interest for us is likely to be the PM's bilateral with Charles Haughey – their first meeting since he made his speeches in the United States. Both Geoffrey Howe and Tom King have tried to calm the atmosphere, and O'Rourke delivered before the weekend a long apologia from Haughey, which won't have helped very much.

29 JUNE 1988

I discussed the Thatcher/Haughey meeting with Percy Cradock, before seeing the record myself. It was predictably hard-hitting, with the PM castigating him for poor security cooperation on the border, and hinting darkly at alternative ways of protecting it (i.e. by sealing the border, which would be formidably difficult). But the atmosphere evidently ended better than it had started, and they agreed quite an up-beat communiqué. The background of Airey Neave's murder and the Brighton bombing adds a passion to Margaret Thatcher's views, which very easily ignites her approach. Haughey, on the other hand, obviously feels misunderstood and aggrieved.

30 JUNE 1988

I was summoned to see David Mellor – fussed about the coincidence of visits to Morocco by Trefgarne and himself, and wanted me to get the Trefgarne visit called off. I pointed out that this could hardly be feasible, but found a compromise which Mellor has accepted. I also discussed security in

Tel Aviv, on which Mellor is spoiling for a fight with Avner, and I have had to restrain him. He really does *loathe* the Israelis.

1 JULY 1988

Judge Webster of the CIA arrived three quarters of an hour late for his call on Geoffrey Howe, having been detained by the PM. Geoffrey told him that he assumed that Webster had been doing all the talking!

4 JULY 1988

I lunched with Julian Amery at the Connaught – an extraordinary fossil, but with some remarkable memories, including seeing King Carol of Romania leaving Bucharest in 1940. He recalled how Denis Greenhill as PUS had tried to sell him the idea of a lease-back for the Falklands, on the grounds that if a right-winger like himself espoused it, it would have wide parliamentary support; he had rejected it out of hand.

7 JULY 1988

We went to No. 10 for Peter Carrington's farewell dinner, at which both the PM and Peter Carrington made excellent speeches, with the PM telling the story of her meeting with the Chinese, at which the latter spoke non-stop for two hours, and Carrington passed her a note saying: 'Margaret, you are talking too much' – an occasion which Carrington himself once described to me as the only time he had seen Margaret Thatcher get the giggles. (When I saw Carrington a few days later, he complained about her speech at his farewell dinner, saying: 'Why does she always have to snipe at the Foreign Office?' [I later saw the text of the speech by Robert Rhodes James, with some very complimentary remarks about the diplomatic service, and criticising his Conservative colleagues for not being more appreciative.)]

12 JULY 1988

I went to Chris and Lavender Patten's drinks party – what a nice couple they are; perhaps too nice to succeed in politics? I was much taken by Cyril Townsend's wife, who told me I was far too young to be a PUS! An interesting comment in view of Tony Blair's later government letting it be known that they were looking for PUSs who were under forty-five.

13 JULY 1988

My bilateral today with Geoffrey Howe was Tony Galsworthy's last appearance as Geoffrey private secretary. I entered the room with a Fijian greeting, kneeling on one knee and clapping three times, since Tony's father was a Ratu from his days in the colonial service.

18 JULY 1988

I lunched with Greville Janner, who repeated, almost word for word, Avner's comment on the expulsion of the Israeli information officer, saying that it left him 'naked' – on the grounds that the Israeli Intelligence Service had succeeded with Arab terrorists in the way that the British evidently could not. I decided not to point out the anomaly of a British Member of Parliament relying on a foreign Intelligence Service for protection.

19 JULY 1988

Geoffrey Howe's speech at his farewell drinks for the Galsworthys included a reference to the *Financial Times* description of Christopher Meyer as 'the thinking man's Bernard Ingham', describing Tony Galsworthy as 'the common man's Charles Powell'. Tony in turn quoted someone as saying 'happy is the man whose wife tells him what to do, and who has a secretary to do it'. I was not sure that Elspeth was totally amused.

21 JULY 1988

I attended the opening of the arms control heads of mission conference, at which David Mellor made a particularly unfortunate reference to the 'awful possibility' of a Dukakis victory – in front of four academics invited to join the conference. I have also heard that Denis Thatcher is alleged to have been making disobliging comments about Dukakis to an American journalist.

Humphrey Maud called before his departure for Nicosia, gloomy about Personnel Department's proposals to change much of his staff soon after his arrival (which reminded me of Dick Beaumont's response to Personnel Department's invitation to him, for the third time in succession, to ask his head of chancery in Cairo (i.e. me) to keep 'a careful eye' on some junior member of staff: 'May I remind you that my head of chancery, unlike Cerberus, has only two eyes.')

25 JULY 1988

Geoffrey Howe called me down to tell me that David Mellor was about to be moved in a ministerial reshuffle, and would be replaced by William Waldegrave. I pointed out to Geoffrey that there would inevitably be speculation that Mellor had been kicked out for his pro-Arab views, particularly on the very day when the press are reporting that the Israelis had pulled five intelligence officers out of London. Perfect material for some Arab conspiracy theories! Geoffrey then spoke to Nigel Wicks, suggesting that the timing of the move might be reconsidered. He apparently reverted to this twice more, provoking an irritated call to me from Nigel this evening.

But the move has gone ahead, and Waldegrave will appear in the office tomorrow. Mellor was contacted in a public telephone booth in Italy, but is evidently delighted by his new job in the Ministry of Health, which can at least be presented as promotion to be deputy to a new Secretary of State, Kenneth Clarke. I am fairly certain that the move is indeed related to Mellor's pro-Arab attitude, and recall that Charles Powell told me on Friday that 'Mellor really has gone too far this time'. A pity to move someone after one year, when he has established excellent contacts in the Arab world. But he has become a bit unbalanced about the Israelis, and shows it.

26 JULY 1988

I called on William Waldegrave, and found him rather bemused by his grand office and commenting, like all new ministers, that he was suffering from a slight hangover, having celebrated his appointment last night. He told me that his previous Secretary of State, Nicholas Ridley, had told him, as a fellow younger son of a peer, that he had found the FCO full of older sons (precise meaning obscure?). I told William that Nicholas Ridley had recently told me that he had not in fact enjoyed his time in the FCO – no doubt partly because of the Falklands debacle.

Waldegrave seems very nice and intelligent, though I wonder if he quite realises what the pace of work is likely to be. He is hoping to start with a five-week holiday.

I received a warm and appreciative letter from Virginia Bottomley – the third of Geoffrey Howe's PPSs to get promotion in the reshuffle (the others being Kenneth Clarke and Richard Ryder). On the whole, the press have presented Mellor's appointment as a promotion, though Hella Pick had a piece in *The Guardian* suggesting that he had been removed for his anti-Israeli views.

29 JULY 1988

At my farewell lunch for Rodric Braithwaite (to Moscow), Simon Jenkins of the *Sunday Times* talked to me about ministerial visits abroad, claiming (rather ludicrously) that the FCO misused their ministers, who should devote their attention to the House of Commons, and that only ministerial Lords should travel. I pointed out that this would severely reduce ministers' credibility with their foreign contacts. Simon responded by saying that contact-making was for diplomats, not ministers – fairly ripe from a journalist who has claimed in the past that ministerial activity has virtually made the diplomatic service redundant!

8 SEPTEMBER 1988

Geoffrey Howe discussed with me the PM's increasing tendency to keep work to herself and not to consult her colleagues. There has just been a ridiculous incident about a military paper on an Ireland commissioner from the Ministry of Defence, which No. 10 has commanded is not to be seen by anyone else. As Geoffrey commented, this is the way that bad mistakes happen.

9 SEPTEMBER 1988

We received today our six-month delivery of a haunch of venison – given to permanent secretaries and, I think, certain Cabinet ministers, on condition that we pay for the delivery charges.

12 SEPTEMBER 1988

I was telephoned by Tim Eggar about an incident today where a Cuban diplomat fired a gun in the street – following closely after a major row with the Vietnamese, whose gun-toting third secretary was expelled. Tim has decided that, on this occasion, the Cuban ambassador should be chucked out. The incident hit the headlines two days later. (When Geoffrey Howe returned from Africa eight days later, he was put out that Tim Eggar had not consulted him, even though he was technically in charge of the office during his absence, and had consulted No. 10 instead.)

14 SEPTEMBER 1988

An interesting side-light on Margaret Thatcher today from Rodric Braithwaite, who saw her yesterday before returning to Moscow. When he discussed dates for Gorbachev's visit next spring, a reference was made to the PM's tenth anniversary in May, at which she commented: 'If I'm still around.' Everyone was mystified, but she appeared to be serious – presumably from superstition about the risk of assassination. I remember that Nigel Wicks once told me privately that there were rumours (unexplained) that the PM did not think she would be at No. 10 beyond next spring (see p. 104, 13 June, above).

19 SEPTEMBER 1988

My morning meeting was largely taken up with a discussion about Tim Eggar's campaign against diplomats' use of guns, and non-payment of fines, which has got massive press coverage, but which threatens to turn into a declaration of war against the diplomatic corps. I have advised that we should cool it, particularly since further action against one embassy is going to be needed this week.

20 SEPTEMBER 1988

The PM spoke today in Bruges – the culmination of a lot of drafting and redrafting. John Kerr managed to achieve about 80 per cent of our proposed changes to Charles Powell's draft (which had earlier been compared to *The Jimmy Young Show!*); but it is still a pretty harsh statement of the PM's attitude to federalism in Europe, coloured by her strong personal resentment of Delors, whose appearance at the Trades Union Conference will have done nothing to assuage (although John Weston pointed out today that the PM had almost certainly not read his speech in full, since it contained several well-planted olive branches).

21 SEPTEMBER 1988

The PM's Bruges speech is again widely covered in the press, most of it critical. Bruce Anderson in the *Telegraph* says it was clearly written by Charles Powell, and that No. 10 would not have asked the FCO to write it, since it is known how different their views are on Europe. But most commentators have pointed out that it is her style that is wrong. The PM herself is no doubt delighted by the storm she has caused, and by comparisons drawn with de Gaulle. A few days later, Charles Powell told me that the PM's dinner with the Belgian Prime Minister over dinner in Brussels had been pretty rough, and that she had thoroughly enjoyed a good row over the future of Europe.

22 SEPTEMBER 1988

I summoned the Czech ambassador today to expel three of his staff for espionage – about the fourth expulsion of diplomats within a few weeks. Tim Eggar tomorrow summons a group of ambassadors to talk to them about fire-arms and parking fines. I asked today for proper guidance to be sent to posts, to reassure governments that we have not declared war on the diplomatic corps. (I later record that the diplomatic corps were very steamed up about Tim Eggar, and that the Cypriot doyen had asked to call on Geoffrey Howe about it.)

The Japanese ambassador called this afternoon on instructions to hand over letters of 'astonishment and aversion' to the editors of *The Sun* and the *Star* at their outrageous editorials on Emperor Hirohito (who is dying).

The Sun said that he should go to hell, and that many Britons would gladly dance on his grave. Apparently, the embassy telephoned one of the papers, but got someone whose father had been on the Burma Railway, and who was extremely rude.

4 OCTOBER 1988

I reported today to William Waldegrave on David Mellor's conversation with me last night about his Middle East contacts, having told me that he hoped that the FCO agreed that he should not let them drop. I encouraged him, but asked him to bear in mind William Waldegrave's position, since the Arabs are all too prone to develop one point of contact and influence.

6 OCTOBER 1988

I lunched with John Blelloch, and had a useful talk on Northern Ireland. He had at first found Tom King quite difficult, though they have now got used to each other. He told me that John Stanley (who was sacked in the last reshuffle) had made a row because his mail in the House of Commons is not being scanned for security. He also insisted, while in Northern Ireland, on his private secretary travelling in a separate car. As his private secretary was a girl, John had assumed that Stanley did not want it thought he was too intimate with her. The real reason (revealed by John Stanley's detectives) was that when they stopped at traffic lights, he always lay on the floor.

7 OCTOBER 1988

Chris Patten is writing Geoffrey Howe's Foreign Affairs speech for Brighton. Geoffrey is not proposing to show it to the PM in advance.

10 OCTOBER 1988

I gave Lynda Chalker lunch today at Lockett's (with the dreadful Alfred Sherman from No. 10 at the next table). Lynda is still very worried about her future, and was probing to see if I thought she was likely to reach the Cabinet in the next reshuffle. I have no idea, but rather doubt it.

11 OCTOBER 1988

A poisonous document surfaced today on British foreign policy, published by the 'Committee for a Free Britain' (an extreme right-wing organisation), illustrated by a photograph of Geoffrey Howe apparently giving a Marxist salute in Mozambique. I advised Geoffrey that there was no future in his suggestion of showing them despatches or submissions designed to correct their impressions of the office. There might be advantage in getting some of them round for a talk. But their document will have several ready ears at the Brighton conference this week.

Quite an interesting discussion with DUSs this morning about developing relations with Taiwan, on which there is fairly consistent pressure from the business community. I had to turn down a suggestion this week from Ray Whitney that I, or another FCO official, should meet the Taiwanese Foreign Minister, who is here on a private visit.

12 OCTOBER 1988

John Boyd and I attended a meeting in Robin Butler's office to prepare a brief for the three ministers (Geoffrey Howe, George Younger and Douglas Hurd) who will have to argue with the chief secretary on agency finances. Robin (himself an ex-Treasury official) is taking a splendidly robust anti-Treasury line, including advice to keep the front page of their brief well covered from peering Treasury officials.

I got into trouble today through Catherine Pestell passing on to Tim Eggar a comment which Lynda Chalker had made to me about the British Council in Helsinki. Tim immediately complained that Lynda was interfering in his business, and Lynda was cross with me for having passed it on. They all squabble like children.

13 OCTOBER 1988

Whitehall dining club this evening, at which I sat between Jeremy Morse and John Baring, discussing Europe and the Prime Minister – a subject much in the news today, following Ted Heath's intervention at the party conference in Brighton.

30 OCTOBER 1988

Jet-lagged and short of sleep from our visits to New Zealand and Australia, I received a haggard and nervous Simon McDonald in the drawing room this afternoon (while [my daughter] Olivia took Virginia off to the garden) and was asked, rather formally, if he could marry Olivia. Great news; they both seem blissfully happy.

3 NOVEMBER 1988

David Harris, the MP for St Ives and Geoffrey Howe's new PPS (succeeding Virginia Bottomley), called on me this morning, and then attended my morning meeting. An ex-journalist who is still finding his way round the office, he made quite a useful contribution on events in the House of Commons this week (when the government was nearly defeated on eye tests).

I briefly attended a counter-terrorism exercise, under Simon Glenarthur's chairmanship, in the Cabinet Office briefing room – a joint exercise with Barbados, for which William Waldegrave has flown to the island. Rather inconveniently, a real (though minor) crisis occurred today with a coup in the Maldives, with a request to us, the Americans and the Indians to intervene. Archie Hamilton, the Minister of State in the Ministry of Defence, asked me this evening if we had a military commitment to the Maldives. I confirmed that we had not, and told him in confidence that we had recently discovered that we *do* have some sort of commitment to one other Commonwealth country, though we do not think that their government is aware of it!

9 NOVEMBER 1988

The results of the US presidential election came through during the night. The PM telephoned George Bush early this morning to congratulate him (no doubt greatly relieved that it is not Dukakis). James Baker was quickly appointed Secretary of State, and Geoffrey Howe sent him a comradely message as an ex-Chancellor of the Exchequer.

10 NOVEMBER 1988

Virginia and I went to the President of Senegal, Diouf's, return banquet in the RAC's very splendid dining room. I was told by Bill Heseltine that he was proposing to wear the boutonnière of the Ordre du Lion (which we had both been allowed to receive), so I did likewise. Bill was mocked for wearing it, so he removed it, as did Ken Scott. Paul Greening (the Master of the Household) had meanwhile seen mine and put his on, as did two others who had seen Ken Scott's. A scene from a French farce?

15 NOVEMBER 1988

A bombshell today from Nicholas Ridley's officials in the PSA, who revealed that Ridley was about to write to Sonny Ramphal confirming that he proposes to take off the top floor of Marlborough House, which would mean that it would be another five or six years before the Commonwealth Secretariat could reoccupy it. I held a meeting to arrange for a minute to be drafted for Geoffrey Howe to send to Ridley pointing out the snags. The PSA tend to be an unguided missile, and Ridley is particularly resistant to advice from the FCO, having had unhappy memories of his time as an FCO minister (Falklands and all that).

21 NOVEMBER 1988

William Waldegrave gave me lunch at Le Poule au Pot. He is very worried about *The Times*'s correspondence on the FCO, and the question of alternative foreign policy advice; he is convinced that Geoffrey Howe was mistaken to weigh in on Monday with his very robust letter. There were two very unhelpful letters today from Andrew Gilchrist and Louis Heren – both tending to confirm the impression that the FCO pursues its own policies regardless of ministerial direction. This really is rubbish, particularly with our present ministerial team.

28 NOVEMBER 1988

A large FCO and ODA ministerial and official meeting today to discuss the geographical distribution of aid. Geoffrey Howe passed me a note at the beginning of the meeting saying that he found the subject matter 'ineffably tedious'. Basically, the problem is how far the ODA are prepared to use aid money for political, rather than developmental, purposes, though when I said this at the meeting, I was howled down by the ODA participants.

5 DECEMBER 1988

The press is still full of articles criticising the Prime Minister for her handling of the Belgians and the Irish over the Patrick Regan extradition case, including some surprising attacks in the *Daily Mail*, claiming that she is not making adequate use of Foreign Office advice. In fact, the Belgians have behaved outrageously, and fully deserve the public rebuke that the PM gave to Maartens at the European Council in Paris.

I discussed with Peter Gregson (PUS at the Department of Energy) some complications over ministerial visits to Peking, with both Lord Young and Peter Morrison planning to visit simultaneously, when Alan Donald is away on leave.

6 DECEMBER 1988

Following a talk I had with Geoffrey Howe yesterday about human rights and Gorbachev, Jim Callaghan told me today that a television interview that he had given a few weeks ago about Soviet prisoners of conscience had been followed by a heavy postbag from young people in this country, arguing that we should look at the beam in our own eye before talking about motes in others. I mentioned this to Geoffrey this evening.

[A later entry, dated 31 August 1999, records a comment made by Valerie Strachan of Customs and Excise that one of the troubles of having such a young group of Cabinet ministers was that they tended to ignore the advice of their senior officials and permanent secretaries, on the grounds that anyone over fifty was over the top. Robert Cooper had also told me that he didn't think that Robin Cook trusted any of his officials; but neither did any of Robin Cook's officials trust him!]

14 DECEMBER 1988

I discussed with Geoffrey Howe Lord Young's behaviour over BP and the Kuwait Investment Office, on which he has grossly failed to consult either the FCO or the Department of Energy in talking directly to the Kuwaitis.

Geoffrey sounds thoroughly fed up with him, and commented that he is beginning to doubt the value of their private meetings, since 'he seems to have no political instincts'.

16 DECEMBER 1988

David Mellor was to have given a talk today on his year in the FCO, but had to cancel with Edwina Currie's resignation over salmonella in eggs (leaving him in the sole glare of publicity at the Department of Health).

1989

5 JANUARY 1989

Ministers seem to have been fairly quiet over Christmas, with not too much jostling for the television screens (though William Waldegrave has not done badly over the PLO and the Chemical Weapons Convention in Paris).

9 JANUARY 1989

I put forward to Geoffrey Howe for his return this week a paper on top appointments for 1990–92. [Interestingly, nearly all of them turned out to be wrong, with the exception of John Weston for NATO. My forecast for PUS (also wrong) was, at this stage, Robin Renwick.]

11 JANUARY 1989

Geoffrey Howe returned from his Arabian visits this morning – a good trip, with some warm and encouraging discussions in the Gulf. But he was furious at being kept waiting five hours by King Fahd. Both he and Stephen Wall were all for leaving without seeing him. Not surprisingly,

Stephen Egerton and David Gore-Booth had talked him out of it, at the cost of getting some stick for being 'typically camel corps'.

12 JANUARY 1989

I lunched with Peter Middleton at the Reform Club. He thinks Nigel Lawson would like to be Foreign Secretary, but his wife Therese refuses to fly; she seems to have spent much of his career travelling to and fro on long-distance liners. Peter also admitted that Lawson does not like foreigners. We both agreed that Cecil Parkinson was unlikely to be made Chancellor of the Exchequer.

George Soros called on me at noon, to describe his initiative to inject capitalism, as he put it, into the Soviet Union. An extraordinary man, of Hungarian origin, who started life as a waiter in a Wheeler's restaurant. He is now a multi-billionaire, with good connections in Hungary and the Soviet Union of Armand Hammer proportions. I found him very nice. A curious, and unusual, blend of extreme enthusiasm and originality, with realism about the economic prospects in the Soviet Union, which he regards as a catastrophe. He was here to solicit the Prime Minister's interest and support for his ideas when she meets Gorbachev.

16 JANUARY 1989

William Waldegrave's call on Arafat in Tunis, and his reference to Shamir's past as a 'terrorist', has led to a renewed storm in the press about FO twits and anti-Semitism. The PM was said to be furious (no doubt with her Finchley constituents in mind), and has issued an instruction that there are to be no more statements, and clarifying her own views as: a) that we do not accept the idea of a Palestinian State; b) that we still believe in the idea of a Palestinian confederation with Jordan; and c) that she has no intention of receiving Arafat himself.

17 JANUARY 1989

William Waldegrave asked me to call, primarily in order to seek reassurance about his remarks in Tunis. I told him that any minister seen shaking hands with Arafat on television could have expected similar flak. I added that I did not personally disagree with one word he had said. I also pointed out the illogicality of accepting the idea of a confederation with Jordan, but not the concept of a Palestinian State. What else would Jordan be confederated with?

William had to answer a Private Notice Question (PNQ) in the House this afternoon, and got about 95 per cent support from MPs, with only two hostile questions from Greville Janner and Ivan Lawrence. The PM stayed behind on the bench, and much improved William's morale by saying 'well done' at the end.

When Charles Powell called this afternoon, he told me that the PM's real objection to William's remarks about Shamir was that it was 'bad diplomacy', and not designed to encourage the Israelis to be more forthcoming. I take this with a grain of salt (and why not encourage Arafat to be more forthcoming by agreeing to receive him?). When I later congratulated William on his performance in the House of Commons, he was clearly much relieved, commenting that he had at least lived to fight another day.

18 JANUARY 1989

I joined Simon Glenarthur and Janet Young for a meeting to discuss the foreign affairs debate next week in the House of Lords, at which Janet wants to speak helpfully about the service. I gave her some ideas, and will probably also talk to Denis Greenhill, who has offered to help. The debate has been sparked off by Roy Jenkins, and is probably designed to reveal, or invent, splits between No. 10 and the FCO on European policies.

22 JANUARY 1989

I spent all day demolishing two boxes, on my return from visits to East and West Berlin, including a brief report from Geoffrey Howe of his talk with the PM about top appointments in the service. She seems determined to keep Antony Acland in Washington beyond his sixtieth birthday, which throws our scenario into some disarray, unless David Hannay becomes PUS and Robin Renwick goes to Washington in, say, 1991 or 1992.

23 JANUARY 1989

A series of fairly wild telegrams from Stephen Day in Tunis about Arab/Israel and the PLO. William Waldegrave is nevertheless (or should I say therefore?) much impressed by him, and commented that the office was not exactly over-full of people so full of new ideas.

I later joined John Fretwell for a talk with Lieutenant General Vernon Walters, the US ambassador-designate to Bonn. I tried to encourage him to listen to John Fretwell (since he claimed to be calling in order to seek our wisdom and advice on Germany, rather than simply regale us with garrulous stories). An entertaining man; but a bit over the top.

A worrying letter today from David Goodall about Peter Morrison [now Minister of State for Energy, and ex-chairman of the Conservative Party], who got drunk in David's residence and poured out offensive attacks against the FCO, saying that we were all useless wimps; hated throughout the Conservative Party; and despised by the PM, 'for whom Charles Powell was the only useful member of the service'. David received some apologies from him next morning. But, *in vodka veritas*?

24 JANUARY 1989

I received a group of French parliamentarians, of different political parties, to discuss the implications of 1992 on the civil service and the diplomatic service. The three socialists tended to argue that there should be a European public service, with total interchange between nationalities; while the Gaullist and UDF (Union for French Democracy) members looked sceptical. In response to their question, I told them that I was *pretty* certain that there would still be a British diplomatic service in 1993; but that I was *totally* certain there would still be a French diplomatic service!

I lunched at *The Observer*, as the guest of Donald Trelford, who had just returned from Tehran with Tiny Rowland, who appears to be doing vast amounts of business with the Iranians, including developing their tea business, with Kenyan advice. Trelford himself had seen Velayati, who had claimed to be put out by his talks with William Waldegrave in Paris, on the grounds that two major powers with worldwide interests should have more to discuss than one British prisoner in Iran, or three British hostages in Lebanon. Trelford seems, from his own account, to have responded well.

25 JANUARY 1989

I had a drink with William Waldegrave, who is very worried by reports of Tiny Rowland's activities in Iran, and warned me against Donald Trelford, whom he distrusts.

26 JANUARY 1989

Chris Patten called this evening to describe an encounter with Peter Morrison in the House of Commons, who had launched a vicious attack on the FCO in general, and David Goodall in particular; he said that he usually gave heads of mission two out of ten, but that David Goodall deserved zero out of ten. He also criticised the aid programme, saying that it was a waste of money. Chris claims that he replied that if he or Peter Morrison ended their careers having done as much for British national interests as David Goodall, they should be happy. I read Chris Patten extracts from David Goodall's personal letter, explaining that I had given Geoffrey Howe an account without revealing David Goodall's identity. I pointed out that at least Peter Morrison launched his attacks against heads of mission known to be outstandingly good.

I paid a quick visit to Australia House for their annual reception, and congratulated Simon Glenarthur on his speech in the House of Lords debate, at which both Denis Greenhill and Janet Young had spoken up well.

7 FEBRUARY 1989

Geoffrey Howe was very pleased with his meeting today with Velayati, and impressed by him 'as a man you can do business with' – the PM's description of Gorbachev. David Gore-Booth is a bit worried that Geoffrey may have been too nice to Velayati in discussing the Iran/Iraq War.

12 FEBRUARY 1989

Secretary of State Baker's first visit to London, as part of an initial tour of NATO countries in eight days. Discussion was mainly on East–West relations and Strategic Nuclear Forces. Geoffrey Howe put up a strong marker on the need to resist sanctions against South Africa, and our hope that the new administration would give priority to Arab/Israel. A very cautious reaction on the latter suggests that Baker has no wish to move at all fast.

20 FEBRUARY 1989

After a weekend of conflicting statements out of Iran on whether Salman Rushdie was still 'condemned to death', EC foreign ministers met in Brussels this afternoon to discuss their reactions. The French, having withheld their ambassador from returning to Tehran, proposed that all EC heads of mission should be withdrawn in protest at Ayatollah Khomeini's latest outburst. This puts us in difficulty, since Nick Browne had already recommended on security grounds that it would increase the risk to the rest of his staff if he was withdrawn. There were complicated negotiations by telephone between William Waldegrave and David Gore-Booth in London, and Geoffrey Howe and Rob Young in Brussels. These were interrupted by the Prime Minister in Frankfurt (for the Anglo-German summit) to say that all UK staff should be withdrawn, and Akhunzada-Basti, the Iranian diplomatic representative, told to leave London. (She apparently told Geoffrey Howe that if any of them were harmed, she would hold him personally responsible.) A sad development, just as we were trying to get back to more normal relations; but hardly surprising, given Iranian behaviour (and some intelligence that the Iranians were actually trying to put assassins to work).

21 FEBRUARY 1989

I am worried by our increasing tendency to close embassies at precisely the moment when you need someone in post. The staff in Tehran will be in a fairly demoralised state; for one or two of them, their heavy luggage and cars only arrived in Iranian customs this week. *The Independent* later had an uncomfortable account of discussions in Brussels, with a fairly accurate version of the PM's telephone call to Geoffrey Howe, together with a claim that our eleven European partners were chortling at having wiped out the British presence in Tehran again.

28 FEBRUARY 1989

Problems have arisen over the PM's visit to Africa at the end of March. The Home Secretary is pressing for the introduction of visas for Turkey and the Maghreb (including Morocco) – a longstanding case that will cause us both political and administrative problems. On the Sudan, the Joint Intelligence

Committee (JIC) have produced a paper on its security and stability, which will almost certainly lead the PM not to go there. She is keen to go to Namibia instead (arriving on the first day of the United Nations presence), and Geoffrey Howe is disinclined to argue against. The department would have preferred her to go to Cairo, and William Waldegrave has dropped a major brick by giving the Egyptian ambassador the impression that she wants to go there, which David Gore-Booth has had to unscramble.

My talks with the Austrian PUS, Thomas Klestil [one of the few of my opposite numbers who went on to become Head of State], were mainly, as expected, about Austria's application to join the European Community (on which Margaret Thatcher was already showing her dislike of the thought of 'another German' joining the club). The community is in no mood to absorb any new applicants, with Turkey already in the queue. Klestil made the point that Austria had saved Europe from Turkey in 1683, and would find it difficult now to be beaten into Europe by the Turks.

1 MARCH 1989

William Waldegrave is in Israel (having been preceded by stories of snubs from Shamir, who has refused to see him). He circulated yesterday the draft of a speech which he proposes to deliver in Israel on Sunday, entirely on the Arab/Israel question – quite a flamboyant and personalised piece, on which he has invited comments (with a clear message that he wants minimum changes). Geoffrey Howe only saw it this morning, and was much alarmed by it. He has sent William a telegram, after discussion with me, warning him that a speech by a British minister exclusively on Arab/Israel, and made in Israel, would be very controversial in Parliament here, and that he really should widen the theme. William will be dismayed, particularly since he sent it to Geoffrey with a personal note, saying that he hoped Geoffrey would discourage officials from changing it.

10 MARCH 1989

With Geoffrey Howe's agreement, I spoke to Charles Powell today about the PM's contacts with the Israelis. Moshe Arens, as Foreign Minister, has recently sent a message to her which Charles has asked the office not to reveal to the Israeli ambassador. I pointed out that this was playing the Israeli game of trying to drive wedges between the PM and her Foreign Office ministers. Charles predictably said that the PM would not want to cut off this sort of direct contact and channel; and at least we could be sure (!) that Charles would keep us informed – unlike David Wolfson, who used to be the PM's channel to Peres. Charles suggested that Geoffrey Howe might want to raise the issue directly with the PM – commenting that he was prepared to bet that he wouldn't!

16 MARCH 1989

I had a cheerful bilateral with Geoffrey Howe – chortling at his own wit in referring to a PUS bilateral as a 'two-sided cat' (he always addressed notes to me under the heading of PUSS).

29 MARCH 1989

Both the Prime Minister and Geoffrey Howe are travelling – the PM having now completed the Moroccan and Nigerian legs of her African tour. Both visits seem to have gone well, though the press have literally invented a story that King Hassan kept her waiting for an hour (with some highly offensive editorials suggesting that sleazy little monarchs should learn better manners). He was in fact scrupulously punctual throughout.

Geoffrey Howe has completed his visit to Pakistan, where he had good talks with Benazir Bhutto. Here again, the press have played up the very dignified protests he received about Salman Rushdie, as if he had been caught in a riot.

31 MARCH 1989

A great flurry over the House of Fraser affair, with *The Observer* producing a special mid-week edition on Mohamed Al-Fayed – subsequently blocked by an injunction (but only after it had appeared widely). The DTI totally failed to let us know what was happening until I telephoned Brian Hayes last night, to enable us at least to brief Roger Westbrook in Brunei. Simon Glenarthur telephoned from Scotland this evening, obviously put out that he had not been kept *au courant* (not surprisingly, since David Colvin had tactlessly, and incorrectly, hinted to him that he had not been kept informed because of his friendship with interested parties). I reassured him that the only reason for excluding anyone from full knowledge of the affair was extreme DTI sensitivity, and that Geoffrey Howe had ruled that it was only to be handled by the absolute minimum of officials.

3 APRIL 1989

Both the Prime Minister and Geoffrey Howe returned from their travels over the weekend – the PM's visit to Namibia coinciding with a massive incursion of SWAPO guerrillas from Angola. This created a major crisis, which the PM seems to have handled with extraordinary skill and firmness, virtually taking charge of the entire UN operation, and speaking very firmly to Pik Botha in Windhoek. She really has made an extraordinary impact wherever she went.

5 APRIL 1989

Easter banquet this evening, at which I pointed out to Tim Eggar that the menu contained a list of Lord Mayors, including one thirteenth-century mayor 'permitted to retire by command of the King'. I told him that I thought this might be a new formula for resolving diplomatic service structural problems!

6 APRIL 1989

The first day of Gorbachev's visit, marred by a furious letter from No. 10 about an alleged shambles at Heathrow last night on his arrival. The main problem seems to have been Leonid Zamyatin's failure to introduce or control the Soviet delegations and swarms of Russian delegates, and security and the press got in the way.

7 APRIL 1989

I drove with Geoffrey Howe to the Guildhall for Gorbachev's speech, and the Prime Minister's reply. A glittering occasion, and superbly organised. I was added to the procession, in order to catch the cavalcade to Windsor for the Queen's lunch.

A very select lunch list, with myself sitting between Denis Thatcher and Trevor Holdsworth (president of the CBI). The setting at Windsor was superb, with the Coldstream Guard of Honour in their Crimean great-coats. A fascinating exhibition had been laid out in the drawing room, with exchanges of telegrams between George V and Kalinin on the gift of the Sword of Stalingrad, together with masses of photographs, documents and Fabergé items (including an open diary by a member of the royal family who attended a Tsarist wedding anniversary in the 1850s).

18 APRIL 1989

A ten-day visit to the United States, joining Geoffrey Howe in Washington on my last day, for a call on the House Foreign Affairs Committee; a call on Vice-President Quayle – much more impressive and self-confident that I had been led to expect; two hours at the State Department with Baker, Kimmitt and others; a press conference and TV interviews before a call on the Senate Foreign Relations Committee; and a call on President Bush, with

Baker, Scowcroft, Bob Gates and Roz Ridgway, while twenty photographers and journalists shouted questions at the President, which he totally ignored, as he spoke to Geoffrey. It is apparently a well-accepted ritual that Bush never answers any questions in these circumstances.

But it was a relaxed discussion, with Geoffrey Howe covering all the points on his checklist, with Bush himself seeming to be totally in command of every subject covered. We went on later for a third session at the White House, with Scowcroft and Gates – mainly on SNF and Germany. None of this appeared visibly to exhaust Geoffrey, who was looking impatiently for work to do on the aircraft later.

20 APRIL 1989

Lunch at Carlton Gardens for the Federal Secretary for Yugoslavia, Lončar. One of the guests was Cibi Stewart, widow of my boss in Cairo, Dugald Stewart, and a heroine of Tito's partisans. When asked by the waiter if she wanted red wine, she was heard to say: 'I'm ready to try anything – even incest.' The waiter looked a trifle startled. Presumably a reflection of Churchill's alleged advice that you should try everything in life, except for country dancing and incest?

26 APRIL 1989

Percy Cradock called, worrying about Europe, and the risk that the Prime Minister is again isolating herself over the Delors report and Economic and Monetary Union (EMU). Practically everyone in Whitehall and the City thinks that we should join the European Exchange Rate Mechanism (ERM) except for Margaret Thatcher. [An interesting comment, in view of subsequent developments over 'Black Wednesday' and the rows sparked off by the Lamont and Major autobiographies.]

27 APRIL 1989

I called on David Howell at the House of Commons, to brief him very privately on the new SIS headquarters, which is concealed in the FCO estimates, and on which the Foreign Affairs Committee may well press me at their hearing next week.

Alan Donald wrote to me today to say that Peter Morrison's visit to Peking had gone very well; I had confirmation from Peter Gregson that Morrison had much enjoyed it – particularly riding round Peking with Janet Donald on bicycles!

2 MAY 1989

The Prime Minister had three successive meetings over the weekend with her Dutch, Italian and German opposite numbers (Lubbers, De Mita and Kohl). She clearly enraged her interlocutors by the dogmatic and dismissive way in which she pressed her arguments on SNF, telling De Mita that she was coming to the conclusion that Kohl was no longer a reliable ally (a remark which will certainly get back to him).

Geoffrey Howe told me at Chevening this morning that he was very worried by the way in which she was now going over the top, and fears that, on the substance, the Americans may be tempted to do a deal with the Germans, leaving the PM stranded. As usual, Geoffrey bemoaned the fact that, on such crucial arms control questions, there had been no structured ministerial discussion at all. I told him that I thought it was unfair and inefficient that the burden was all on him, in his bilaterals with her, to tug her back from excessive Euro-bashing. She is still steamed up about the Delors Report on EMU, on which Nigel Lawson is trying to edge her back from slamming all the doors.

The Prime Minister is showing increasing signs of hype – perhaps because of her tenth anniversary this week. But the press is almost unanimously critical, including even Tory writers like Peregrine Worsthorne in the *Sunday Telegraph*.

I asked Perry Rhodes today about press reports of David Mellor's misbehaviour at his Nordic conference, which I addressed last month. It appears that Mellor grossly insulted the Swedes, by offensive references to their neutrality in the war. But Perry commented that it was a bit difficult to be too fierce about it, since all the other Scandinavians present obviously shared his sentiments.

3 MAY 1989

I had two hours in front of the Foreign Affairs Committee this morning, with much concentration on why people are resigning (a particularly alarming figure of eight fast-stream new entrants last year). Some quite useful points on pay and accommodation, though I had to steer a careful course between appearing to lobby the Treasury via the FAC or I might have seemed to be complacent (with members of the staff side present, and taking notes).

4 MAY 1989

The press today were full of blasts against the European Commission, which heightened the impression of a train running out of control, combined with all the hype surrounding the PM's tenth anniversary today. I discussed this with Geoffrey Howe this morning, who is working quietly with Nigel Lawson to find ways of cooling the atmosphere, and trying to arrange sensible corporate discussion. It is astonishing that OD has never once met to discuss SNF and arms control, let alone wider political relations with Europe. (Have they completely forgotten the criticisms of the Franks committee, and the failure to convene Cabinet committees?)

8 MAY 1989

In the intervals of a meeting at Chevening with the Ministry of Defence, I discussed with Geoffrey Howe and William Waldegrave the handling of Rafsanjani's latest threats, inviting the Palestinians to kill five Americans, French or Brits for every Palestinian killed in the Intifada. We are hoping to mobilise the French, Russians and Japanese into some effective condemnation (and later summoned both the Russians and the Chinese to the office). The PLO has already issued a very good statement after Bassam Abu Sharif had telephoned William Waldegrave at home over the weekend.

Ray Seitz has, most unusually, given William Waldegrave copies of two telegrams he has sent to the State Department, summing up the changes in Britain over the past ten years – moving, as he put it, from being a 'diplomatic leg-iron' to an effective and energetic ally.

9 MAY 1989

I lunch with Tom McNally, now working for Hill+Knowlton. He is still an active Liberal Democrat, and a member of their federal executive. He claims to be optimistic about the chances of the centre parties, but he would, wouldn't he? Their performance at the recent Welsh by-election was pretty calamitous.

I asked Robin Butler today whether he thought the renewed press stories that Geoffrey Howe was about to be sacked were well-founded. He replied that the PM had almost certainly taken no decisions yet, but commented that, while listening to Geoffrey giving a very moving and lucid tribute to the PM's anniversary at Cabinet last week, he was reminded of the harsh cold world of politics; there are now only four members of the PM's original Cabinet left.

Virginia and I went to the state banquet at Buckingham Palace for the Nigerians this evening. One senior Nigerian only arrived after dinner, apologising to the Queen for having missed the President's aircraft because he didn't have a wife, and had therefore not been woken up in time. We both sat next to the Lawsons – she is a rather naïve, young Catholic, and talked a bit about her religion (with a husband who is an agnostic Jew). She clearly does not enjoy official life or travel.

10 MAY 1989

Following confirmation of a firm raft of top appointments with Geoffrey Howe, he discussed it today with the Prime Minister, resulting in practically all the agreed appointments going prematurely awry.

11 MAY 1989

We went to the Nigerian return banquet at Claridge's this evening, at which one British guest said to me, while we were walking in to dinner: 'How nice to see Jack Gowon here. What a wonderful man he is. He has never been known to say a nasty thing about any of his successors.' This was said loudly in the hearing of Ted Heath, who must have thought it was pointed at him.

15 MAY 1989

John Kerr came to see me this morning to discuss his very private drafting sessions with Tim Lankester at the Treasury on European Monetary System (EMS). Both Geoffrey Howe and Nigel Lawson have asked them to prepare a paper designed to persuade the PM to change her mind. John tells me that they were both in a very macho mood last week, and were talking about EMS as a resigning matter. When I commented that I hoped Geoffrey was taking care to bind Nigel Lawson closely to him, John said that he did not trust Lawson at all, and thought that Geoffrey could well find himself provoking the PM into sacking him. John is understandably nervous about his own role in this.

David Hannay told me today that Peter Morrison had told him that Geoffrey Howe would definitely be removed in July, and that Cecil Parkinson would take his place (though I doubt whether even Morrison yet knows the PM's real plans). The row over Europe intensified today, with Michael Heseltine and Ted Heath weighing in with powerful speeches for the European elections. When I lunched today with EC heads of mission, they were all anxious to know why the PM has suddenly decided to handbag the community so violently. Several of them agreed that Delors's appearance at the TUC conference in Bournemouth had enraged her (though in fact what he said had not been at all bad – see p. 113, above).

16 MAY 1989

Geoffrey Howe made the annual speech to the CBI this evening. It is noticeable that his criticism of Ted Heath for lack of 'generosity' (he had originally wanted to add the word 'gallantry') received spontaneous applause from the CBI. He later addressed community heads of mission, commenting, on the new American administration, that the change from Shultz to Baker was likely to be far more significant than the switch from Reagan to Bush. Geoffrey clearly still feels uneasy with Baker, and his tendency to 'UDI' (Rhodesian Unilateral Declaration of Independence), as he puts it. Baker's reputation in the State Department was well illustrated by a savage lampoon in an April Fool's Day issue of the State Department's staff magazine, which claimed that Baker was working on his management relations, and was about to be introduced to his own personal secretary.

Later in the month there was an article by Jeremy Campbell in the *Evening Standard*, arguing that Bush had deliberately turned away from the special relationship that Reagan had enjoyed with Margaret Thatcher, and that American priorities had moved to Japan. John Whitehead told me, during my visit to Tokyo this month, that he and his German colleague had nearly walked out of some function at which the former United States ambassador, Senator Mansfield, had described Japan as America's leading partner, and that Europe now took second place.

19 MAY 1989

This week has illustrated the extent to which international affairs are now dominated by problems of the movement of people – whether it is Turks pouring into Hackney, or Vietnamese boat people swamping Hong Kong.

I think that the Home Office will have to face up to the need for effective post-entry controls, which in turn would require compulsory identity cards – described by the PM in the *Daily Mail* as 'totally repugnant' (though a quick poll at my morning meeting revealed that not one of them, like myself, would in the least mind being forced to carry identity cards – nor would my driver, when I asked him today). But perhaps this is not a typical cross-section!

31 MAY 1989

Renewed stories in the press that the PM is about to sack Geoffrey Howe seem to have done some good. The PM is said to be furious about them. Having confirmed that the stories did not come from No. 10, she said loudly in Brussels that it must have been the work of aspiring promotees. She then went out of her way to say nice things about Geoffrey at her press conference, some of which were reflected in today's press, including a story that there will be no senior reshuffle this summer, though I think that Lynda Chalker and Tim Eggar are almost certain to move.

To No. 10 for a dinner for Prince Sultan of Saudi Arabia. [My diary records an earlier occasion when I had attended a dinner for Prince Sultan, when I was home on leave from Saudi Arabia. I had received a message to say that Mrs Thatcher would like me to be at the front door to help her receive the Prince.

When I turned up, she asked her private secretary for the placement. Having looked at it, she said: 'Sir Patrick is sitting far too low down the table. As an ambassador, he should be much higher.' To which I told her that I had once been told by my ambassador in Washington that an ambassador at home has as little status as a bishop abroad, at which she snorted: 'As far as I am concerned, bishops at home don't have any status'.]

At the end of the evening, I had a discussion with the Prime Minister about Syria and Hafez al-Assad, in the company of Peter Holmes, chairman of Shell, and Roger Tomkys, a former ambassador to Syria who was now an Assistant Under-Secretary. She looked slightly alarmed to find herself in the company of three Syrophiles. Shell now does a lot of business in Syria (through their American subsidiary, Pecten) and Margaret Thatcher is one of the very few British politicians who has seen Assad from time to time.

1 JUNE 1989

I went over to 12 Downing Street with John Fretwell, David Gillmore and Paul Lever for Geoffrey Howe's meeting with Jim Baker, while the PM started her *tête-à-tête* with Bush. The press again were full of stories about the diminished special relationship, which Bush did some good work to correct publicly.

But a series of DUSs have been to see me to express their concern at the way the Prime Minister has left our relations with Europe in a state of disarray. Geoffrey Howe has asked John Kerr and John Goulden to write up a paper to send to No. 10 before the Madrid summit. But it will not be easy to write, and I doubt whether Geoffrey will in fact issue it.

At the Queen's lunch for the Bushes, Virginia and I had a talk with

Elspeth Howe about the possible sacking of Geoffrey, about which she seems pretty fatalistic, saying that they only need to get their domestic arrangements in place. 'It's bound to happen sooner or later.'

2 JUNE 1989

William Waldegrave was in the soup today, having had to admit that it was he who told a journalist that the Russians had tried to suborn Labour MPs (on which there has been an exchange of correspondence and PQs between the Prime Minister and Neil Kinnock – with the PM denying that the government had ever claimed this). I thought William might well have to resign, but it looks as though he may have got away with it. It will increase Geoffrey Howe's sensitivity to junior ministers a) talking to the press; and b) dealing with intelligence questions.

8 JUNE 1989

The problem of Vietnamese boat people was discussed, rather unsatisfactorily, at OD this afternoon. The Prime Minister was said to have been at her worst, simply failing to listen to any arguments she disagreed with. In a later discussion with Geoffrey Howe, he told me that the Prime Minister is very impatient at what she sees as the FCO's failure to think up solutions, and is moving towards a policy of 'pushing off' – apparently oblivious of the appalling implications, with photographs reminiscent of Palestinians and Jews in 1947 in sinking boats and drowning children.

The press are now claiming that neither Geoffrey Howe nor Nigel Lawson is to be sacked. I walked round the park this morning with Peter Middleton; we both agreed that nobody really knows, though Nigel Lawson is said to be in a very jumpy mood.

9 JUNE 1989

Joe Haines wrote an article in today's *Daily Mirror*, following my statement that 'I was sure that any [eavesdropping] devices had no connection with the British government', commenting that I was the sort of person able to convince a naked man that he had egg on his tie!

12 JUNE 1989

I gave lunch today to William Waldegrave, who is still very anxious about his row with the BBC (following John Sergeant's report that Soviet expellees had been trying to suborn Labour MPs), and obviously came near to resignation last week. He clearly thinks his chances of promotion have been damaged.

Robin Butler today delivered the expected bombshell, telling me that the Prime Minister had 'decided' that Charles Powell should stay on at No. 10; that he had been disgracefully treated by the FCO ('though not by Patrick Wright, who has always been a loyal supporter'); that he needed a more political job, like political director; and that he might succeed Robin Renwick in South Africa if (or when) Robin becomes PUS. Robin Butler had to make it a condition of talking to me that nothing would be said to Geoffrey Howe, of whom she had made some very disparaging remarks. I pointed out that, at the very least, I would have to discuss with the Foreign Secretary alternative candidates for Madrid. After Andrew Turnbull had joined us, we arranged to have a 'trilateral' meeting with the Prime Minister tomorrow.

13 JUNE 1989

Robin Butler called on me at 8.30 a.m. to say that he had just come from a private meeting with the Prime Minister, at which he had taken a very tough line on Charles Powell's future.

Andrew Turnbull, Robin and I met in the PM's study at 4 p.m. for a full hour of very tough talking. Robin and I put forward very strongly our advice that Charles should resume his diplomatic career; that the PM had already agreed (in writing) to the destination and timing of his next post, after three changes of post and six changes of timing; that talk of Charles being 'crucified' (the PM's word) was ridiculous; and that Carla had been stirring up trouble, and claiming to me that the FCO 'had it in' for them both.

I pointed out, particularly in comparison with the postings of Charles's predecessors (Luxembourg, Vienna, Amman and Budapest), that Charles was getting a highly prestigious and important job. The PM lashed out savagely, accusing Robin Butler of twisting the constitutional position – saying that she was not bound to accept either his advice or mine. She several times implied that she could not go on without Charles, and that she might resign herself. At another point, she said that it would be either Charles or Geoffrey Howe. She also said that she would simply not work with any successor, and she knew that there was no one of Charles's character; this gave me a chance to say that we had two candidates in mind, one of whom was a very experienced speech-writer, and the other described by Antony Acland as the best diplomatic service officer he knew – the last point made her look a little thoughtful for the moment.

The PM railed against the FCO, saying that its watchwords were negotiation and compromise; that she had had to fight them all the way on Rhodesia, Falklands, Hong Kong, Europe and NATO. The only good advice had come from Charles. I reminded her that we had given her three first-class private secretaries, and would do so again. She quoted Philip de Zulueta as someone who had been allowed to stay on for seven years, and no one had dared to fight Macmillan. Why were we fighting her? I pointed out that the FCO had, at that time, thought that de Zulueta was damaging his FCO career, as indeed he did. Robin tellingly added that de Zulueta had regretted his departure from the service all his life.

At one point, the PM misinterpreted me as saying that she had forced Nicky Gordon Lennox out of Madrid, and added mysteriously that she would be quite happy to see him come back as PUS. (A Freudian slip, reflecting her thinking about Charles's future after Madrid? Or perhaps a comment on her plans for me?) Throughout this meeting, she was moderately polite to me personally, saying that she knew I was a 'loyal friend' of Charles.

After the meeting, Robin, Andrew and I spent half an hour in the Cabinet room discussing the fallout of this discussion. Robin really does seem to be serious about his position; he told Andrew that he felt that his reputation as Cabinet Secretary was at stake, having conveyed to me a written assurance that Charles Powell would be released for Madrid.

14 JUNE 1989

Permanent secretaries had an interesting discussion this morning about style of government, with widespread criticism of the way in which the PM is attacking everything and everyone – Europe, NATO, the economy etc. – without proper ministerial discussion or strategic thinking.

16 JUNE 1989

I took the opportunity of a private meeting with Geoffrey Howe today, after our 'bilateral', to give him a full account of my meeting with the Prime Minister. This led on to a discussion about the PM's attitudes, and her current tendency to attack everyone and everything. Geoffrey seemed quite grateful that I had taken the brunt, particularly since (as Robin Butler had mentioned to me) he and Nigel Lawson have just put in a minute on EMS, referred to by John Kerr as 'the resignation minute' – i.e. virtually saying 'accept that the time is getting near to join, or we shall both resign'.

18 JUNE 1989

John Kerr telephoned me late this evening about the EMS Paper, on which the PM has apparently (and typically) tasked Charles Powell and Alan Walters to produce a reply. One theory is that she may agree to an earlier move on EMS, provided all talk of a social dimension is dropped – a ludicrously unattainable objective. Her first reactions to the Paper are said to have been very bad.

19 JUNE 1989

Virginia and I went to Geoffrey Howe's diplomatic banquet in the Duveen Gallery at the British Museum – discreet checks having been made to confirm that the Greek ambassador did not object violently to eating next to the Elgin Marbles. Adam Fergusson (Geoffrey's PPS) buttonholed me after dinner to ask if anyone had yet checked with the Spanish to see if they would actually accept Charles Powell. The Spanish have broken away from the Conservatives in the European Parliament, and Adam thought there was a serious likelihood that they would refuse. That really would be an ironic twist to a long-running saga!

20 JUNE 1989

The Charles Powell saga continued today with a visit from Robin Butler to tell me that the PM had rejected our advice, and had told him that only his resignation would force her to release Charles. Robin showed me his minute in reply, saying that it was not right to base her actions on a threat. He strongly reiterated his advice, and rehearsed at length the timetable of events over Charles's postings (for which I had spent a weekend going over Charles's personal file, and preparing a paper for Robin). The next crunch will come with Geoffrey Howe, who told me this afternoon that he was not prepared to let Charles stay on. I am not at all sure what my own position is, since ultimately it is presumably open to the PM to decide what to do.

21 JUNE 1989

I told Geoffrey Howe the latest news about Charles Powell, and he asked where that left him. He was not at all sure that he should not regard it as a case of Charles or himself. He described his meeting with the PM and the Chancellor last night on EMS, and said gloomily that even if the PM was prepared to indicate some shift in her position at Madrid, she would certainly do it with such bad grace, and setting such impossible conditions, that all negotiating advantage would be lost. He was about to see Nigel Lawson, and told me (very privately) that both of them were getting very near to resignation. He was seriously worried about the PM's state of mind, and the damage it was doing to the nation. He frankly wondered if Douglas Hurd or Cecil Parkinson could do the job better.

I said that I hoped he would not do anything in a hurry, and that he would make sure that Nigel Lawson kept firm. I pointed out that Lawson was probably readier to leave politics for the City than Geoffrey himself; he acknowledged that this was probably true. But for the first time ever, he told me it was not much fun, and that all his dealings with No. 10 had become a perpetual hassle. I said that I was personally glad that I had at least been able to take one hour of abuse off his shoulders last week.

John Kerr tells me that, following the meeting between Geoffrey Howe and Nigel Lawson with the PM, Lynda Chalker had asked Geoffrey how it had gone, to which he replied: 'None of your business.' Not surprisingly, she is on poor form at present.

22 JUNE 1989

Resignations are still in the air today. Tony Fanshawe told me at lunch that Lord Young had handed in his resignation to the Prime Minister last night because he was 'fed up', though it was not clear what with. Geoffrey and Nigel Lawson have meanwhile decided to return to the charge on EMS after their recent meeting, and Geoffrey appears to be in a fairly robust mood today.

Virginia lunched with Elspeth Howe this afternoon, who told her that Margaret Thatcher was totally impossible. 'We should all stick together, and to our guns.' She said that it was a pity that all this could not be leaked.

Geoffrey Howe discussed Hong Kong with me today, wondering whether he should have gone on *Panorama*. I said that several people had told me they thought it was a mistake, but I had seldom seen a politician put in such a difficult position. I would certainly have advised him beforehand to do it, given the need to get across the government's case. He is thinking of writing to John Birt about the programme, which I think is probably a mistake.

23 JUNE 1989

Andrew Turnbull telephoned me at 5.30 p.m. to say that the Prime Minister had reached her verdict on Charles Powell, and wished to keep him. He asked me to let Geoffrey Howe know, before he and the PM meet 'over the weekend'. Andrew asked me if I wished to see Charles this evening. I said rather stiffly that I saw no need. Charles knew well enough what my views were on where and when he should go.

I then talked to Robin Butler, who had already heard the news, and was in deep gloom about it. I said that I had not yet told the Foreign Secretary the news, but would feel bound to rehearse in full the arguments which Robin and I had put to the PM. Robin said that this was entirely reasonable.

I then had three telephone conversations with Geoffrey (two of them from his car), who became more and more determined to oppose the decision. I warned him that the PM was almost certainly immovable on the subject, and I really saw no alternative to going along with it, unless Geoffrey felt he could deploy the political dangers for the PM, and the government, of the decision. I pointed out that the constitutional arguments were not strong (though it is theoretically open to the Foreign Secretary to refuse to recommend Charles for further ambassadorial appointments).

I talked also to Stephen Wall, who agreed with me that a real confrontation with the PM was more likely to lead to Geoffrey's departure – either by resignation, or by being sacked. I set out the arguments in a long minute, including (at Geoffrey's request) the de Zulueta precedent and parliamentary handling. Tam Dalyell and David Winnick will have a field day when the news breaks, as will Michael Heseltine, whose resignation was of course closely tied up with Westland and Charles Powell's involvement.

Robin Butler tells me that he does not think he can continue to work with Charles Powell, and must look forward to a possible seven years with the Prime Minister with some trepidation.

I had a meeting with Geoffrey Howe to discuss the very difficult decision of whether to allow BAE to sell Hawk Trainers to Iraq, which Geoffrey (quite rightly) wants to put to OD.

1 JULY 1989

On return from a visit to Khartoum (just in time, since a coup nearly delayed our departure, which would have made us miss Marcus, my eldest son, and Rebecca's wedding), I discovered that Geoffrey Howe had not yet sent his minute to the PM about Charles Powell, having been advised (probably rightly) that the tough draft that I had produced last week was too confrontational, and might even precipitate Geoffrey's departure from the government. Stephen Wall had produced a more emollient draft, which Geoffrey had not liked either. I therefore sat down at 5 a.m. and produced a third draft, which was collected from a neighbour's house in East Sheen and taken to Chevening (after we had departed for the wedding at the registry office in the Marylebone Road, and for Stuart Bates's wedding breakfast in the Savoy).

3 JULY 1989

A telegram arrived from Geoffrey Howe in Hong Kong (where he is having a tough time trying to explain government policy on the right of abode), giving a slightly revised version of my draft minute, which I later showed to Lynda Chalker, after it had been issued. Lynda told me that an MEP friend of hers and Robin Butler's had told her that Robin was in a more depressed mood than he had ever seen; and that Robin had allegedly said that he was ready to accept a good offer of outside employment. I did not comment on this.

I later called on Robin, who is still agonising over what to do. I sympathised, and said that any suggestion that he might resign would have made his continuing relationship with Margaret Thatcher very awkward. He commented that, given her personality, it might actually have increased her respect for him. Winning battles over her opponents does not increase her respect for them.

5 JULY 1989

An early start for breakfast with Lynda Chalker at the Royal Horseguards. She expects a reshuffle on 17 July, but not involving major Cabinet posts. She was visibly unsettled to see a group of Cabinet ministers (David Young, John MacGregor, Tony Newton and Francis Maude) also breakfasting, and was madly trying to work out why. She is very jealous of her ministerial colleagues, and particularly William Waldegrave.

William Waldegrave asked me to call to try to find some money for the Hungarians, where he is visiting next week. He has caught the PM's disease of wanting to hand out goodies on every overseas visit – a tendency that has already distorted the aid programme. When I explained the difficulty of getting more than minimal sums, he admitted that he was not used to working in a department with such a small budget.

I am worried about David Gore-Booth's overenthusiasm for the Arab cause, and his tendency to infuriate the Americans unnecessarily. Not surprisingly, there are signs that the Jewish lobby are starting a campaign against him. He needs to watch it.

Tim Lankester paid his first call since succeeding John Caines as PUS of the ODA. I briefed him on FCO/ODA relations, and the relationship of both of us with No. 10, who have leaked some wild remarks by the PM on moving the ODA right out of London – related, as I told him, to the PM's neurosis about being surrounded by too much Foreign Office.

I accompanied Geoffrey Howe to lunch with Sultan Qaboos of Oman at one of his adjacent houses in Upper Brook Street. On arrival, we were ushered into a large salon with two, apparently original, Canalettos on the wall. I told Geoffrey they must be photographs, but he discovered later that they are indeed genuine. After waiting for ten minutes, and having been offered orange juice, I asked whether the Sultan knew we were there, and was told that he was still with George Younger upstairs. After a further delay, we were ushered into the street, and into the next-door house, where again nobody seemed to know what was happening. It finally emerged that we were supposed to be in a third house (also adjoining), where Qaboos had just arrived. Gin and tonics, and champagne, were then served for us both (though not for the Sultan or Hussein bin Ali).

A very nice and interesting lunch party followed, including Robert Alston, Tim Landon and David Gore-Booth. All cutlery was gold plated and each guest was given the choice of five main courses, following lobster and caviar served in vast quantities. Qaboos was fairly relaxed about Soviet–Iranian relations, following Rafsanjani's visit to Moscow, on the grounds that they are not natural allies, and on both political and religious grounds Iran is more likely, in due course, to mend her fences with the West.

I called Robin Butler to discuss Nico Henderson's diaries, which he has submitted in unedited form for pre-publication clearance. I shall have to tell Nico that they are simply not on; they break almost every rule in the book in his comments on ministerial relationships, royal conversations and official advice. I expect to have a tough time with Nico, who will argue, with some justification (as did Christopher Meyer many years later, in connection with his book *DC Confidential*) that he has not done anything which many ministers have been allowed to do. [Nico finally only got clearance for the publication of his memoirs by appealing to Douglas Hurd after my retirement – Douglas himself having strong (and not totally objective) views about the Radcliffe rules, and indeed the rules restricting intelligence records.]

7 JULY 1989

Further talk of reshuffles today. Geoffrey Howe told me that Simon Glenarthur has decided to leave government. Simon himself invited me to call, saying that he could no longer support his children's schooling on a ministerial salary. I expressed suitable regret and appreciation for the interest he has taken in the service.

At Geoffrey's request, I asked Denis Greenhill to call after lunch, to sound him on possible ministerial talent in the Lords, and in particular on Lord Caithness. Denis confirmed that Caithness is a very popular and effective minister (for the Environment). He also commended Baroness Hooper and Baroness Elles, though Geoffrey later told me he did not think the latter would do – far too powerful a personality. I would like to see Janet Young back again, but she is probably much too dug in to her private life, and would find it difficult to accept junior ministerial rank again, having once been in the Cabinet.

When Charles Powell called, and I had suggested that we regard the dossier about his future closed for the time being, I put in a plug for more access to No. 10 for FCO under-secretaries, saying that the PM had twice told me she would welcome this. When I asked about reshuffles, he said (no doubt correctly) that he knew too much. [A sign of the times; in my day, reshuffles were handled exclusively by the principal private secretary and the Cabinet Secretary.] He did however tell me, very privately, that the FCO would have quite an extensive, if not total, reshuffle, and that he regarded Geoffrey Howe's departure as 'not impossible'. On that, he says, the PM's mind is not yet made up.

Otherwise, he thought nearly all the jobs would change: Lynda Chalker to the ODA, to be replaced by Francis Maude; and that Glenarthur would 'probably' leave (he was clearly not aware of Simon's own decision).

I gave lunch to John Blelloch – a relationship that needs constant attention, given Tom King's desire to keep all Northern Ireland affairs to himself. Tom will almost certainly move on, perhaps to be replaced by Chris Patten?

10 JULY 1989

A poisonous editorial in *The Independent* on Hong Kong, claiming in effect that the PM wants to do the decent thing, but that Geoffrey and the FCO are stopping her. It calls for Geoffrey to go. In any other paper, I would have assumed that this was inspired from No. 10; but I doubt whether *The Independent* (which, like *The Guardian*, has opted out of the lobby system) is susceptible to this.

I telephoned Denis Greenhill to tell him that Lord Cairns (formerly Simon Garmoyle) had put his name to No. 10 as an interested ministerial candidate. As ex-head of VSO (Voluntary Service Overseas), he might well be a plausible candidate.

11 JULY 1989

I asked the US ambassador to call at 4 p.m., to receive a wigging on US attitudes to Vietnam boat people, on which they have been very obstructive and unhelpful. Henry Catto explained the domestic sensitivities on anything to do with Vietnam; but I pointed out that this hardly justified unhelpful lobbying against us in Geneva. I also drew a contrast with the Americans' treatment of asylum seekers from Haiti, Mexico and El Salvador. They have forcibly returned some 19,000 Haitians since their agreement with 'Baby Doc' in 1981.

13 JULY 1989

Tristan Garel-Jones tells me he thinks the reshuffle will be on 24 July, and that Geoffrey will not be moved, since the PM could only get rid of the 'big three' if she was seen to promote younger people, of comparable status and ability, in their place; and that none had been identified. He agreed that Chris Patten was being strongly pushed forward; No. 10 had apparently planted some questions in the House this week to enable the PM to heap praise on him. But he could hardly be Foreign Secretary yet – perhaps Transport?

I met the Israeli ambassador at the garden party (having failed to recognise him), and he asked if it was true that Geoffrey Howe had today met Bassam Abu Sharif of the PLO. I knew that this had been the plan, Bassam having been invited to come to London to see William Waldegrave; but I found it difficult to confirm, beyond saying that it was quite possible that Geoffrey had met him briefly. We are playing this down; but it is in fact the first time that a Cabinet minister has met a senior PLO figure, apart from a rather frosty and coincidental meeting between Margaret Thatcher and Arafat at Tito's funeral. The PM is adamant that she will never meet Arafat again – but never say never?

14 JULY 1989

Bastille Day, and the economic summit in Paris, preceded by interviews with the PM on French radio, casting fairly offensive doubt on the value of the French Revolution, and claiming in effect that Magna Carta had thought of it first! Why does she always have to go to meetings facing, or provoking, a row? It will not have done her much good, particularly with pictures of her looking grim in the third row, between Gandhi and poor Mr Uno (said to be terrified that Mrs Thatcher would not shake his hand because of his trouble with geishas).

17 JULY 1989

Reports on the economic summit at my morning meeting revealed that the PM had appeared to be in a sunny mood throughout, concluding with a very warm meeting with Mitterrand, at which he himself suggested that he should fly over to see her before too long, and complained that the press on both sides of the Channel seemed to work hard to invent difficulties between France and Britain. The French planners told Robert Cooper last week that all their planning papers ended with recommendations that France should draw closer to Britain, but nothing ever seemed to happen.

18 JULY 1989

I discussed with Geoffrey Howe the Prince of Wales's visit to Hong Kong, which David Wilson has recommended should be postponed. I told Geoffrey that he could not advise against postponement, if the governor had advised otherwise. We have today sought confirmation from David Wilson that his advice still holds, and that the government can quote him publicly.

19 JULY 1989

Speculation today that the Prime Minister may appoint a special Cabinet minister for Europe, with Lord Young's name mentioned in several papers. Neither the idea, nor the personality, would be at all welcome to Geoffrey Howe, but it may be pure guesswork, and Lord Young is widely thought to be leaving government.

The call by Bassam Abu Sharif on Sheikh Zayed at Buckingham Palace broke in the *Evening Standard* today. William Waldegrave told me that one newspaper had described Abu Sharif as one of Arafat's leading advisers, and William himself as one of Abu Sharif's advisers! There have been more attacks against William in the *Mail on Sunday* ('Upper class twit and tool of the FCO's Arabists').

I attended a meeting this morning with Lynda Chalker and Elspeth Howe on one side, and Mark Russell on the other, about women in the service. Tension between the two sides became quite intense, rather unfairly, since Mark has in fact done a great deal to improve the lot of women during his time as chief clerk. I pointed out that many of the proposals and practices – e.g. work-sharing – cost money that we simply could not get under the present running cost regime.

20 JULY 1989

Michael Quinlan called to tell me very privately that George Younger is leaving government to become chairman of the Bank of Scotland, and to consult me about the Soviet Defence Minister's visit beginning on Tuesday morning, with the reshuffle set for Monday evening. After consulting Geoffrey Howe, I later passed on his advice that he and George Younger's successor (whom Geoffrey, by a slip of the tongue, revealed as Tom King) should both take part in the visit. An odd arrangement, but probably better than trying to put off the visit at this stage. Otherwise, no further news on reshuffles, though the press speculated that either Alan Clark (of 'Bongo Bongo Land' fame) or Peter Tapsell might become the second FCO Cabinet minister.

21 JULY 1989

Robin Butler told me very privately that Geoffrey Howe will go in the reshuffle on Monday, and be replaced by John Major. Geoffrey will get ostensible promotion as Leader of the House (and Deputy Prime Minister), but he will be very sad to leave the FCO. Lynda Chalker, who was visibly nervous and worried at the no. 1 board this morning, goes to the ODA, but not with Cabinet rank. Francis Maude joins us on promotion (good for him).

Simon Glenarthur is, of course, leaving, but I do not yet know who replaces him. The PM is said to have resisted the idea of Simon Cairns. Next week should be fun! There is also the complication of the Yazov visit, on which it looks as though George Younger's succession will be delayed for a week or two to enable him to act as Yazov's host, with his successor taking occasional part.

23 JULY 1989

Virginia and I went to Glyndebourne this evening to see Britten's *A Midsummer Night's Dream* as guests of Clifford and Pamela Chetwood (of Wimpey's). I had earlier forecast that, with reshuffles in the wind, the one category we would not see this evening were Conservative politicians – all of whom would certainly be glued to their telephones, waiting for a call for tomorrow's reshuffle. At dinner, however, we saw David and Lita Young, who told me he was now an ex-politician, having today left for the private sector.

24 JULY 1989

Geoffrey Howe was summoned to No. 10 at 9.10 a.m., to be told (without any prior warning) that he was to leave the FCO, and offered either the Home Office or leadership of the House. He told the PM that he did not want the Home Office, but wanted time to think. The PM apparently made it clear that one of her reasons for moving him was the way in which he had played their disagreement over EMS in the run-up to the Madrid summit last month.

Stephen Wall called me at 9.45 a.m. to tell me that Geoffrey had returned to the office in distress, and had left immediately for Carlton Gardens to confer with Elspeth. I saw Geoffrey at about 11 – obviously stunned by the news, and deeply offended, both by the lack of any warning and by the PM's failure to inform him about his successor. (I have not revealed to anyone that I have known the successor's identity for three days.) Geoffrey had drafted a letter to the PM expressing his dismay; setting out various important foreign affairs questions on which he is engaged; and telling her he did not want either of the jobs on offer [i.e. a fairly tough resignation letter which would have done the PM no good at all, and a foretaste of the resignation speech which was later to bring Margaret Thatcher down].

I advised Geoffrey not to tell his junior ministers until he had seen the PM's reaction to his letter. In fact, Geoffrey read out the letter to the Chief Whip, who reported it orally to the PM. He was later invited back to No. 10, and offered the leadership plus the deputy premiership, which he accepted.

Other moves also emerged during the day, and I wrote farewell letters to Tim Eggar (moved to Employment) and to Simon Glenarthur. Lynda Chalker is still in Turkey until Wednesday afternoon. Geoffrey Adams and I had to negotiate the somewhat delicate problem of Francis Maude wanting (quite understandably) to move in to her office tomorrow morning.

John Major invited Stephen Wall to call this afternoon to discuss immediate moves, and later telephoned me in response to a message of welcome I had sent him. He has said that Geoffrey Howe can stay in Carlton Gardens for the time being, but John has to host a dinner there tomorrow for the premier of St Vincent.

News of the full reshuffle did not emerge publicly until 7 p.m.; astonishingly, the row over Geoffrey's move has not yet emerged. All the press were taking the line this morning that Geoffrey would not be moved. They also curiously failed to forecast George Younger's departure. It has in fact been a massive reshuffle (which of course included John Major's appointment as Foreign Secretary), and the FCO will have great difficulty in inducting four new ministers, with only William Waldegrave remaining. He is already asking me, very nervously, whether Francis Maude (who was previously his assistant whip) will outrank him.

29 JULY 1989

William Waldegrave sent me an early telephone message to say that he needed to speak to me urgently before John Major arrived. The latter in fact turned up ten minutes early, before Stephen Wall and myself were there to greet him (thereby causing him to make a remark to the press about fooling 'the mandarins' – for which he later apologised).

William Waldegrave meanwhile turned up, looking very worried, and anxious that he should not lose any of his present portfolio, having allegedly heard Francis Maude announcing that he would be dealing with both the European Community and East/West relations. I calmed him down, and asked if he would like to add Africa to his portfolio? He said that he would be happy to add anything, provided he didn't lose anything.

Stephen Wall and I had half an hour with John Major, reaching quite quick agreement on portfolios, though suspending a decision, at my request, on which minister should sit on the no. 1 board. I want first to test the new personalities, though Francis Maude told me later that he was very keen to do it. [A foretaste of his campaign, many years later, as minister for the Cabinet Office, to allow ministers to remove and select their permanent secretaries?]

John Major has a very easy manner, and admitted that he was feeling fairly daunted by it all, having – like Geoffrey Howe – had no warning at all before yesterday morning. This is not what John says in his autobiography, where he claims that Tristan Garel-Jones had tipped him off three days earlier – as indeed had Robin Butler to me; but John had not believed him!

He is likely to go cautiously at first, and obviously wants to brief himself very thoroughly before making speeches or meeting his opposite numbers. I had another two and a half hours with him this afternoon, mainly discussing Hong Kong and Cambodia (with David Gillmore also present). But we also had a general discussion on how he wants to do the job. He is very conscious of press comment and told us both that the PM had no idea what his views are on Europe (though he is reputed to be strongly Thatcherite on EMS); and that he did not want to ask No. 10 for approval unnecessarily, though it would be tactically important to keep them up to speed. He was curiously adamant that he will not report to Cabinet this week on his proposed meeting with the Chinese Foreign Minister in Paris this weekend.

I asked if Norma Major would want to involve herself in his travels, and with the service, on which he gave a fairly negative reply. They live in Huntingdon and have two children at school. He has been offered Chevening, and Geoffrey Howe has been offered Dorneywood, though it seems very unlikely that he will use Chevening in the way the Howes did.

I had half an hour with William Waldegrave and Francis Maude separately this afternoon. William is now fussed that his office (both staff and space-wise) will be inadequate for his expanded portfolio. Their respective seniority is clear, though Lynda Chalker is no longer Deputy Foreign Secretary – just Minister for Overseas Development – with, in declining order, William, Francis, Lord Brabazon and Tim Sainsbury.

As for Lord Brabazon, I have succeeded in concentrating all administration

– minus personnel operations department – in his portfolio, which should diminish the extent of ministerial interference in the running of the service.

Tim Sainsbury was the last minister to be appointed, and reported to John Major at 5 p.m. John Major told me this morning that he expects great difficulty with Tim, both as the oldest and most experienced of his junior ministers, but nevertheless the most junior – at fifty-seven, he is eleven years older than the Foreign Secretary, and about fifteen years older than either William or Francis. He has also just had a major row (no pun intended) with the Treasury, having virtually told them to jump in a lake. I met him later; he certainly seems perfectly civil and friendly. William Waldegrave speaks very highly of him, particularly on his performance in the House of Commons.

Virginia and I had arranged a farewell drink for Mark Russell this evening, but turned it into a joint farewell also for Geoffrey Howe, Simon Glenarthur and Tim Eggar. I also invited John Major, who considerately said it would be easier for Geoffrey and myself if he stayed away.

I later received the following letter from Geoffrey, having also sent all three departing ministers an appropriate letter of farewell:

My dear Patrick,

It was very good of you to write as you did, even before the end of Black Monday – and then to speak so kindly when you allowed me to gate-crash Mark Russell's party.

Elspeth and I have greatly appreciated all the kindnesses we have enjoyed from Virginia and yourself. They have helped to turn fascination with the job into fun as well. And we really have valued the sheer professionalism, zeal & loyalty of all with whom we have dealt in the Service – most particularly, perhaps, in private office and news department. (PUSs are in a class of their own, of course.)

I must say it's a funny world in which so many 'partnerships' can be called up at such disastrously short notice; yet there's so much achieved that's worth trying to preserve.

My warmest thanks for all your help & understanding.
As ever,
GEOFFREY

Charles Powell said that Geoffrey Howe had had it coming to him ever since the morning of Madrid, when he'd had the gall to threaten to resign. When I said that it was surely an honest difference of policy, Charles was extremely dismissive, accusing Geoffrey Howe of leaking yesterday's row in the press, and saying that I at least now had a Foreign Secretary on the way up, rather than one on the way down. I said that I thought Geoffrey had been treated disgracefully, and that while John Major was clearly a delightful and able man, I very much regretted Geoffrey's departure. Could the PM, I asked, not even have had the courtesy to warn Geoffrey in advance? Charles asked, in reply, what good that would have done.

26 JULY 1989

The press is full of speculation today about the motives behind the reshuffle, with much talk about the attempt to get the FCO in order, and to bring Foreign Office policies on Europe more in line with the PM's thinking. There is much speculation in the press that John Major is closer to Margaret Thatcher on European policies, and that he had got one over on his officials (i.e. Stephen Wall, Christopher Meyer and me) by arriving early at the Foreign Office yesterday. He told me that he had slept last night for five and a half hours but was still worried about the press, including their hounding of Norma, who had been pursued while distributing Meals on Wheels. A Huntingdon journalist has apparently camped outside their house for two days.

I tried today to sort out the problems of precedence among Foreign Office ministers, on which the press are taking an intense interest, particularly since *The Independent* published the list with Francis Maude as no. 1 and Lynda Chalker as no. 4! After checking with both Charles Powell and Robin Butler, I have recommended that William Waldegrave should stand in for the Foreign Secretary at Cabinet, where necessary, and not Lynda. I received a message from her at Heathrow today, on her return from Ankara, to say that she needed to talk to me urgently about the supervision of Personnel Operations Department, I told her later that the Secretary of State had not yet taken a decision on this. But I have in fact advised John Major not to give it to Lynda – not because she does it badly, but because she is, after all, a minister in charge of a home civil service department.

As John Major came to us from being Chief Secretary, I asked him whether he could tell me anything about the prospects for the diplomatic service bid in the public expenditure exercise. He told me yesterday that unfortunately his move had been so rapid that he could not remember the Treasury's fallback position on the FCO bid. John Anson, Second Permanent Under-Secretary at the Treasury, had told me yesterday that John Major had shown no particular interest in the FCO; John Major himself told me that he had confidently expected to get Transport.

He also told me how successful Geoffrey Howe had been with the FCO bid through sheer doggedness and refusal to give in. I said that I hoped he would do likewise.

27 JULY 1989

Lynda Chalker called on me this morning to talk about her visit to Ankara, and about her own position. On the latter, she pressed her case to supervise Personnel Operations Department, and to remain on the no. 1 board. I said I was doubtful about this, since it would look very odd, both in the FCO and the ODA, to have a minister in charge of a civil service department sitting on a diplomatic promotions board. I later discussed this again with John Major, who is attracted by the idea (presumably to be kind to Lynda, who is still feeling very bruised), but agreed to suspend a decision until after the holidays. My present preference would be Tim Sainsbury; but I shall have to discuss this with the board.

Tony Favell, John Major's PPS, called on me at 10 a.m. and stayed on for my morning meeting. John Major later described him to me as someone he had inherited from his Treasury predecessor – 'a nice and friendly man'. I scored a bit of a coup with him by contradicting him when he said that he well understood that the FCO's main objective was to develop and maintain good relations with foreign countries; I pointed out that the FCO saw its role as promoting British interests abroad, and that good relations were sometimes (but not always e.g. Romania) a means of achieving that. He seemed quite agreeably startled to hear this from an FCO mandarin!

The press today was almost universally critical of the PM's handling of the reshuffle, and her spiteful treatment of Geoffrey Howe. John Major told me, at our bilateral this afternoon, that he was worried by the implications in the press that he had been sent to the FCO to change Community Policy in an anti-European direction. He said that this was quite false (at least as far as he was concerned), though he might want to be a bit robust on occasions. I pointed out quite sternly that the FCO itself was often very robust, in spite of press allegations to the contrary.

John Major is still feeling very new, and the pile-up of paper, and decisions waiting to be taken, is formidable. I think he has no idea what his programme is going to look like when he gets going properly. [It later occurred to me that the Foreign Secretary's programme, apart from travel, can frequently involve up to twelve separate meetings a day – for all of which a degree of briefing is required; whereas the Chief Secretary probably has far fewer meetings, and probably the time to focus on one departmental meeting on public expenditure in one day.]

When I suggested that he might hold some Carlton Gardens-type of seminar on broad foreign policy issues, he welcomed the idea, saying that we might have one a week in September. I warned him that this might be a little difficult. But he is very easy and informal to work with, and he has the reputation of being a formidably hard worker. When Tony Favell told my morning meeting that he had never known anyone to work so hard, I asked him how well he had known Geoffrey Howe.

It does not look as though Norma Major is going to play much part in the service, or on his travels. He is also going to find it very difficult to spend as much time with his family as he would like.

28 JULY 1989

When I told the morning meeting today that John Major had said that he had not been sent to the FCO to change our European policies, Mark Lyall Grant (Francis Maude's private secretary) said that Maude had claimed that that was *his* mission!

4 SEPTEMBER 1989

[Summer leave, including Olivia's wedding to Simon McDonald at St Bride's.] I returned to the office today, after a weekend of catching up with paper. The main preoccupations over the holidays have been Colombia drugs, and aid for the new non-Communist government in Poland. The PM's talk with Mitterrand on Friday went well, with Mitterrand stressing his wish to avoid rows with us. They had a long and very private talk on Germany, on which both share considerable worries, particularly with Eastern Europe in turmoil. John Major seems to have performed well with Dumas, though he is clearly finding the welter of paper intimidating, and has complained (as did Jim Callaghan during my time in No. 10) that it leaves him no time to think.

The Howes are still in Carlton Gardens, having moved out of Chevening, and John Major has given instructions that no efforts should be made to hurry them out (though Elspeth told us at the British Museum this evening that they will be out by the end of this month). John Major is himself staying in the resident clerks' flat, to the despair of the private office.

The PM had given instructions this morning that President Menem's brother (the Speaker of the Argentinian Parliament, who is here for the IPU conference) was not to meet the Queen or herself, nor any senior ministers. On arrival at the Royal Gallery, I was immediately nobbled by David Montgomery, and introduced to Menem.

I saw a stream of under-secretaries today, including John Kerr, who is (wrongly) chastising himself for what he sees as his role in Geoffrey Howe's departure, and who, like David Hannay (whom I also saw), is pretty gloomy about the future of community work, particularly given a very weak new team in the Department of Trade.

Lynda Chalker is still lobbying hard to stay on the no. 1 board, but seems to have over-sold her case with John Major last week. I will try to persuade John Major to select Tim Sainsbury for the job, but may have to fall back on Lord Brabazon.

Otherwise, I have gathered few impressions yet of the new team. Francis Maude has shown he is both bright and susceptible to advice. But he clearly regards himself as the PM's spy in the camp, and told John Kerr that he proposed to continue his practice in the Department of Trade of calling fortnightly on Charles Powell.

5 SEPTEMBER 1989

A long bilateral with John Major this afternoon. He was in expansive form, and kept me for nearly two hours. Lynda Chalker had telephoned him about six times, mainly no doubt about her seat on the no. 1 board. Although John was initially inclined to think it didn't matter if it looked odd, he suggested, before I did, that Tim Sainsbury would do it best. He clearly did not want either William Waldegrave or Francis Maude to do it. William was one of the ministers whose political judgement could be said to be erratic. He is nevertheless keen to delegate more to his junior ministers – secretaries of state always start off by saying that! – and accepts that occasional misjudgements might be made. I pointed out to him the risk of the PM occasionally raising things with him that he had not heard about.

John Kerr tells me that John Major had a reputation in the Treasury for tunnel vision – i.e. briefing himself fully on the subject in hand, but not more broadly. John Major virtually admitted this to me, describing William Waldegrave as a 'conceptual thinker', unlike himself. He is still worried about his lack of background knowledge, though I told him that a constant reading of telegrams would quickly build up a good base. He is also very worried about his visit to Washington this weekend, and rather suspicious of Jim Baker (who he thinks leaked unhelpful accounts of their meeting in Paris).

John Major is also worried that the press will be looking for opportunities to contrast him with Geoffrey Howe. For this reason, Stephen Wall tells me he has hesitated to invite me to accompany him to the States, since it would look as though a new Foreign Secretary was being guarded by his mandarins.

He is keen to use Carlton Gardens effectively, but made no mention of Geoffrey Howe's continued occupancy. He has suggested that junior ministers should also use it for their entertaining, and readily agreed that I could occasionally. When I suggested that, as an exception, he might be prepared to meet my French opposite number, François Scheer, when he comes next month for talks and lunch, he rather horrified Stephen Wall by suggesting that he and I might jointly give Scheer lunch in Carlton Gardens *à trois*. I expressed suitable thanks, but suggested that he would have his hands full looking after foreign ministers, without entertaining secretaries general. He was happy to leave it to my judgement, but stressed that the importance of Anglo-French relations made him quite ready to stand by his offer.

I lunched with Max Hastings of the *Daily Telegraph*. Having recently appointed Julia Langdon of the *Daily Mirror* as the political leader writer, he told me that Conrad Black, the proprietor, had received two complaints: one from Alistair McAlpine, the Conservative Party mogul; the other from Charles Powell, saying he hoped she would not bring her left-wing views to the *Telegraph*. Possibly in order to test my reaction, Max said he was outraged that a civil servant should speak like that, and claimed that dislike of Charles Powell was the one factor that united all Cabinet meetings.

Max Hastings was very critical of Geoffrey Howe's performance over the reshuffle, though he blamed Elspeth for extensive leaking over Madrid etc. He quoted G. K. Chesterton as saying that there were 'Big Great Men', who make those around them feel great; and 'Little Great Men', who do the opposite. He thought Margaret Thatcher fell into the second category, with her contemptuous treatment of her Cabinet colleagues.

7 SEPTEMBER 1989

There are signs of strain in the private office, with Stephen Wall resisting John Major's suggestion of office meetings at 9.30 p.m. before he retires to the resident clerks' flat. Stephen also issued a cross minute today, criticising the briefing for Washington as inadequate. John Major likes to have the full story, which is going to result in vast briefs, which will put quite a strain on both the office and the Foreign Secretary.

Charles Powell called this afternoon, describing the Prime Minister as 'incorrigible' over Argentina. When Michael Marshall tried to persuade her just to shake Speaker Menem's hand at the IPU conference, she replied: 'I don't shake hands with our enemies.' The Madrid negotiations are *not* going to be easy.

1–13 SEPTEMBER 1989:
VISITS TO WASHINGTON AND NEW YORK

This was John Major's first major visit abroad (apart from his short trip to Paris for the Cambodia conference). He was very nervous, both because of his inexperience, and from his fear that the press would draw unfavourable contrasts with Geoffrey Howe ('Was it for this that the PM had a reshuffle etc. etc.?'). In fact he did very well, and seemed to be totally in command of his brief. His manner is far more direct than Geoffrey's, and he comes across as a straightforward and friendly person. He also overcame his reservations about being accompanied by mandarins (see above), and agreed that I should accompany him.

The press were fairly critical of his speech to the Economic Club of New York, claiming that he had said nothing new. But the speech went down well with a very prestigious audience of about 800 of New York's richest Americans. After the speech, John said he wanted to go to the hotel bar 'to relax and meet some real people'. He admitted that he had been very reserved about my accompanying him to the States, since he (repeat he!) thought the purpose was to keep an eye on him. He seemed genuinely grateful for my help, and particularly for my encouragement. When I congratulated him on his speech, but said: 'I can't go on congratulating you like this,' he replied: 'I don't see why not. I like it!'

His call on President George Bush ranged quite widely over drugs in Colombia, Arab/Israel and Poland; though Bush seemed more preoccupied, and less at ease, than when I had accompanied Geoffrey Howe a year ago. Vice-President Quayle, on the other hand, was again impressive (perhaps in contrast to his earlier reputation), and talked confidently, and well-briefed.

The working lunch with Jim Baker at the State Department covered a few quite sharp Anglo-American disagreements (e.g. Vietnamese boat people and the broadcasting directive); but John Major handled both subjects well, and visibly impressed the Americans by his grasp of detail when discussing the Conventional Forces in Europe (CFE) negotiations.

I skipped the call on Defence Secretary Cheney at the Pentagon in order to have an hour alone with Bob Kimmitt at the State Department – mainly to discuss ways of improving multilateral consultation with Japan, and how to use the Economic Seven without offending French doctrinal objections.

14 SEPTEMBER 1989

A DUSs' meeting today, mainly to prepare for a series of seminars that John Major has agreed to hold at Carlton Gardens on foreign policy, starting with arms control and defence next week, in preparation for the PM's seminar at Chequers at the end of the month. It will be interesting to see if John Major is any readier than Geoffrey Howe was to allow the FCO to produce think-pieces on the future of the European Community, for example, which Geoffrey discouraged (understandably) in view of the row that papers of that sort were likely to provoke in No. 10.

The planners have produced a paper on EC enlargement, taking a fairly unorthodox view in favour of extra enlargement, and which has caused a stir in the office. Everyone subscribes to the theory that the planners should produce provocative papers, but always object when they do so on their own subject!

15 SEPTEMBER 1989

I called on Lord Brabazon, as the first of my courtesy calls after the break. Not easy, though his private secretary, Robert Court, told Geoffrey Adams afterwards that he did not think his minister had been on top form.

18 SEPTEMBER 1989

A good booklet has been published on 'Britain in Southern Africa', only spoilt by prominent photographs of Charles Powell with the PM on her African trips. Geoffrey Adams pointed out that, under the rules in No. 10 in my time (whereby we were required to contribute a bottle of wine to the No. 10 bar for every private secretarial photograph that appeared), this should cost Charles several thousand bottles! There is also a nauseating article, with a full-page picture of Charles, accompanying a piece arguing for a Prime Minister's foreign affairs unit – 'better value than the £7 billion FCO budget'!

9 SEPTEMBER 1989

John Major had his first PESC bilateral today with his successor, Norman Lamont, on the diplomatic wing, the aid wing and the Intelligence Services. No agreement on any of them (predictably). John told me that he didn't enjoy the experience of gamekeeper-turned-poacher, though he did manage to read Lamont's brief upside down, and could see what the Treasury's fallback position was. He thinks we are safe on running costs, but will be cut back hard on programme expenditure.

At my bilateral with him this afternoon, he showed himself to be very fussed about the pile of work and appointments, and has clearly been giving the private office a hard time, though mainly because he doesn't feel fully briefed. When discussing his meeting with Genscher in Cologne tomorrow, he asked why he needed to go to a museum with him. I explained that the purpose of his visit was primarily to get on good personal terms with Genscher, given the deep and obvious hostility between Genscher and Margaret Thatcher (who deeply insulted him by some very contemptuous remarks about 'European Liberals' in the House of Commons last year).

Christian Adams, on loan to the DTI in their projects division, took up a longstanding invitation to call on me today. He was reassuring about rumours that the DTI want to take over export promotion from the FCO, adding that Nicholas Ridley, the new Secretary of State, does not believe in export promotion at all!

20 SEPTEMBER 1989

Robin Butler told me today that John Major had commented that Douglas Hurd would make a good ambassador in Washington, if he ever gave up the Home Office. When he had commented that Margaret Thatcher might want Charles Powell to do it, John Major has said that that would be another Peter Jay; South Africa would be a much better choice. That is increasingly my own view of how to resolve the problem of Charles Powell's future.

21 SEPTEMBER 1989

Nico Henderson called to discuss a letter I had written him about his memoirs. He is naturally disappointed, both through pride of authorship, and because he thinks his memoirs would reflect well on the service, to whom he owes his loyalty (as opposed to Mrs Thatcher, to whom he owes very little, and of whose policies on Europe he is very critical). He reluctantly conceded that my arguments were well founded, though he contested, with some justification, whether ministers were subject to such strict constraints. But he agrees that he will simply have to put his memoirs aside for several more years, i.e. for the Radcliffe-recommended gap of fifteen years.

A disturbing letter today from Michael Alexander at NATO, reporting a conversation with Bob Blackwill of the National Security Council, claiming that the PM's treatment of Mitterrand and Kohl (and their resentment of it) was having a damaging effect on her relationship with President Bush.

This touches on the broader question of whether the PM's apparent lack of commitment to Europe weakens the 'special relationship' – a point which was incorporated in the paper prepared for Geoffrey Howe to put to OD just before the reshuffle. I marked Michael's letter, with his agreement, to John Major, saying I would like a word sometime about it, rather than any covering minute, which would merely have added to the alarming pile of paper waiting in the private office.

22 SEPTEMBER 1989

Today was the first of John Major's seminars at Carlton Gardens – this one mainly to prepare for next Friday's seminar at Chequers on defence policy, to which to the PM has invited several Americans, which worries John Major, as he thinks it will constrain discussion.

John Major and I had a private word about Michael Alexander's letter, and agreed that ways must be found to put the problem to Margaret Thatcher. He is rightly conscious of the need not to appear 'captured' by the FCO – he was described in the *Daily Express* this week as being treated by the PM as her idiot son, without the balm of maternal forgiveness! He is also worried by the impression in the press that he is a Thatcher clone, and asked me if this worried the office. I said that I had been asked by a few people if it was so, and told him, in reply to his question, that I had replied with his own words: that he had come to the FCO with very little foreign affairs experience, and had yet to form his own ideas; but that he had no preconceived attitudes.

We invited both John and Norma Major to sit at our table at the Diplomatic Service Wives Association ball this evening. John is a non-dancer, because of a leg injury; but he was very shy about leaving early – nicely worried that people would think he wasn't doing his duty.

He drew me aside at one point and asked me to be nice to Norma, who was only just coming to realise that the office were actually quite normal people, without horns! She is obviously still finding it all very difficult, and a bit fussed about leaving the children with her mother. But she is going with him to New York for the UN General Assembly next week.

As a postscript to John Major's programme on his first day as Foreign Secretary, Rob Young later reminded me that he had accompanied John Major on his call on Sheikh Zayed, armed with a brief and an atlas. As they were shown into the presence, it immediately became clear to Rob (though possibly not to John Major) that Zayed had been told to expect a call from the Foreign Secretary, and was therefore expecting Geoffrey Howe. There was a look of total mystification on Zayed's face, which John Major may have interpreted as the look which Arab Sheikhs always put on when receiving distinguished visitors, and which nearly reduced Rob to hopeless giggles.

25 SEPTEMBER 1989

I did a round of ministers, following the summer leave. William Waldegrave still looks very down in the dumps; he is alleged, by the correspondent in one of this Sunday's papers, to have been bitterly disappointed by his non-promotion in the reshuffle. He is obviously finding the additional burden of African business quite heavy, if only in terms of ambassadorial calls and receptions. He told me that he thought Charles Powell (with whom he is very close) had found his job much diminished with John Major as Secretary of State, and that Charles would certainly not be able to treat John Major in the way he had treated Geoffrey Howe. He thought Charles might well be looking for a diplomatic posting before long, and hoped that I had good successors in mind. I said that I had rather given up thinking about successors to Charles, having identified several in the past three years.

Francis Maude is obviously pleased with his recent visit to Hong Kong, though worried that it may have increased expectations of a government resettlement package.

I also used my call on Francis Maude as an opportunity to put up a marker about diplomatic service work on export promotion, having heard rumours that Lord Trefgarne had got Francis Maude's agreement that the Department of Trade should take it over. If so, Francis concealed it; but he seemed quite impressed by my arguments about the need to involve ambassadors and others in trade and investment promotion.

I called on Tim Sainsbury, who is suffering from shingles. I urged him to cut down his programme in the West Indies, where he goes this week. He is also suffering from his son's nearly fatal accident in the United States this summer, in which his girlfriend was killed and he suffered minor, but allegedly repairable, brain damage. I took Tim through the procedures for ministerial consultation on the No. 1 board, suggesting that he should consult Lynda Chalker rather more than he might otherwise, given her hopes of staying on the board.

26 SEPTEMBER 1989

I had one of my regular heads of department meetings this morning, at which I spoke at length about the new ministerial team and their working methods. Less grumbling than usual and quite a good discussion about management and training. There are a lot of new faces since March.

John Major has had some good bilaterals in New York, including a hard-hitting talk with Arens of Israel. David Gore-Booth and the department are delighted.

Crispin Tickell has (as I hoped) reacted with dismay at John Major's amendments to the brief for the Madrid talks with the Argentinians; I hope I shall be able to soften John Major up for the discussion in OD next week. I also encouraged David Gillmore to talk again to Tim Sainsbury, who clearly felt that the original brief did not give enough leeway on the Falklands protection zone. We are, incidentally, about to face problems with Rex Hunt's memoirs, which, as Robin Butler has pointed out, will have to be treated in the same way as Nico Henderson's. But Rex Hunt is much less likely to comply, and will have a powerful ally to lobby in Margaret Thatcher.

28 SEPTEMBER 1989

Some to-ing and fro-ing today on the Falklands papers for next week's OD. Having asked for the negotiating brief to be stiffened, John Major discussed the question with Crispin Tickell, who telephoned the department from New York to say that John Major now wanted the paper softened beyond the original version! Meanwhile, we received a stern rebuke from No. 10 on the line that John Major had taken on sovereignty in his talk with the Argentine Foreign Minister. So no doubt he will now veer back again to a tougher line. I warned Robin Butler at dinner this evening that the paper was unlikely to be in by this weekend.

John Major has received quite a good press and coverage on his New York speech, and on his meetings in the States. So he should be pleased.

29 SEPTEMBER 1989

When Charles Powell called this morning, I referred to two sharply worded minutes from No. 10 this week: one on John Major's talk with the Argentine Foreign Minister (see above), and one on the Prime Minister's worries about American attitudes to arms control. John Major has authorised some admirably robust and un-Howe-like responses to both letters.

Charles also claims that the press coverage on the PM's proposed visit to South Africa did not reflect official briefing from No. 10 (though Patrick Fairweather has been told by a journalist that it comes from the PM herself).

Margaret Thatcher has also been showing signs of her Germanophobia over the past few weeks, and has very unwisely discussed the Germans both with Mitterrand and (as seen from a very closely kept part of the record) with Gorbachev. This phobia also colours her attitude to community enlargement, since she regards the Austrians as another sort of German (see p. 128, above), and seems to be obsessed by a feeling that German speakers are going to dominate the community. She is also, of course, deeply suspicious of Genscher; any talk of German reunification is anathema to her.

There is a debate going on in the office about aid to India, with several people, including William Waldegrave, arguing that India's international misbehaviour does not warrant such a large aid programme, and that we should switch some of it to Poland and Hungary. There has been a fierce counter-blast from South Asian Department, and probably from the ODA.

4 OCTOBER 1989

I called on Lynda Chalker at the ODA, who gave the speech of thanks for Geoffrey Howe at his 'farewell party' in the Lord President's office this evening. Lynda is still talking about the blow to morale in the FCO caused by her own and Geoffrey's departure, though she told me she thought it was getting better. She has accepted her non-membership of the no. 1 board, and gave me the impression that she was in any case constantly consulted by John Major on all matters, including senior appointments.

Geoffrey Adams told me today that Lynda had apparently very much irritated John Major at the Foreign Affairs Council in Luxembourg this week by asking him rather bossily if he had covered all the points in his brief. John had apparently snapped back: 'No, none of them. Perhaps you had better do it all next time.'

Geoffrey Howe himself made a good speech, without any signs of rancour; he quoted Claude Cheysson as saying that the French diplomatic service was the second best in the world after the British. He also made some nice references to me as 'no ordinary PUS'.

David Dell tells me that Lord Trefgarne is still pushing the idea of an overseas trade service on the lines of the Defence Export Services Organisation (for which he claims to have Francis Maude's support). David did not think it would run, but promised to keep me informed.

5 OCTOBER 1989

I had a long session with John Major, who had had two good OD meetings (on Hong Kong boat people and the Falklands). He is still getting on well with the PM, and is pleased about it. He is being quite forthright in giving the PM advice, and hard-headed about Charles Powell.

Stephen Wall told me this week that John Major's reaction to Charles Powell's two rebukes on the Falklands and arms control had been: 'I'm damned if I'm going to be chased round the world by preposterous letters from Charles Powell.' But John Major told me (sensibly) that the PM is 'politically in bed' with Charles, and that there is no point in pushing it – this said in response to my expression of hope that he would see more of the PM, and be able to brief her at CHOGM more than Geoffrey was able to do at Vancouver.

Curiously, John Major told me today that the PM was much more tired than she appears, and he thought it not impossible that she might give up in a year's time. I told him that there had been some odd rumours last year that she might give up in the spring, but that I had found both stories difficult to credit. John admitted that it was just as likely that she would want another four years in office.

But John Major is still desperately worried about next week's party conference speech, since he has to speak on Europe, and knows that the press will be drawing comparisons with Geoffrey Howe (who he thinks may well get a standing ovation). Stephen Wall confirmed to me that John still needs constant reassurance, and had even passed him a note during his talk with the Chinese Foreign Minister, asking how he was doing. He is also very fussed about Vietnamese boat people, which he described as potentially his political suicide. He is also clearly uncertain about his junior ministers.

I held a businessmen's lunch today, at which one participant produced a series of stories about the lack of help received in Tokyo and Moscow. Luckily, several other members present said that they had found both these embassies particularly helpful. But it nevertheless left a bad taste. There was then quite a lively discussion, at the end of which the original complainant actually moved a vote of thanks!

William Waldegrave had (as he told me at the time) been shaken by his non-promotion at the reshuffle, having (as I pointed out to him) only been led to expect it by constant stories in the press that William and Chris Patten were 'the two men to watch'. Chris had once been present at some occasion when William Waldegrave had been summoned to the telephone to take a call from No. 10, and he had been so consumed by jealousy that he had had to go for a walk!

John Major told me this afternoon that Chris Patten was making himself very unpopular with Nigel Lawson over his enormous PESC bid; and with Nicholas Ridley, having overturned a major planning decision on Foxley Wood. Meanwhile, John Major seems to have pulled off a very respectable PESC bid for the FCO.

Given John Major's reported dislike of the grandeur of Antony Acland's residence in Washington, and his resistance to working in the Foreign Secretary's grand office overlooking St James's Park, we face an interesting conflict between the Prime Minister's liking for grand ambassadorial residences, and our present position, which is to get rid of the Morisa Toreza residence in Moscow. I told John Major today that we could certainly try to negotiate the retention of the Moscow residence, but that it would cost an extra £27 million at least. I also reminded him that a very public competition had been held for a new residence. But John himself has no doubt that we shall have to go ahead with the Prime Minister's pronouncement that we 'must keep that residence in Moscow'.

We still don't know if the Russians will allow us to stay; but the whole issue has been revived by Gorbachev saying to the Prime Minister in April: 'Why on earth do you want to leave your residence in Moscow?' Rodric Braithwaite is also lobbying hard for it (though Charles Powell claims that Rodric did not put the Prime Minister up to it).

6 OCTOBER 1989

I chaired an appeal board this afternoon for a young counsellor, who alleges that he only discovered his homosexual tendencies through a chance encounter at the age of thirty-eight. There seems to be little alternative, under the current regulations, to withdrawing his positive vetting (PV) certificate. But this raises again the whole question of homosexuality and positive vetting. John Major may well be sympathetic to a change in the rules; he had to be dissuaded from sending a note of sympathy to the young man when the news broke. But it would have to go to the Prime Minister, who is unlikely to be sympathetic.

10 OCTOBER 1989

Having decided to uphold the PV decision, I wrote to the young man, and later received an appreciative letter from him, commenting on 'the sensitive and sympathetic way' I had handled his hearing – generous of him, considering his career is now in tatters.

11 OCTOBER 1989

The office was fairly quiet today, with most ministers away at Blackpool. John Major was making his conference speech, nervous that he would be upstaged by Geoffrey Howe, who was addressing a fringe meeting this morning, calling for a new look in the Conservative Party.

12 OCTOBER 1989

A two-and-a-half-hour meeting of the board of management discussing, among other things, the division of the PESC round, on which the Treasury has made a very good offer. I have written a private letter to John Major, congratulating and thanking him for getting both the office and the British Council an excellent deal – even better than last year's. Quite an achievement in a year when expenditure – e.g. on the poll tax – seems to be spinning out of control.

13 OCTOBER 1989

The Prime Minister has predictably not yet begun to concentrate on next week's CHOGM in Kuala Lumpur, for which I leave shortly for a day of preliminary meetings of senior officials. John Major is to travel out with the PM, in spite of his fierce attempts to avoid it. He told me at our bilateral last week that he could not imagine anything worse than a twelve-hour flight on the PM's aircraft. As it turned out, I was booked for the return on the PM's flight, joining her dinner with the ruler of Qatar en route.

I talked to Charles Powell about the need to issue appropriate warnings to the Prime Minister about security in the hotel rooms in Kuala Lumpur. His main worry is what Denis will have to say about the other Commonwealth leaders!

The following is extracted from a paper which I prepared on 29 October 1989, on my return from Malaysia.

> The Prime Minister remained throughout as excluded from official contact as she had at Vancouver; but at least this time she saw a lot of her Foreign Secretary. Unlike Geoffrey Howe at Vancouver, John Major was invited almost every day to have lunch or dinner with the Thatchers in their Shangri-La suite. John showed signs of independence. At one

point, when I pointed out that the PM might object to something, he blurted out: 'If the PM doesn't like it, she can bloody well come and renegotiate it herself.'

There were healthy signs also of recognition that the relationship with Charles Powell is not a healthy one. When I had discussed this with John Major before CHOGM, he had said that we should try to get to a more sensible way of briefing the PM, but that we all had to realise the extent to which Charles had become her 'political bedfellow', and that he did not intend to push it.

[What other recollections of CHOGM? The great row, of course, was over the PM's separate statement, issued simultaneously with the CHOGM communique on South Africa. There is a slight mystery as to how this originated; but it seems to have been a brainchild of, and drafted by, Charles Powell at the Langkawi retreat. He later told me that he had gone to the other side of the island to draft it. The result carried the clear implication that it not only repudiated the CHOGM communique (or 'peed all over it', as Patrick Fairweather graphically described it), but also repudiated John Major's share in drafting it. Hurried redrafting was negotiated by Stephen Wall, to get across the points on which we agreed with the CHOGM communique, and to emphasise the fact that it was a joint communique or statement by both John Major and Margaret Thatcher. Not that this stopped the British press seeing it as a humiliation of John Major.]

There was my row, partly simulated, with Yacovou, the Cypriot Foreign Minister, and Tassos Panayides, their High Commissioner in London, about the Cypriot draft passage for the communique, which they stolidly refused to show us before it issued. And the unexpectedly heavy opposition to the draft passage on Hong Kong, led by the Tanzanians and Ghanaians, but joined in by the Indians ('the only problem of confidence in Hong Kong relates to the 1962 British Nationalities Act') and most notably the Pakistanis, who had obviously been nobbled, as the Indians told us they had been, by the Chinese.

Happily, I sat next to Yaqub Khan at dinner on the last night (with Dato' Kamil of the Malysian MFA [Ministry of Foreign Affairs] on my other side, supplying us with whisky for an otherwise dry official dinner), and persuaded him to keep Pakistan's reservations to the Hong Kong part of the communique to a private letter written subsequently to the Commonwealth secretariat.

26 OCTOBER 1989

My diaries do not give much detail on John Major's transfer from the Foreign Office to the Treasury, or on Nigel Lawson's departure as Chancellor, beyond the fact that John telephoned me from No. 10 this evening to ask me if I was sitting down, before telling me the news. His call on a Thursday evening was followed by intense speculation about who his successor would be, with the names of Nicholas Ridley, Cecil Parkinson and Norman Fowler being mooted, as I stood drinking a stiff whisky in the private office with Stephen Wall and Maurice Fraser. Eventually, the call from Charles Powell came through, telling us it was to be Douglas Hurd, with Charles's comment: 'I had to work hard to save you from Cecil Parkinson.'

Earlier rumours that Parkinson was the most likely successor to Geoffrey Howe had caused a minor panic in Personnel Department, since one of the potential private secretaries in the private office was the husband of the twin sister of Parkinson's girlfriend, Sara Keays.

27 OCTOBER 1989

This morning, Stephen Wall, Andrew Burns and I saw John Major off the premises and welcomed Douglas Hurd. In a private word with John before he left, I offered my congratulations and good wishes on a formidable task ahead as Chancellor of the Exchequer, during which he again showed familiar sensitivity about being portrayed as a prime ministerial cypher.

He also commented on how 'friendly' he had found the FCO. When I later mentioned this to Clive Whitmore, Clive said that this comment did not at all surprise him, coming from an ex-Treasury minister – recalling that at any PES negotiations he had attended, he had felt that there was more empathy between the Chief Secretary and those with whom he was negotiating than with the officials on his own side of the table.

30 OCTOBER 1989

Douglas Hurd's first week as Foreign Secretary (but not, of course, his first ministerial post in the Foreign Office, having been Minister of State from 1979 to 1983). I attended two of his meetings today: the first on Hong Kong (democracy, boat people and right of abode), on which the FCO had an appalling weekend press. There was a really savage attack on Percy Cradock in a *Sunday Times* editorial; but there were several other sneering articles today, claiming that the FCO does not understand the suffering of 'real people'.

The second meeting was on EMU, on which Douglas was questioned on *Panorama* this evening. He stuck closely to the Madrid Agreement; but John Kerr was very depressed this morning at the damage that the PM's interview yesterday with Brian Walden would have done to our position in the community.

I sent Douglas a very personal minute today on the impact that our community attitudes are having on the Americans, as well as a personal note on Margaret Thatcher's attitude to Germany. She again talked about German reunification at CHOGM, though I got it removed from the record.

[Although not recorded in my diaries, I remember also sending Douglas a note suggesting that (partly to please his Conservative political allies) he should consider referring to himself as Foreign and Commonwealth Secretary, rather than just Foreign Secretary – a suggestion he sharply rejected.]

I called on Peter Gregson at the DTI to remind him of the FCO's interest in the House of Fraser affair, on which the Attorney General is about to decide whether to prosecute or not. Nicholas Ridley is apparently very grumpy about the affair, taking the view that the government should never have become involved. Peter also talked to me about Lord Trefgarne's idea for an export agency to conduct export promotion, which Peter hopes to suppress.

After lunching at the Security Service, I joined John Boyd for a talk with Douglas Hurd about personnel questions. He assumed that Charles Powell would 'do a de Zulueta', and revealed that Geoffrey Howe had been to see him on Saturday for a long talk about Charles, and about the difficulties I have had over his postings. Helpful.

31 OCTOBER 1989

Marcus's thirtieth birthday and the investiture for my GCMG. I talked to my fellow honorand, Helen Suzman, who was very nervous, but went quite pink with pleasure when I pointed out to her that she had broken two records: first, as an honorary recipient getting her award personally from the Queen (not unique, but rare); and secondly, having her award announced in a speech at the United Nations.

It looks as though Douglas Hurd's working methods may be more economical with paper than for either of his predecessors (he claimed to me that the load of paper in the Home Office was heavier than in the Foreign Office – see p. 72, above). He likes short, sharp minutes, followed by discussion; he prefers to take his decisions at meetings.

1 NOVEMBER 1989

Stephen Wall told me today that the choices to succeed John Major as Foreign Secretary had first been Cecil Parkinson, but that John Major had himself dissuaded the Prime Minister from that. She had then wanted to appoint Tom King, and Charles Powell had talked her out of that. So, Douglas Hurd was her third choice (and in my view, undoubtedly the best).

The row over the reshuffle still simmers on, with a fairly provocative statement by Nigel Lawson in the House yesterday. Lawson himself came up to me at the Palace this morning and said: 'You have got a first class Foreign Secretary.'

Geoffrey Howe, Douglas Hurd and others were also waiting for a meeting of the Privy Council. Geoffrey seemed keen for a gossip, but I had to dash for the Finnish lunch at No. 10.

My first bilateral with Douglas Hurd this afternoon. He confirmed that he wants to delegate more to his ministers of state (having no doubt suffered from non-delegation himself). He asked me about Ivon Brabazon, whose performance on Cambodia appeared on television last night. But it looks as though there is a real chance of reducing paperwork, as Douglas much prefers meeting to reading.

Christopher Mallaby looked in, having seen the PM today. He commented on the extraordinary mix of dottiness and good sense. At one point, she blurted out: 'I hate Europe and wish we had never left EFTA. [the European Free Trade Association.]' The trouble is that this attitude is all too obvious to the Europeans and the Americans.

2 NOVEMBER 1989

Stephen Wall told Geoffrey Adams privately today that Douglas is planning to put himself forward to accompany the Prime Minister to Camp David later this month. It will be interesting to see if she (or Charles) accepts this. Geoffrey Howe never tackled the question directly, but twice asked me to raise it with Charles – with predictable results.

3 NOVEMBER 1989

I called on Lord Brabazon today, who complained about the pile-up of submissions on Fridays, evidently hoping to avoid boxes at the weekend. I pointed out the impossibility of this, particularly if Douglas Hurd, like John Major, is determined to delegate more to his junior ministers.

Percy Cradock called, confirming Christopher Mallaby's account of the PM's obsessions about the European Community and Germany. Percy commented that there are signs of her obsessions becoming policy. I later discussed with John Fretwell and David Ratford how to handle the briefing for the PM's visit to Camp David in three weeks' time, in order to divert her from launching her obsessions on Bush. Both obsessions could have a very damaging effect.

Stephen Egerton called in advance of his posting to Rome, incidentally confirming that the confusion over decorations exchanged during King Fahd's state visit (in which I appeared to have received a higher Saudi decoration than other recipients) had certainly arisen from Fahd's deliberate decision to downgrade the Saudi honours list (except for mine, for which he had signed the warrant, three years before) because of our refusal to give his young son a GCMG.

5 NOVEMBER 1989

Nigel Lawson appeared on the Brian Walden show today, stating quite clearly that he had given the Prime Minister until Christmas to get rid of Alan Walters – thus contradicting the PM's similar appearance last week, when she claimed that she did not know why Nigel Lawson had resigned.

At least one of the draft minutes that Geoffrey Howe never sent Margaret Thatcher about Charles came near to a threat by Geoffrey also to leave. I now think that Geoffrey's unsuccessful attempts to move Charles (and some press articles which the PM attributed personally to Geoffrey) played a major role in his removal from the FCO.

6 NOVEMBER 1989

Charles Powell called at 9 a.m., having spent much of the weekend dealing with the Lawson affair and its ramifications. No. 10 put out a statement today saying that there was no contradiction between what the PM and Lawson had said respectively on television. Charles told me that, just after Lawson had resigned, he received a telephone call from Julian Amery, reminding the PM that, in the 1920s, Lord Reading had been called in, as a very senior member of the party, and that he, Julian Amery, was available – presumably to be Foreign Secretary? [A story which, many years later, I passed on to Amery's biographer, Richard Bassett, even though Amery himself presumably tells the story in his diaries.]

I talked to Charles about the PM's visit to Camp David, trying to alert him to the dangers of the PM Euro-bashing in front of President Bush.

My lunch today with Norman St John-Stevas, and my drink this evening with Ray Whitney at the House of Commons, revealed that both of them are deeply disturbed by the PM's current attitude towards Europe, and that both feared that we were allowing Britain to become marginalised. Her interview in the *Sunday Correspondent* yesterday is an extraordinary document, revealing a lot of her obsessions about the Community, and again hinting, à la Bruges, that she would like to see a much expanded Europe, including EFTA and others. Also some hilarious use of the first person plural (immortalised in her famous announcement outside No. 10: 'We have become a grandmother'). 'One realised that we were becoming very tired.'

7 NOVEMBER 1989

The FCO has received quite a battering this week, both on Vietnamese boat people (with a particularly offensive article in *The Spectator* by Auberon Waugh), and on hostages (with a programme on ITN last night claiming, rather implausibly, that Britain is the only country to have mishandled their hostage problem).

Tim Lankester called for our regular FCO/ODA round-up. He seems quite shaken by the experience of Kuala Lumpur, and the extent to which the Prime Minister has withdrawn into her private circle, compared with when Tim was at No. 10 as the Treasury private secretary.

Douglas Hurd seems to have handled his first Foreign Affairs Council very skilfully, and had a good dinner with Delors, announcing at his subsequent press conference that, in his view, there was a 'natural alliance' between Britain and the Commission – not the sort of thing one hears much from No. 10!

8 NOVEMBER 1989

I attended Douglas Hurd's meeting on China and Hong Kong, with Alan Donald present. Douglas's style of holding meetings is a joy compared to Geoffrey Howe's. At the end of Geoffrey's meetings, I was never clear what had been decided, if anything; I used to read the private secretary's records with interest, as if I had not been there. Douglas's own summing up of some of his meetings was so clear that the record could almost have been turned, word for word, into telegrams of instructions.

Douglas told me today that he wants to experiment with a weekly meeting of all his ministers, PPSs and whips, including myself and the private secretary, to discuss parliamentary and public handling of foreign affairs issues, in the lines of meetings he apparently held as Home Secretary.

I also discussed with Douglas today the handling of the PM's visit to

Camp David later this month – both on European issues and on Germany. Helmut Kohl rather ostentatiously today singled out Bush and Mitterrand for their line on the problem of East Germany – with no mention of Margaret Thatcher. The situation in East Germany changes at an astounding pace, with both the government and the politburo having resigned this week.

9 NOVEMBER 1989

I had to leave a meeting early to see Francis Maude, to whom some MPs have complained about 'sloppy briefing' on the United Nations from the department. I got Duncan Slater to sort it out and to brief Maude himself; but Francis pointed out that antagonising a few MPs could set back all the hard work we have done to overcome basic antagonism towards the FCO in parts of the Tory Party.

10 NOVEMBER 1989

I spent much of today discussing the extraordinary developments in Berlin, and the Prime Minister's response to it. She was apparently appalled to see pictures of the Bundestag singing 'Deutschland Über Alles', which she described as 'a dagger in my heart'. She was persuaded to put out a welcoming statement in her name at 11 a.m., which was passed to the Germans. The government also agreed today to offer the use of our military camps and installations for the use of refugees from East Germany. But the PM was apparently strongly opposed to the idea at Cabinet yesterday.

I have tried to ensure that Margaret Thatcher's speech at the Lord Mayor's banquet on Monday contains warm references to Helmut Kohl; Charles Powell's present draft contains warm references only to the Prime Minister herself, Reagan and Bush. I have put up a note to Douglas Hurd, with a line for him to take with the PM next week, before her visit to Camp David. But it seems very doubtful whether anyone can persuade her to conceal her strong distaste for Germans.

13 NOVEMBER 1989

After an extraordinary weekend, with the breaking down of parts of the Berlin Wall and the sacking of Zhivkov in Bulgaria, I had three and a half hours of talks with Bob Kimmitt, who is also visiting Brussels, Paris and Bonn this week.

In a private, opening half hour, he mentioned some concern in Washington at what they thought was anxiety here over a lessening of the special relationship. He assured me that although the Thatcher/Reagan relationship had been one of 'the heart', Bush saw his relationship with her as more 'intellectual', and thought he had already established it as Vice-President. He also indirectly raised the PM's remarks in Kuala Lumpur about American hypocrisy over the Vietnamese boat people (when she had referred to American deportations to Haiti, Mexico and so on), and passed on a plea from Larry Eagleburger that we should not air our differences in public. I countered by expressing our hope that the Americans would also keep quiet about their disagreements with us on Vietnamese boat people, and not lobby against us with the United Nations High Commissioner for Refugees.

Otherwise, we had a good session of talks, covering East–West relations; arms control; Hong Kong; Iraq; Lebanon; and South Africa. Kimmitt is impressive, and spoke without a single note (unlike myself, who had been given vast briefing folders).

Virginia and I went to the Lord Mayor's banquet this evening, at which Margaret Thatcher delivered her speech (see above). At drinks afterwards at the Mansion House, she was anxious to discover whether I had got 'the message' of her speech, by which she presumably meant her veiled warn-ings against German reunification. But it was a good and witty speech, well delivered (with much joking about the fact that both she and the new Lord Mayor, Hugh Bidwell, are grocers). [Many years later, I met the headmistress of Norwich High School for Girls, Valerie Bidwell, on a Swan Hellenic Cruise, and asked her husband, Jim, whether he was related to Hugh Bidwell. His answer was: 'No. Hugh is from the Grocer side of the family.']

15 NOVEMBER 1989

I attended the first of Douglas Hurd's new meetings with ministers, whips and PPSs, with Robert Cooper, Andrew Burns and Stephen Wall. A useful discussion on the follow-up to Douglas's meeting yesterday with the PM on Eastern Europe and Germany. I later held a meeting myself, to dish out the work, involving messages to Gorbachev and Bush. Douglas thinks he is more or less in line with the PM on her approach to Saturday's dinner in Paris, though No. 10 have unwisely been putting it about that the PM wants discussion of Eastern Europe to swamp any discussion of EMU and the Social Charter at Strasbourg.

Charles Powell told Stephen Wall that the PM was less happy with the meeting, and suspects Douglas of peddling an independent line; she had also muttered to him darkly about FCO 'treachery' at Madrid, telling Douglas that she would tell him about it one day. I fear that this is a reference to David Hannay, to whom she said at Madrid: 'Are you working for me, or against me?'

Credentials this morning were followed by a farewell audience for six retiring heads of mission and their wives, whose conversation in the ante-room during the credentials ceremony reminded me that when heads of mission and their wives get together, it becomes a cross between a cocktail party and a Diplomatic Service Wives' Association coffee party.

16 NOVEMBER 1989

I joined Tim Sainsbury for an early meeting to brief David Orr and John Hanson on the extra £5 million which the British Council has got this year. David Orr was (for him) very generous about it, saying that even the chaps on the desks had been excited by the news.

17 NOVEMBER 1989

In a secret and personal letter to the service, dated today, I wrote the following about Douglas Hurd and John Major:

> The press have predictably tried to probe the extent to which Douglas Hurd is his own man, or whether foreign policy is ultimately decided by the Prime Minister. In reply to just that question, he told the BBC World Service last week that the Prime Minister had an important part in foreign policy, particularly nowadays when there are a great many summits, and when heads of government are pitchforked into foreign affairs in a way which was not so when he himself joined the Foreign Service in 1952. What was crucial was that both sides of Downing Street should work closely and confidently together. He went on to say that he had worked with the Prime Minister in his last two ministerial offices, and had never found any difficulty in getting a relationship which was not subservient, 'where we swap ideas and occasionally arguments, and in the end of that an agreement is reached which we both respect'. In response to a later question about the updating of our policy on Cambodia, and whether this was the Prime Minister's or his own initiative, Douglas Hurd replied: 'Of course it is my initiative. I am the Foreign Secretary, and here was an area of policy which seemed to me to need updating.'
>
> Few of you will probably need any introduction to Douglas Hurd. He came into the job with great enthusiasm, revealing the extent to

which he has kept himself very well informed on foreign affairs since he was last in the office as a Minister of State in 1983… In any case, Douglas Hurd comes to his new responsibilities with the experience shared with his Permanent Under-Secretary of having served as private secretary to the PUS!

On John Major, I wrote:

I was personally sad to see him leave the office, and I think that he was genuinely coming round to realise that this was a job which he could enjoy. Indeed he told me so, in the rather unpropitious circumstances of Kuala Lumpur. There is no doubt that the first, and as it turned out the only, three months of his time as Foreign Secretary had been difficult for him in terms of the steepness of the learning curve required, though I can report that his sense of humour was well up to enjoying *Private Eye*'s lampooning of his inexperience in their diary about his visit to the United States.

When I went to say goodbye to him on that Friday morning in the Secretary of State's office before his final return to the Treasury, John Major said some kind things about the way in which he had been received by the office and by the service. He particularly emphasised, as he had before, the friendliness which he and Norma Major had found from all of those (sadly too few) members of the service they had met. So I should hope! But it has made me wonder quite what they were both expecting?

20–25 NOVEMBER 1989:
VISITS TO PRAGUE, SOFIA AND BUDAPEST

[This is not the place for a detailed account of the visits that Virginia and I paid to these three European capitals. But they came at such an extraordinary moment of political change in all three governments that the following snippets may be worth recording here.]

An excellent programme had been arranged for us in Prague, including a call on Pavel Sadovsky, the Secretary General at the Foreign Ministry, with whom I had been delegated to raise a human rights question on behalf of CSCE (Commission on Security and Cooperation in Europe) – a hard-faced communist apparatchik, flanked by three officials (sitting directly opposite me) who barely tried to conceal their agreement with all my arguments. The young man concerned was in fact released two days later – thereby constituting the only tangible diplomatic success of my career!

Our conversation in the Foreign Ministry was in full earshot of the students demonstrating in Wenceslas Square, and our ambassador and I later joined them (though we were not, I think, identified).

On Sofia, my most striking memory is of a call which ambassadors were invited to pay, and which I joined, on the new non-Communist President Mladenov and his Foreign Minister (the second of whom asked me to pass on particularly warm greetings to Douglas Hurd).

In Budapest, I recall particularly my discussion with László Kovács, the Secretary General at the Foreign Ministry, who was astonishingly frank about anti-Russian sentiment in Hungary, and their resentment at the continuing presence of Russian troops.

27 NOVEMBER 1989

The Prime Minister's meeting with President Bush at Camp David (not accompanied by Douglas Hurd) seems to have been quite hard pounding, with Bush pressing her both on defence questions and on her attitude to the European Community. Meanwhile, Vietnamese boat people are receiving vast coverage in the press, in expectation of early repatriation.

28 NOVEMBER 1989

Douglas Hurd and I attended the memorial service at St Margaret's Westminster for Derek Inchyra (for whom Douglas had worked as his private secretary, see page 134, above), with Alec Douglas-Home sitting on my other side. A large congregation of very old diplomats, including Lord Gladwyn and several half-forgotten faces from the 1950s. Inchyra's heir, Robin Inchyra, told me he had had to tell his father that I was unavailable abroad, since he was in a rather wandering state, and had some worry about Italy and kept asking to see me. Robin thought that his father remembered having disobeyed some instruction during the war, and that it was preying on his mind.

29 NOVEMBER 1989

I attended Douglas Hurd's weekly meeting of ministers and PPSs, at which there was a good discussion on German reunification, following Kohl's speech in the Bundestag yesterday. Horst Teltschik, Kohl's private secretary, briefed Christopher Mallaby and his French and American colleagues last night, revealing significantly that Kohl had been in close contact with Bush, Mitterrand, Gorbachev and Egon Krenz, but not Mrs Thatcher. She was due to see Genscher this afternoon, and Douglas tried to have a word with her beforehand to advise her on the line to take with him. When Stephen Wall proposed this to Charles Powell, the latter replied: 'The Prime Minister knows perfectly well what line to take; but I suppose if the Foreign Secretary insists on seeing her first, that is his prerogative.'

I have also discussed with Douglas Hurd and William Waldegrave the embassy in Beirut, which the Prime Minister wants to pull out to Cyprus, in view of the high risk of a Syrian attack against General Aoun. I have persuaded Douglas to contest the PM's decision; but an assessment by the JIC today makes it probable that she will insist on it. I am depressed (as is Douglas) at the thought of emptying yet another mission in the Middle East; Kabul, Damascus, Tehran and Tripoli are already without ambassadors.

30 NOVEMBER 1989

Douglas Hurd continued to fight today against the Prime Minister's wish to close Beirut, and has gained at least another few days. He is being quite impressively tough with her. He told me this morning that she had again reverted to 'FCO perfidy' in Madrid, with explicit criticism of David Hannay. He had argued strongly that he knew David well, and that he had never heard him utter a word of criticism against her; on the contrary, David had fought staunchly for British interests. I have agreed to put a submission to him on top appointments before Christmas; but he is a joy to work with.

1 DECEMBER 1989

Charles Powell arrived late for his bilateral this evening, having had to cope with tantrums from the PM. He did not reveal what they were about; but Douglas Hurd told me yesterday that he thought the leadership election was fussing her more than she would admit. She is also following a ludicrously full programme. Even on foreign affairs, she has had a major appointment every day this week, including Wałęsa tomorrow, and Brussels (for Bush's debriefing on the Malta summit with Gorbachev) on Sunday.

Percy Cradock called this evening, in near despair about the Prime Minister's working methods. He says that meetings get worse and worse, though Douglas Hurd is considerably more effective at putting forward arguments than Geoffrey Howe was. He acknowledged that Douglas has put up a much stronger and more effective counter-argument about Beirut than Geoffrey would ever have agreed to do.

5 DECEMBER 1989

Michael Alexander called and gave me an account of yesterday and the post-mortem briefing by Bush in Brussels. The PM had been very upset by Bush's second intervention on Europe, in which he called for greater 'integration', and appeared also to be supporting German reunification, and a follow-on meeting on CFE – all of them bugbears for Margaret Thatcher. She was apparently very angry when they left the meeting, muttering that this was the thanks one got for being a loyal ally.

She was also distinctly cool with Chancellor Kohl, looking extremely glum when he came up to greet her. Michael thinks that her anti-German obsession is very worrying, and that she really is in danger of marginalising us in Europe (though events in Germany this week certainly justify some concern over the German problem). Bush later telephoned her, having evidently been alerted by Henry Catto (who in turn had been alerted by Charles Powell), and reassured her that his remarks on integration were not intended to interfere in a European argument, but were purely designed to support the 1992 process.

The result of the leadership election this evening produced fifty-seven abstentions or votes against Margaret Thatcher – a result which most of the press, other than the *Mirror*, interpret as fairly good for her. But there is quite widespread feeling that she is losing her touch.

6 DECEMBER 1989

Douglas Hurd had a preparatory talk with Dumas in Paris yesterday (in advance of the European Council in Strasbourg), and later made a vivid impression by giving a rare British ministerial interview in French, having already impressed the Italians as Home Secretary by conducting talks in Italian.

President Egon Krenz of the GDR (German Democratic Republic) was sacked this afternoon, with a non-Communist appointed in his place; there were also reports of people breaking in to army barracks to steal arms.

Messages today about Vietnamese boat people from both Henry Catto and Antony Acland, arguing strongly against going ahead with mandatory repatriation, followed by a further, strongly worded message from Antony of the 'grave damage' to our image in the United States. I think we shall have to call off the first aircraft load scheduled for next week, particularly since Jim Baker is now due here on Monday.

7 DECEMBER 1989

Douglas held an early meeting to discuss Antony Acland's advice on Vietnamese boat people, initially inclined to accept our official advice. But ministerial opinion won the day, largely on the grounds of the likely reaction in Hong Kong to further indecision in London. Douglas cleared this decision with the Prime Minister after Cabinet today.

Virginia went to a wives meeting at Lancaster House, to which the Duchess of York was invited. Judy Hurd did well, and spoke nicely.

8 DECEMBER 1989

At the European Council in Strasbourg today, the Prime Minister tried hard to whip up support for a meeting of the 'Berlin Powers' – though it was not clear whether this included the Russians or the Germans (i.e. the occupying powers or the Quadripartite Committee).

Meanwhile, the Soviet embassy telephoned me and read out a message from Shevardnadze, suggesting an urgent meeting of the 'Berlin ambassadors'. It is clear that the Russians are very steamed up about potential chaos in East Germany, and early moves towards reunification.

Michael Alexander sent me a message today, reporting Bob Blackwill of the White House as again warning us that the United States government does not want Britain to appear isolated from the European Community, or from the integration process in Europe. The handling of Germany is now likely to preoccupy ministers even more than Vietnam, Hong Kong or Cambodia. But the pressures on the office at present are horrendous, and not made easier by the flu epidemic. We have received 16,000 letters this week on Cambodia alone.

I lunched with Robin Butler, mainly to gossip about the Prime Minister, who has been sweetness and light since the leadership election earlier this week. We discussed the possibility that she might give up in the spring, and I reminded Robin that John Major had twice referred to that possibility with me. Robin recounted a curious story that Denis Thatcher had said that once a leader was challenged, there was unlikely to be any turning back – as if he expected an early departure.

11 DECEMBER 1989

Although business at the European Council in Germany has been conducted with remarkably good humour (Margaret Thatcher even winning a round of applause for some gracious remarks she made about the European Community), she is very steamed up about German reunification, and the danger of violent reactions in East Germany.

I joined Douglas Hurd's talks with Jim Baker over lunch today. Baker opened with a deliberate statement about the special relationship (following the PM's reaction to Bush's remarks about European integration in Brussels). Charles Powell told me later that she had been pretty cool with Baker, when he repeated his statement to Douglas. But she is obviously working hard to soften her image, following the leadership elections.

12 DECEMBER 1989

Douglas Hurd's meeting with ministers and PPSs was mainly concerned with Vietnamese boat people. In spite of TV shots of screaming refugees, and predictable allegations of 'shameful behaviour' in press and Parliament, the operation in fact went off very smoothly, with all fifty-eight boarding and leaving the aircraft without any show of force, or even persuasion. Tim Raison and David Ennals are to visit Hanoi shortly to monitor their condition.

Robin Butler called this afternoon to urge that John Weston should keep in close touch with the Cabinet Office over Eastern Europe. John is being very resistant to the idea that the FCO (and particularly himself) should lose control of the subject. I spoke to him at the News Department Christmas party this evening, but also told Stephen Wall that I thought that both John Weston and William Waldegrave (whom Douglas has asked to take control of the German question) would need frequent injections of 'Basingstoke'. [This is a reference to W. S. Gilbert's *Ruddigore*, where Mad Margaret can be calmed by shouting 'Basingstoke', and which I was surprised to discover, when I joined the board of De La Rue, meeting in Basingstoke, several years later, was unknown to any other member of the board.]

15 DECEMBER 1989

Right of abode for Hong Kongers has blown up into a political row in the Conservative Party, with the right wing, led by Norman Tebbit, stirring up opposition to any grant of citizenship. The decision by OD(K) to grant citizenship to about 230,000 against the wish of the Home Office will go to Cabinet on Wednesday.

Douglas Hurd seems to have had excellent quadripartite talks in Brussels, obviously establishing good relationships with Dumas and Genscher; the latter is particularly important, given the PM's poor relationship with Kohl. I had a word today with John Weston about a potential conflict between departments on dealing with Eastern Europe and Germany, as well as Waldegrave's tendency to harness Assistant Under-Secretaries, as he has with David Gore-Booth. The Waldegrave–Gore-Booth mafia needs to be watched.

Michael does not find Tom King a particularly thoughtful or effective Defence Secretary, though better than his earlier experience of him in Employment had led him to expect. Michael welcomed the idea of another Chevening meeting.

19 DECEMBER 1989

Trouble has broken out in Romania this week, with what our ambassador, Michael Atkinson, described as a massacre in one of the mainly Hungarian towns near the Hungarian border. William Waldegrave went slightly over the top this evening, calling for all countries to help bring down Ceauşescu's regime. I asked for the text to be flashed to Michael Atkinson, since it would, for most governments, be a pretext to break relations, or at least to chuck out the ambassador. When I went to William's Christmas party in the Durbar Court this evening, William looked distinctly nervous, asking me if he had got us into trouble; he probably has, though his remarks will be widely applauded.

20 DECEMBER 1989

The Americans invaded Panama overnight, in an attempt to capture Noriega; but the bird had flown. Bush telephoned the PM early this morning, who characteristically expressed immediate and full support (though legal adviser Arthur Watts pointed out later that it was very difficult to give any clear legal justification for what they had done). No other European or other government expressed support at all, and some (such as Spain) came out with quite strong condemnation.

I submitted two pieces of Christmas reading to Douglas Hurd today: one a selection of papers on German reunification, CFE and European architecture; the second a massive paper by John Boyd on top appointments, for discussion on 3 January.

Percy Cradock spoke to me very privately today about Margaret Thatcher's health and mood; he suspects that she is taking pills or vitamins for her perpetual colds (one of which we had witnessed when she visited us in Luxembourg in the late 1970s), and combining this with occasional drinks. He is finding her much less lucid than usual.

I went to a series of Christmas parties, including lunch with Tim Sainsbury. He told a nice story about his grandfather, who was a keen huntsman, and was once serving behind the counter in Sainsbury's store in Kensington High Street, when a smart hunting woman came into the shop and said, very haughtily: 'Mr Sainsbury, I'm surprised to see you serving in a shop,' to which he replied: 'I'm surprised to see you doing your own shopping.'

21 DECEMBER 1989

Romania appeared to be going up in flames today, with pro-government demonstrations turning, as in Prague, into protests against the President and the police. The Prime Minister and Douglas Hurd decided today to recommend removal of Ceauşescu's GCB – the first such case since the Emperor of Japan during the war.

Douglas commented again on the PM's more relaxed mood, saying that she kept mentioning the need for 'diplomacy' in the present crisis, and has been giving a lot of thought on how to handle Kohl. The trouble is that her gut dislike of Germans is far too obvious, though Kohl was quoted in the press today as making some very complimentary remarks about her.

Virginia joined me this evening for Mike Shingler's Christmas spectacular in the Durbar Court – an extremely well organised affair, with some very good singing and readings (including by both Douglas Hurd and William Waldegrave). I accompanied 'Jingle Bells' on an electronic piano towards the end, while Father Christmas appeared on successive balconies of the court. [Shingler is a born impresario, who was later to organise my retirement party, also in the Durbar Court, in June 1991.]

22 DECEMBER 1989

Romania flared up again today, and it was clear by late morning that Ceauşescu had fallen and fled. Fierce fighting continued in Bucharest and elsewhere. The Romanian ambassador, Soare, had asked to call on John Fretwell at 11.30 a.m. to deliver a long complaint about British statements and alleged interference in Romanian internal affairs. John Fretwell countered by informing the ambassador a) that his President was being stripped of his GCB; and b) that his government had fallen. The ambassador appeared not to have heard the news, and again complained that John's remarks were unwarranted interference. (Soare, having appeared on TV at Heathrow, on leaving London for home, later appealed for medical help for the victims of the uprising – a confused gentleman!)

The rapid fall of Ceauşescu has confounded most of the forecasts, including my own, who told several people earlier this week that I thought Ceauşescu could hang on until death; ironically, a Christmas card arrived today from Hugh Arbuthnott (formerly ambassador in Bucharest, and now in Lisbon) saying that he did not think Romania would go the way of the other 'reformers'.

The Prime Minister was persuaded last night to send a message to Gorbachev to ask for his support for a Security Council debate on Romania, and to bring his influence to bear on Ceauşescu – another first.

Panama meanwhile looks bad; ironic that American action on the Canal should coincide with a major upsurge in Eastern Europe – compare Suez and Hungary in 1956, though in that case Suez blanketed the Hungarian uprising, at least in the British media.

1990

CHRISTMAS AND NEW YEAR
2 JANUARY 1990

Virginia telephoned Veronica Atkinson, who was evacuated from Bucharest with other dependents, having spent hours in the residence cellar with three children, and the Securitate tramping around upstairs, shouting and looting, until they were rescued by the German embassy. The residence was later badly damaged by fire, with the Atkinsons losing most of their belongings.

Douglas Hurd called a meeting this afternoon to discuss the objectives for 1990 and his diary for the next month or so. Life is likely still to be dominated by Europe and Hong Kong, though I have reminded Douglas of the need to continue to pay attention to Japan, India and Australia. He shows some resistance to Japan, while acknowledging its importance. This may again be a generational thing; even someone only one year older than myself may tend to be more anti-Japanese from the war. Margaret Thatcher shows marked signs of such a bias, as did Harold Wilson.

3 JANUARY 1990

Nicky Gordon Lennox called on retirement from Madrid, and gossiped with me about the Prime Minister and Denis Thatcher. He had been struck by how heavily Denis was now drinking, and referred to worries among Margaret Thatcher's close circle that this could become a reason for her to give up early.

In the context of a discussion about top appointments, Stephen Wall claimed that the Prime Minister is opposed to David Hannay 'because there would be too much rapid machine-gun fire from the FCO'. Douglas Hurd asked me jokingly whether my own machine-gun fire had much worried the Prime Minister. I replied that my machine gun had been sited much too far away, during my whole time as PUS, for it to worry Margaret Thatcher.

9 JANUARY 1990

The Prime Minister has reacted very angrily to a telegram from Christopher Mallaby in Bonn about German attitudes to our stance on reunification, saying that she is 'alarmed' that he can be so wrong on our line. Percy Cradock commented to me that the PM has a distressing tendency to shoot the messenger, and to form rapid prejudices, combined with the memory of an elephant.

10 JANUARY 1990

I called on William Waldegrave today to try to persuade him to accept one of Personnel Department's two candidates as his private secretary, both of whom have East European and Middle East experience, in succession to his previous private secretary who has had to be moved because of a liaison with the no. 2 in the PLO office in London. The Gore-Booth machine has already been hard at work trying to identify other candidates, which will infuriate Personnel Department. I have told David Gore-Booth to lay off. And now it emerges that William has been to the private office, and mentioned it to Douglas Hurd, who has undertaken to raise it with me. Dear God!

Douglas Hurd told me that, in the course of a talk with the Prime Minister about senior appointments, she agreed to see one senior appointee before his posting, mentioning that she had seen Crispin Tickell before his posting 'and look how well he has done'. More seriously, she complained about the FCO's failure to follow through with imaginative ideas, claiming that the French always outdo us with initiatives – a bee in her bonnet, which Douglas is not inclined to take too tragically.

I attended a small meeting chaired by Robin Butler, at my suggestion, to discuss Whitehall coordination on drugs work. Rather surprisingly, he got Clive Whitmore's agreement to transfer the drugs committee from the Home Office to the Cabinet committee. When I reported this later to Douglas Hurd, he was very surprised, and thought David Mellor would resist very strongly, having just got his teeth into drugs work.

11 JANUARY 1990

A two-hour seminar at Carlton Gardens on Germany, CFE and European Architecture. There is slight gloom among the troops who have prepared extensive papers for the Chequers seminar on 28 January, since Douglas now thinks – perhaps in response to the Prime Minister's recent grumbles – that he should produce three punchy minutes, rather than sending departmental papers. I later pointed out him, as he readily accepted, that it was a pity to suppress some extensive and imaginative work by the department, thereby fuelling the Prime Minister's belief that no one in the FCO ever produces any ideas.

Meanwhile, Alan Clark (now a minister at the MOD) has put forward some personal ideas (well covered in his subsequent diaries) about major reductions in BAOR (the British Army of the Rhine), which will be attractive to the Prime Minister as a supposed 'lever' against reunification (which of course it is not).

Hermann von Richthofen called at noon to deliver a message from Genscher, revealing – rather oddly – that the Russians have made slightly different proposals, suggesting to the Americans meetings at Foreign Minister level, but ambassadorial or Special Envoy level to ourselves. The aim of both proposals is primarily to discuss FRG/GDR relations. We shall need (as Genscher has asked) to keep very close to the Germans on this, since they will be very sensitive to any four-power discussion on anything other than Berlin. There is also the risk that the Prime Minister is likely to share, and will want to respond to, Soviet anxieties. In her present mood, she gives the impression of trusting Gorbachev more than Kohl.

I attended one of Douglas Hurd's ministerial meetings this morning, at which he underlined the importance of not letting Hong Kong swamp all other foreign policy questions. There is a lot of sensitivity in the third world about super-power preoccupation with Europe; and there is a danger of British ministers thinking only of Europe and Hong Kong at present. William Waldegrave, in particular, is reluctant to pay any attention to Africa, other than South Africa.

12 JANUARY 1990

A long bilateral with Douglas Hurd today before his departure for Hong Kong and my own departure for East Africa next week. Douglas does not want us to take any specific action following the Prime Minister's recent rebuke to the FCO for our failure to follow up ideas, though I pointed out the lack of contact between the PM and middle-ranking officials in the FCO.

I also spoke with him about the continued protection arrangements for Henry Catto that I discussed yesterday with Tim Sainsbury, who has minuted strongly on the subject. Henry faces a 'unique risk' and should have appropriate protection. Douglas, as an ex-Home Secretary, is very reluctant to argue the case against his old department, but has agreed to talk to David Waddington about it next week.

UKDEL Vienna have just discovered that the French, Italian and German foreign ministers have got together to speak at the forthcoming

CFE conference without telling us. A sign of the times, with the UK being marginalised, or perhaps treated as 'the United States' anchor to windward', on which Antony Acland has just sent in a powerful warning from Washington.

Douglas Hurd also mentioned to me his dinner last night with Julian Amery, whom he described as 'a sort of Foreign Secretary in exile'. He asked me if Julian had been a nuisance in the office; I said that, on the contrary, he was sometimes quite useful, e.g. in arranging for officials to meet Savimbi.

There were more astounding developments today in Eastern Europe, with the Romanians tonight outlawing the Communist Party, and Gorbachev telling the Lithuanians this morning that he had ordered legislation to be prepared to enable them to break away as an independent state, if that was what they wanted.

16–23 JANUARY 1990: VISITS TO EAST AFRICA
24 JANUARY 1990

Home for the inevitable pile-up of paper, including an extraordinary report from Harare of the Zimbabwe Foreign Minister commiserating with a group of East European ambassadors on the terrible upheaval which the Imperialist West is creating in Eastern Europe, and expressing the hope that all will return to normal again! The ambassadors tried, but failed, to persuade him that it was nothing whatsoever to do with the West, and that they were all delighted at what was happening.

25 JANUARY 1990

I called on Lynda Chalker, mainly to report on my Africa trip (where she is shortly going again), but also to remedy the long gap since I last saw her *à deux*. She raised with me the arrangements for aid to Eastern

Europe, where she rightly wants more ODA involvement. But she seems to have had a good meeting with William Waldegrave, and has reached an understanding with him.

I also discussed this with Douglas Hurd this evening, and got his support for the idea of a Cabinet Committee on Eastern Europe at both ministerial and official level. He is showing that he is already far more self-confident that John Major was (for understandable reasons); but he takes little interest in personnel questions, or the no. 1 board, and seems happy to accept our advice.

27-30 JANUARY 1990: VISIT TO WASHINGTON

Much of Douglas Hurd's visit, and my own talks with Bob Zoellick and Bob Blackwill in Washington, dealt with Germany, on which there are new developments daily. [I was told, many years later, that the FCO could find no trace of a long reporting telegram which I sent from the embassy; but which was eventually looked for, at my suggestion, and found in No. 10's papers.]

Hans Modrow, the new Prime Minister of the GDR, has brought forward the elections to March, and Gorbachev has been quoted as saying that he would now accept German reunification. There is, of course, a lot of work to be done on various implications for NATO, the European Community, CSCE and our Four-Power status in Berlin. The Americans have thrown the Prime Minister into a state by telling her on Saturday that Bush intends to announce, in his State of the Union message, further considerable reductions of US troops in Germany.

Eagleburger and Gates were sent over to discuss all this with the Prime Minister, while Douglas and I were still in Washington. The PM told them that she would support Bush publicly ('as is our habit'), but that she took strong issue with the apparent failure to consider the strategic implications. It certainly seems to have been handled in Washington in an entirely 'political' way; the only person in the Pentagon who was told was the Defence Secretary.

31 JANUARY 1990

I attended Douglas Hurd's ministerial meeting, at which there was general agreement that we need to do something to correct the image that we are the most opposed to reunification. But it won't be easy; the PM still speaks pretty incautiously to all and sundry.

David Hannay called, worried about our isolation in the community on the line we are taking over Eastern Europe – i.e. that we are the only member who does not believe that the thaw in the East calls for a tighter and more 'Federal' community. I also talked to him about the PM's views on Germany, on which we have seen some further, very hurt, German comment (though Ewen Fergusson reported today that François Scheer thinks that the French are equally in the doghouse, if not more so).

My bilateral with Douglas Hurd this afternoon was quite jolly, though I find him a much less open, or jokey, person than either Geoffrey Howe or John Major. I discussed him with Antony Acland during the Washington visit, since Antony and Douglas were exact contemporaries at Eton and Oxford, and are mutual godparents to their children. Although I still find him a very private and bottled-up person, I do find him very easy to work with, and receptive to argument and advice, in spite of his experience and confidence in dealing both with papers and the Prime Minister.

2 FEBRUARY 1990

Stirring events in South Africa today, with promises to release Mandela and un-ban the ANC.

5 FEBRUARY 1990

Stephen Wall had a row with Charles Powell yesterday (Sunday), when Charles telephoned Catharine from Chequers, demanding to talk to Stephen. Stephen told Catharine to say that Richard Gozney was the duty private secretary, and that he should talk to him. Charles refused to do so. (This may be an incidental, and rather unfortunate, result of my telling Stephen that he should delegate more!)

6 FEBRUARY 1990

Geoffrey Howe tells me that the Conservative Party ball, chaired this week by Bridgett Walters, had been totally boycotted by the Jewish community, presumably in protest at Dennis Walters's well-known pro-Arab views. Geoffrey is outraged, and was muttering about the hypocrisy of Jews applying boycotts, when they have consistently tried to get the government to fight the Arab boycott.

7 FEBRUARY 1990

A mixed press for Douglas Hurd's speech in Berlin yesterday, with some commentators describing it as the first real sign of political thinking on Germany by the government; with others trying to draw a distinction with the PM's more critical remarks in Parliament yesterday. The office is still being deluged with letters from No. 10, urging Douglas Hurd to get together with the French and the Americans *à trois*.

8 FEBRUARY 1990

A difficult meeting today with Douglas Hurd and Francis Maude on Hong Kong, to decide how to tackle the extremely tough position the Chinese are taking on constitutional development in Hong Kong. Percy Cradock, who was present, is very worried that Francis Maude's rather gung-ho attitude could lead us into real crisis. It was an interesting example of officials arguing for settlement, with ministers extremely worried about parliamentary accusations of kowtowing. A more or less satisfactory conclusion was reached, that David Wilson should be asked to try to ensure that EXCO support it.

There was apparently a tempestuous Cabinet meeting today. Len Appleyard was later to give us a vivid and amusing account, which led Douglas Hurd to remark: 'Cabinet now consists of three items: parliamentary affairs; home affairs; and xenophobia.' The Prime Minister was said to have been in a very erratic mood, lashing out at our friends and allies, but suggesting at one point that we should be resuming arms sales to Iraq and Iran – a bit ironic, since the Home Office has given its reasons for expelling nine Iranians (without consulting or informing the FCO) that they were supporters of the Iranian regime.

9 FEBRUARY 1990

Talks today with German Permanent Under-Secretary Jürgen Sudhoff, almost entirely dominated by the German question. I started with a private word, trying to correct the impression in Germany that we are the most obstructive and reluctant of Germany's allies on reunification. I read him two extracts from Douglas Hurd's recent speech in Germany, but admitted that Margaret Thatcher was more suspicious. Jürgen said that he entirely understood her feelings; if he were a 65-year-old Brit, he would probably feel the same. But he was full of assurances that no German could ever contemplate making a third ghastly mistake again this century.

When I thanked Sudhoff for keeping to this visit in spite of everything going on (Kohl and Genscher leave for Moscow tomorrow), he said it had caused the only real row he had had with Genscher in three years as his

PUS. But it was a good day of talks, though I was not entirely reassured that Sudhoff had got the message that Germany must consult her allies before taking up firm positions on NATO, the European Community, CSCE and Four-Power status.

There is clearly an overwhelming feeling in the FRG that the GDR is galloping towards chaos and bankruptcy (a word which caused a political row in Germany today), and they simply don't know how to react. Sudhoff himself described Kohl's offer yesterday of Monetary Union as a panic measure; no one, least of all West German bankers, knew what the effect would be.

East Germans are still pouring out at a rate of nearly 3,000 a day, and many factories, hospitals, schools and institutes are closing down. The whole distribution and administrative systems are paralysed.

We have just discovered that Nicholas Ridley has been discussing a revamp and privatisation of export promotion (since John Banham helpfully copied his reply to Ridley to Douglas Hurd!), but has given orders that the FCO are not to be told. It looks as though Douglas himself has some fairly unorthodox views, which we need to discover (and possibly try to correct).

More rumblings today from No. 10 on the PM's views on Germany – nicely summed up in one newspaper headline as: 'Maggie furious on German Unity; says UK must not pay'. Douglas Hurd has meanwhile had some useful talks with Baker, Dumas and Genscher in Ottawa, with more to come.

13 FEBRUARY 1990

Talks in the margins of the Open Skies Conference in Ottawa today seem to have produced a consensus that there should be talks between the two Germanys and the Four Powers fairly soon after the GDR elections. This was blazoned in the *Daily Mail* as a brilliant suggestion by Margaret Thatcher!

The PM continues to bleat about reunification to all her visitors – the Polish Prime Minister being the latest. She is also revelling in being the only politician to argue for the lifting of all sanctions against South Africa; she provoked a blazing row in the House of Commons today by accusing Neil Kinnock of taking his orders from the ANC.

14 FEBRUARY 1990

Douglas Hurd returned from Ottawa this morning, having reached firm agreement on an early meeting of the '4+2' talks, or '2+4' as the Germans prefer to call it, after the GDR elections in March. Genscher flew in from Ottawa today, and saw the PM, in an attempt to reconcile German and British views on reunification. According to von Richthofen, Douglas Hurd's presence was crucial in getting the Prime Minister to declare 'public support' for the German position afterwards, though he told me that the PM was very grudging.

I had my bilateral with Douglas Hurd this evening in the House of Commons, while he was struggling with a bad-tempered debate on South Africa. It emerged that Douglas does indeed have some fairly unorthodox views on trade promotion (see above), though he accepted my argument that we should be very careful not to set back the much greater acceptance in the service that 'trade' is an important part of the job. I suspect that his understandable preoccupation with the great issues of the day may lead him to underestimate the importance of other aspects of diplomatic work.

15 FEBRUARY 1990

William Waldegrave asked to see me to air his worries about a Joint Unit running the East European Knowhow Fund. Part of his trouble is his antipathy to Lynda Chalker and the ODA. He has also apparently had a row with Lynda over who should speak to the Southern African Development Community conference in April. But the Joint Unit is clearly floundering under the weight of enquiries and proposals for ways to help Poland and the other East Europeans.

16 FEBRUARY 1990

The Prime Minister has exploded to Douglas Hurd about press stories earlier this week about relations between No. 10 and the FCO, saying that she is all the sadder since she regarded relations between us as 'particularly good'. According to Stephen Wall, she went on to make complimentary remarks about me, saying that the trouble was with 'those under him' (i.e. quite a lot of people!).

19 FEBRUARY 1990

More press coverage today on the PM's anti-German speech to the Board of Deputies of British Jews. When I had to talk to Julian Bullard this afternoon, to discourage him from accepting an invitation to appear on *Panorama* with Gordievsky, he asked me: 'Can't you stop her talking about Germany?' Douglas Hurd takes a realistic and sensible view, pointing out to me today that she has in fact moved quite a long way in her views. Her meeting with Genscher last week seems to have helped a bit, though Kohl is still her real *bête noire*.

20 FEBRUARY 1990

I lunched at the European Commission offices, chaired by John Drew. The department have a fairly low opinion of his effectiveness, but it can't be easy running an office in the knowledge that the Prime Minister has the lowest opinion of your organisation (and I should know!).

Douglas Hurd spent today in Dublin, wrestling with sanctions, on which we are isolated in our wish to lift the investment ban on South

Africa. Ironically, this is one case in which the Prime Minister is criticised for being too flexible; the press continue to attack her for her inflexibility over Germany. The Germans themselves have got into confusion over the future of German troops in East Germany, with Genscher and the Defence Minister contradicting each other publicly.

21 FEBRUARY 1990

My hearing before the Foreign Affairs Committee went fairly smoothly, and was cut short by Ted Heath's fortieth anniversary lunch, to which all the Conservative members were going – as did his arch-rival Margaret Thatcher. The *Times* correspondent later told News Department that the hearing was not newsworthy 'since Sir Patrick was so open with the committee. There is only news when mandarins are obviously trying to hide things.'

22 FEBRUARY 1990

I gave lunch to Simon Barrington-Ward, the Bishop of Coventry and Prelate of the Order of St Michael and St George, of which I am ex-officio secretary. He has been engaged in some pretty direct and critical correspondence with ministers about sanctions for South Africa. After I had given Simon William Waldegrave's similarly hard-hitting reply, he told me he found himself in a slightly awkward position, leading a Southern African Group; but he assured me that he was not just a 'trendy lefty'. He is an extremely nice and intelligent man (who apparently, like Tony Lloyd, competed with Douglas Hurd for all the prizes at Eton), and a convinced and scholarly Hegelian (which interested me, since I had always understood that the Warden of Merton, Geoffrey Mure, was one of 'the last Hegelians').

23 FEBRUARY 1990

A meeting of DUSs, mainly to discuss immigration and visa policy. We reached general agreement that we may have to adopt a more selective policy (like the Australians, Canadians and Americans), designed to attract more skilled migrants. The single market and open frontiers in the Community are already posing some formidable problems for our immigration policy and visa control, particularly since we rely much less on post-entry control than others. Compulsory identity cards may well have to be introduced. An FCO poll last year seemed to belie the widespread assumption that this would be widely unpopular – a point I have always found difficult to understand, in days when we carry identification in the form of credit and debit cards, security passes and driving licences.

Hermann von Richthofen called to deliver Genscher's bread-and-butter letter after his visit last week, having been instructed to do so at the highest level – clearly a deliberate attempt to counter press stories here and in Bonn of an Anglo-German row. Hermann was very insistent (in marked contrast to von Ploetz at the NATO Council yesterday) that the Germans were keen to consult their friends and allies on the 'external' implications of reunification – a phrase deliberately designed to exclude the future disposition of the Bundeswehr, on which Genscher made some unhelpful remarks this week, in contradiction to his defence colleague, Stoltenberg. I rather formally gave Hermann the text of Douglas Hurd's speech in the House of Commons yesterday, asking him to report it to Bonn.

The Cabinet-Secretary-designate for Namibia (Mbumba), called on me today and asked for a quick resume of what a Foreign Service is and does, which I tried to give him in half an hour!

27 FEBRUARY 1990

Douglas Hurd used his ministerial meeting this morning to talk about

Germany and the Prime Minister's idea of using the CSCE to reassure the Poles. Andrew Wood has reported from Washington that Bob Blackwill's account of the President's reactions to his long conversation with the PM last weekend shows that Bush seems to have become seriously alarmed by the impression that the PM somehow regards the Russians as a bulwark against the Germans. He is also said to be worried by anti-British feeling in Germany, even to the extent of wondering whether Kohl would agree to Britain being included in the '2+4' talks. This is probably an exaggeration, but a sad reflection on the extent of current distrust between Thatcher and Kohl. The PM continues to air her worries about Germany with all and sundry.

A meeting today of my board of management, discussing the possible need to close posts, e.g. in Panama City. But all closures carry heavy penalties, and even closing subsidiary posts raises storms of protest. In the short term, they do not even save money, and we have often – e.g. in Stuttgart – found ourselves needing to reopen after a few years.

I also found that the threat to close posts carried less and less credibility with ministers. [Many years later, Malcolm Rifkind told one of my successors, John Coles, that, as Defence Secretary, he had kept a list in his desk of all the threats made by the chiefs of staff to close down regiments, or even regimental bands. (It used to be said that the last shot in their locker was to abolish the marine band – to which, unfortunately, I could wield no similar threat for foreign secretaries.) Malcolm swore that none of these threats had ever been fulfilled.]

1 MARCH 1990

The government is in increasing difficulty over the poll tax, Hong Kong right of abode, trade figures etc. Douglas Hurd, who is in Budapest this morning, has faced virtual revolt in his constituency over the poll tax.

Jim Callaghan telephoned me about his visit to Portugal next week and commented (as others have done) on the amount of travel Douglas is doing: 'I know he's a young man, but he'll kill himself if he's not careful – you tell him to slow down.'

2 MARCH 1990

I called on Lord Brabazon for one of our regular talks, covering (among other things) homosexuality, on which I have now minuted recommending a switch to home civil service regulations – i.e. considering positive vetting on a case-by-case basis, and no longer an automatic bar. Brabazon looked doubtful and has minuted to Douglas Hurd, rather infelicitously saying he thinks we should 'stand firm'. I doubt whether Douglas will be ready to consider a change of policy, but Frank Berman, the deputy legal adviser, has interestingly pointed out to me that my arguments that security considerations did not any longer justify our policy could put the service in breach of the law, since our only justification would then be discrimination on the basis of sexual preference.

I had a private word today with Douglas Hurd about William Waldegrave's relations with Lynda Chalker, warning him that they could complicate the already difficult functioning of the Knowhow Fund.

Francis Maude has made a bit of an ass of himself this week by briefing the press on the FCO's 'coup' in getting other countries to provide a safety net for Hong Kong. This produced headlines in the *Daily Mail*, most unusually crediting great skill and success to FCO ministers and officials. Douglas Hurd had to issue a comment saying that the story was 'a bit premature' – sadly, it has no foundation at all.

The government are still facing real problems over Hong Kong, and the Prime Minister is now said to be having second thoughts about the Nationality Package – on the grounds that it includes such people as 'artists' and 'social workers'! But the government otherwise is in a mess, with the leak of Peter Walker's imminent retirement yesterday, and the prospect of a diametric reversal in the East Staffordshire by-election. So a defeat on the Nationality Package for Hong Kong (with eighty Tories seriously threatening to vote against it) could be very damaging.

6 MARCH 1990

Chatham House has invited senior civil servants, including Robin Butler and myself, to take part in a poll on attitudes towards the United States. Robin thinks it would be very difficult for us to accept, even anonymously, since it is bound to lead to civil servants commenting on policy. I agree, and discussed it frankly with Jim Eberle this afternoon. It would look fairly odd if the poll result concluded that the most senior civil servants thought that the special relationship had come to an end.

8 MARCH 1990

Two birthdays today: Douglas Hurd (sixty) and Nancy Caccia (eighty). I sent Douglas a card, reminding him that, in other circumstances, he would have retired today, and wishing him many more years in the service.

I have received a ridiculous instruction from ministers that we should strengthen our embassy in Nicaragua. I shall have to tell Douglas Hurd how we have to shift resources; there simply are not enough people to go round.

9 MARCH 1990

Alan Donald called, back from China for the heads of mission conference. I got out the atlas (à la *Yes, Minister*) to look at the map of China with him. He is concerned that we have virtually all our manpower in Peking, in the far north of the country, and none – apart from six people in Shanghai – in the economically important central areas, or in Canton.

Rumours today of a Conservative putsch against Margaret Thatcher, and of her early retirement later this year – causing a drop in sterling and denials from the party (by Geoffrey Howe – how he must hate doing it!).

12 MARCH 1990

A weekend of activity over the Iranian journalist Bazoft, who was sentenced to death on Saturday by Baghdad. Douglas Hurd has decided to fly to Baghdad en route to Oman next week, provided we can be sure that the Iraqis have not carried out the execution before he gets there. But it is a formidable political risk. I discussed it with Jim Callaghan this evening, recalling his flight to Kampala to release Denis Hills.

John Kerr reported to my morning meeting this morning on the Bretton Woods-type negotiations in Paris to set up a European Bank of Reconstruction and Development, commenting that by far the worst negotiators were the Americans, who arrive with their proposals already approved by the President and Congress, and say they cannot budge from them. Even the Russians, Czechs and Hungarians were far more skilful negotiators.

13 MARCH 1990

An early ministerial meeting, at which I warned them about our shortfall in running costs and manpower, particularly first secretaries – and referring specifically to Francis Maude's request for 'three or four good first secretaries' to form a Special Unit on the presentation of our community policies. I also warned them that we are going to need a very large PESC bid this year.

I then attended a long meeting with Douglas Hurd and officials on community enlargement and subsidiarity. There was general agreement that we should adopt a positive attitude towards EFTA and East European Enlargement, but present it in a way to counter accusations that we are merely trying to weaken the community, while others (e.g. the French and the Dutch) are trying to federalise it.

I attended a meeting with Ivon Brabazon and others on homosexuality, concluding that, for presentational and procedural reasons, any change will have to come from the Security Commission, and that Douglas Hurd should be advised to ask the Commission to look at the question again. This will require the Prime Minister's agreement, which may well kill the whole initiative stone dead. We also concluded that ideally we should carry the MOD and the intelligence agencies with us. First indications from the Secret Intelligence Service are positive.

14 MARCH 1990

Douglas Hurd gave me today an account of his talk with the PM about top appointments, which had gone about as disastrously as was possible. The only points worth recording here are that she objected to almost every single proposal carefully worked out by John Boyd and myself; raised the idea of Robin Leigh-Pemberton as ambassador to Washington (presumably on the analogy of Lord Cromer); and very privately aired the thought that Geoffrey Howe might need a diplomatic post (unspecified). Douglas claimed that she had again spoken very warmly about me, saying that she always liked meeting me, and that she admired my sense of 'fair play'. She also complained – believe it or not – that she did not see enough of FCO officials, at which Stephen Wall and I nearly exploded! She also shows constant signs of wanting to extend people beyond sixty (though not me, apparently!), and even talked of extending Antony Acland yet again.

15 MARCH 1990

The Iraqis hanged Farzad Bazoft this morning, having invited the embassy to be represented. Robin Kealy did not actually witness the hanging; but he spent the last half hour with Bazoft, receiving messages for his family, *The Observer*, Saddam Hussein and others.

I attended a short meeting with ministers and the Middle Easterners to discuss Douglas Hurd's statement in the House this afternoon. David Gore-Booth angered Douglas by arguing that Saddam Hussein probably believed that Bazoft was a spy, and had a genuine suspicion of the British. In a curious, and untypical, flash of temper, Douglas said this was ridiculous, and that 'we should never have allowed Saddam Hussein to rule Iraq' – a remark that would have confirmed all Saddam's suspicions of British colonialism! Ministers nevertheless successfully resisted demands to chuck out the Iraqi ambassador, and to cut off credits etc. – all of which would have damaged our interests more than theirs.

16 MARCH 1990

Robert Armstrong told me today that Marie Palliser had never got over Michael's non-peerage. He recalled an incident in Cabinet when virtually no one in the House of Lords had defended some move by the government, at which Margaret Thatcher had exploded with the words: 'I knew I was right to stop giving peerages to ex-bureaucrats' – at which point she had turned to Robert and added: 'Except, of course, to my Cabinet Secretary.' I told Robert that I firmly assumed that neither I nor Antony Acland would get one.

[Three years after my retirement, I was offered, and accepted, a peerage by John Major. When I paid my courtesy call on the Clerk of Parliaments, he told me that when Margaret Thatcher had paid a similar call, Denis Greenhill had put his head round the door. This had provoked her into saying proudly: 'At least that is one thing I managed to stop; peerages for permanent under-secretaries of the Foreign Office.']

The Lord Mayor of London, Hugh Bidwell, called on William Waldegrave today to discuss my idea that the City of London might sponsor a British School in Prague (after Havel had spoken lyrically to William, during his visit to Prague, about the old English Grammar School which Czechs of his generation had fought to attend). I am not sure if Hugh Bidwell will take it up, and there was no opportunity to pursue it further when we dined at the Mansion House this evening.

19 MARCH 1990

William Waldegrave chaired the ministerial meeting this morning in Douglas Hurd's absence in South Africa. The discussion was mainly on Germany (where the East German elections have produced a superb triumph for the CDU and Helmut Kohl); Lithuania (where the FCO are under criticism from both sides for either being too enthusiastic about independence, or not enough – one article in *The Independent* actually managed to criticise us on both scores); and the Bazoft case. It emerged today that Customs and Excise intend to arrest two Iraqis tomorrow. I have been asked to contact the Home Office and Brian Unwin at Customs and Excise, to persuade them not to oppose bail.

20 MARCH 1990

I managed to persuade both Clive Whitmore at the Home Office and Brian Unwin at Customs and Excise that the two Iraqis should be deported, rather than put on trial.

William Waldegrave asked to see me urgently today to consult me on a point about Lithuania, but also to ask for my view on a request from President Havel (conveyed by Harold Pinter) that he should see Salman Rushdie during his visit, and be filmed doing so. I pointed out that the timing could not be worse, with a spate of recent statements from Iran that they want to release their hostages; and that pictures of Havel with Rushdie could expose the Czechs to security threats. William thinks he has since persuaded Pinter that the meeting can be organised, provided there is no publicity. Special Branch is apparently happy to take Rushdie to the embassy.

21 MARCH 1990

William Waldegrave told me, on his return from Heathrow to greet Havel, that he had failed to convince him that any meeting with Salman Rushdie should be unpublicised, and asked me to try again today. I later deployed three arguments based on a) the security of Rushdie himself; b) Czech security; and c) the fate of the hostages (pointing out that we had received more forthcoming messages than ever). Havel appeared to agree; but when Special Branch approached the embassy to fix up a meeting for tomorrow, the Czech diplomat concerned (possibly the new seventy-year-old ambassador Duda) had a fit, and said he would strongly advise Havel not to bring Rushdie to the embassy!

22 MARCH 1990

I went to Northwood for a PUSs' briefing and lunch at Admiralty House with Ben Bathurst. Peter Gregson, who was there, had a word with me about Nicholas Ridley's visit to Poland and the Soviet Union. Ridley had complained to Gregson about bad briefing for the Soviet leg, and had also complained to his private secretary about David Logan, who had allegedly spoken 'disloyally to Mrs Ridley about German reunification'. When I tackled William Waldegrave about this, he said that Ridley had described the embassy in Moscow as 'a bunch of trendy lefties', and would be writing to William. I told William that I would like to give the embassy the chance to present their side of the story, if only because one of my colleagues had very nearly had his career ruined by unfounded accusations of disloyalty reported back to the Prime Minister. Ridley also claimed that the embassy had shown no interest in export promotion, with senior staff saying that they did not regard it as their business.

23 MARCH 1990

I gave lunch to Peter Preston of *The Guardian*. Interestingly, he by no means excluded the possibility of Margaret Thatcher going on to win the next election, though there must be increasing pressure for someone else to take over. He thought that Douglas Hurd would be a possible 'stop-gap' until John Major or Chris Patten was ready to succeed. I pointed out that Douglas's age meant that he could be stopping gaps for at least fifteen years.

Charles Powell claims that morale in No. 10 is surprisingly high, but Rifkind's resignation (which was a damn close thing yesterday) would have been disastrous for the government.

26 MARCH 1990

A tense weekend in Lithuania, with Soviet generals and troops appearing in Vilnius, and speculation that, in spite of Shevardnadze's assurances to Baker in Namibia, the Russians might use force.

Douglas Hurd told me privately that he is worried that the Prime Minister might go back on the Hong Kong Nationality Package, given the current political pressures on her. Percy Cradock does not think this is remotely likely.

Lithuania looks very bad. The Prime Minister had an hour's conversation with Gorbachev today, by which she was not at all reassured. He was very careful not to give cast-iron assurances about the use of force.

29–31 MARCH 1990

I attended a Königswinter Conference at St Catherine's College, Cambridge this weekend. The dinner was addressed by the Prime Minister and

Helmut Kohl – separated on the high table by the chairman, Oliver Wright (apparently on Margaret Thatcher's insistence). Robert Rhodes James, who came up to me halfway through dinner, told me that the PM was being treated disgracefully and that no one was speaking to her. He later made it clear that what was really fussing him was that Kohl and the PM had literally not exchanged a word during dinner.

The PM's speech was much criticised a) for over-emphasising the military aspects of the Anglo-German relationship and (in spite of FCO advice to the contrary) including a reference to keeping nuclear weapons on German soil; and b) because there was no single reference to the European Community. I was sitting opposite Michael Heseltine, who had given a presentation at the afternoon session, widely described as a 'leadership bid'. He had said to me this afternoon: 'You must be careful not to be seen smiling at me,' and ended dinner rather embarrassingly suggesting that he and I should lunch together some time (see also p. 32 above) – which would certainly confirm all the PM's suspicions about the FCO.

3 APRIL 1990

News came through this afternoon that the Russians were expelling Rod Lyne for having contacted Mrs Gordievsky (even though the embassy had been careful to keep the MFA informed). Charles Powell talked to his contact in the Soviet embassy last night, who expressed horror and disbelief at the way 'they' were behaving. Douglas Hurd sent a personal message to Shevardnadze this morning, in the hope that he can get the decision reversed. I suggested to Douglas that he should also invoke the help of Jim Baker, whom Shevardnadze is visiting tomorrow.

5 APRIL 1990

Shevardnadze agreed today to postpone Rod Lyne's departure until after

Douglas Hurd's visit next week. Peter Carrington gossiped with me (after a meeting of the Order of St Michael and St George in my office) about things Margaret Thatcher had said to him about Germany. I told him of her remark to Havel about Munich, saying that she could never bring herself to visit 'that place', at which Peter commented that she had very little understanding of history: 'After all, it is not as though she fought in the war.' He gave me the impression that he thinks she should go, but admitted that it would be difficult for her to do so under current pressure. I told him (rather indiscreetly) about a recent letter to the PM from Patrick Jenkin (about giving up the chairmanship of UK/Japan 2000), in which he had said: 'I always think it is better to go before you are pushed.'

6 APRIL 1990

Charles Powell called this afternoon, claiming that the PM was in a defiant and confident mood, and feeling that her Cabinet were for once pulling together. When I asked whether Denis was upset about the opinion polls (which today record the lowest public support for any Prime Minister since polls began), Charles replied: 'No; merely angry.'

Some signs of give today from the Russians about Rod Lyne's expulsion. The embassy here seem to think it possible that Rod might be allowed to stay on for six months.

9 APRIL 1990

I lunched at the *Financial Times* with Richard Lambert and others, who told me that Helmut Kohl (who had visited the *FT* after his bilateral talks with the PM last month) had given some fairly disobliging imitations of Margaret Thatcher, and that Helmut Schmidt, on another occasion, had been vitriolic about her.

22 APRIL 1990

[After returning from an Easter break] I talked today to Tim Renton (as Chief Whip) about the government's troubles. He thinks that Norman Tebbit has done himself more damage than the Conservative Party by his performance over the Hong Kong bill. He compared his own job to a man running a nuclear power station, hoping meltdown would not happen before the summer. He also hinted strongly that there would be some sort of reshuffle in the summer, but that FCO ministers would not be affected. I spoke warmly about Tim Sainsbury, saying that I thought he was under-promoted.

24 APRIL 1990

I lunched with Michael Palliser at Midland Montagu, who had taken a bet with Malcolm Rutherford of the *Financial Times* that Margaret Thatcher would not resign this year. Malcolm (like others) thinks she will go before the autumn. I now think it more likely that she will go next spring, if at all, before the election. But I told Michael Palliser that I thought it would ultimately depend as much on Denis Thatcher as on the PM herself. [As it happened, none of us was right, since she eventually went in November. But Malcolm Rutherford (who died in December 1999) received considerable tributes in his obituaries for good political judgement, including an early piece of talent-spotting over Ronald Reagan.]

30 APRIL 1990

Tim Lankester told me today that Lynda Chalker had returned from Douglas Hurd's aid policy meeting last week, and had been very angry at the way in which she had been interrupted and ignored by Douglas (who does indeed have a habit of simply talking through people). The trouble is that both

Lynda and William Waldegrave are in a highly sensitive state – the first because she missed having a Cabinet post and knows that she will almost certainly lose her narrow majority at Wallasey in the next election; the second because he sees colleagues (and friends) like Chris Patten getting Cabinet ranks ahead of him, in spite of his own (justified) view of his intellectual abilities (as a Fellow of All Souls).

1 MAY 1990

A British Council board meeting, at which Tim Raison came out with an emotional outburst against Iraq and Iran, arguing that the British Council should not operate in either. I argued strongly against this, pointing out that neither diplomatic nor cultural presence represented support for, or endorsement of, the regimes. A strange line for Tim Raison to take, as an ex-Minister of Overseas Development, who has given aid in the past to quite a lot of undesirable regimes!

Douglas Hurd has decided that we should look again at our relations with Syria. Ministers have deliberately made some mollifying comments on both Iran and Syria in the past week or two (which the Swedes have brought to the attention of the Iranians). But the Rushdie problem still persists, and there is also a risk that the Lockerbie investigation will reveal Syrian complicity.

2 MAY 1990

Douglas Hurd held a meeting to discuss Iran and Syria, and has agreed in principle that we might relax our conditions for resuming relations with Iran (i.e. against either the release of Cooper, or the release of a hostage, but not insisting on both, as at present); and that we should reconsider the idea of an emissary to Damascus – perhaps Donald Maitland, who volunteered himself to me at the Japanese MECAS (Middle East Centre for Arab Studies) party last week.

3 MAY 1990

I went to Lord Maclean's memorial service, at which Archbishop Runcie gave an excellent and witty address, including a charming story about Chips Maclean at a Boy Scout rally, where a diminutive cub had presented a bouquet to the Queen, and was obviously very proud of himself. Maclean, as Chief Scout, later went up to the boy quietly and asked for his autograph!

4 MAY 1990

Geoffrey Holland (Department of Employment) called on me today to explore some ideas for seconding civil servants from his department to employment ministries in Poland, Czechoslovakia and Hungary – an imaginative idea, but an extraordinary illustration of differing levels of resources in large departments. He appeared to have no difficulty in finding either money or people (including something like thirty Polish speakers).

7–18 MAY 1990: VISITS TO BAHRAIN, BOMBAY, PUNE, NEW DELHI AND SEOUL
22 MAY 1990

Having stayed at home yesterday with a heavy cold, I returned to my old office (Downing Street, W16) for the first time in three years today. My cold meant that Virginia and I cut the Saudi–British dinner last night, to which Douglas Hurd had been lured to speak, against the promise that Prince Faisal bin Fahd would also be there. Needless to say, he wasn't.

Geoffrey Adams told me on my return that when Douglas Hurd had informed his ministers privately about David Gillmore's appointment as PUS, he had said that he had deliberately tried to choose a PUS who was as like me as possible!

23 MAY 1990

A ministerial meeting this morning, at which William Waldegrave gave an interesting account of his visit to Paris, where French ministers and officials seemed totally preoccupied with problems of immigration and 'national unity' – as opposed to political cooperation within the European Community. William commented that the French seem to be able to introduce legislation (e.g. to take away voting rights from immigrants) of a sort which no extreme right-wing government in the United Kingdom could get away with.

I gave ministers a brief account of my visits to Bahrain, India and Korea, explaining the growing burden of visa work, and the need to amend the present appeal system. Douglas Hurd (who always opposed this as Home Secretary) seems to be more sympathetic now.

24 MAY 1990

I spent much of the day at Chatham House, chairing the FCO side of a joint seminar on German reunification. Douglas Hurd joined for lunch, and gave a very impressive discourse on the '2+4' talks – apparently his evidence to the Foreign Affairs Committee yesterday was brilliant.

30 MAY 1990

I attended perm secs for the first time in over a month, and found I was about the only person with anything to say. I therefore spoke for twenty minutes on world affairs, including Germany; arms control; the Middle East; and Kashmir. When answering questions, I was again struck by the extraordinary hunger of my home civil service colleagues for news about the outside world. Ken Stowe once told me that I should never underestimate the extent to which even very senior officials at home are starved of reliable information.

31 MAY 1990

I revealed to Virginia today that Douglas Hurd has decided to interview Simon McDonald as his speech-writer, which will mean that Olivia and Simon have to return from Bonn in September. I think that Simon may also be horrified at the thought of working in the office while I am still PUS. I have studiously kept out of the discussion, though Geoffrey Adams has kept me informed.

1 JUNE 1990

Peter Carrington telephoned me early this morning, saying that John Julius Norwich claimed to have been told, either by Stephen Egerton or by the Italian Foreign Minister, De Michelis, that HMG had struck a deal with the Italians to support Venice for EXPO 2000 in exchange for EBRD (European Bank for Reconstruction and Development) being sited in London. I told Peter that there was no truth in the story. But it is an odd affair, since Douglas Hurd did tell Stephen Egerton that he thought we should try to get Italian support for one of our siting claims, and I have a nasty suspicion that De Michelis himself may have been left with the impression that we would support Venice.

4 JUNE 1990

Peter Middleton called to tell me privately of an extraordinary meeting between the Prime Minister and a Treasury team last week, ostensibly to discuss EMS, but ranging over the PM's Germanophobia and Japan. She is obviously searching around for ways of deflecting closer political union in the community, and is accusing everyone of not producing bright ideas. But her loathing of the Germans and the Commission is such that she apparently started to refer to the Commission as being in Bonn. When corrected, she said: 'No. I meant Bonn. After all, the Germans are going to take it all over.'

5 JUNE 1990

A very unfair article in *The Times* today by Vernon Bogdanor, claiming that the FCO not only failed to forecast events in Eastern Europe (who didn't?), but also failed to make any contact with the opposition in advance. William Waldegrave has agreed to sign (and Simon Jenkins to print) a good article, which should appear in *The Times* this week. There have in fact been some very striking cases of British embassies receiving tributes from the new leaders in Eastern Europe for their past contacts.

6 JUNE 1990

The German secondee in the office, just starting his second year in East European Department, called on me today. When I asked whether the two German Foreign Services were yet starting to amalgamate, he pointed out that there are real problems of security: 'We have now discovered that every member of the GDR Foreign Service was 150 per cent Stasi.'

11 JUNE 1990

My morning meeting was largely taken up with discussion of the Prime Minister's visit to the Soviet Union, where she seems to have found Gorbachev in a slightly battered, but still confident, mood. His failure to accompany her to Kiev probably helped to make it an extraordinarily triumphant tour for her, both in Kiev and in Armenia, where she visited the school presented by HMG after the earthquake.

13 JUNE 1990

Peter Gregson talked to me today about Nicholas Ridley's views on export promotion, in advance of Ridley's meeting with Douglas Hurd tomorrow. Ridley seems to have come off his earlier idea of giving all export promotion to the DTI. Luckily, Peter had been in charge (at the London end) of the Saudi–British economic cooperation office in Riyadh in the 1970s, and is convinced that export promotion is better left to diplomats and embassies.

Our presentation to the City in the Midland Bank Theatre this evening went well, under Pat Limerick's chairmanship, with good questions afterwards (mainly on the Knowhow Fund). Then to the Doyen's dinner for the Ramphals, at which Douglas Hurd gave a good speech (not yet drafted by Simon McDonald!).

14 JUNE 1990

An early bilateral with Douglas Hurd, discussing the BBC's offer to do films on the service, in spite of my warning that only one of the six or so films made during my career had been any good (and some a disaster), and strong written advice from Brian Mower. Douglas is very keen to give it a try.

Douglas is cross with the Speaker, Jack Weatherill, who scampered through FCO Questions yesterday in order to reach Teresa Gorman's question on the refurbished FCO staircase and its cost. There are some more snide press articles about it today, and I shall certainly be questioned by the Public Accounts Committee next week. I discovered today that one reason for the refurbishment was that a large chunk of the Foreign Secretary's office ceiling fell down; I have asked the department to collect similar information about disrepair.

18 JUNE 1990

I spent much of today preparing for the Public Accounts Committee hearing on FCO manpower. The hearing turned out to be much the worst I have had so far, with questions hopping from subject to subject. Dale

Campbell-Savours cross-questioned me aggressively on boarding school allowances, on which I was underprepared. The chairman, Robert Sheldon, came partly to my rescue by pointing out that they were not directly connected to manpower; but both Campbell-Savours and Ian Gow (on consular work) were extremely aggressive. After two and a half hours, I felt like a damp rag.

A flurry today over press leaks. The *Financial Times* carries a report on ERM which reads very much like an FCO leak, if only because it referred to Douglas Hurd's breakfast meetings with John Major (about which very few people know). Robin Butler rang me this evening to ask for clues (having been charged by the PM to do so). I told Robin that Douglas had been very angry about the story, and that I found it impossible to believe that he could have been the source. While denying that I was making any accusations, I asked Robin if he had spoken to Peter Middleton (whom John Kerr described to me last week as the leakiest man in Whitehall). It will no doubt remain a mystery (as most leaks do). But it will not have helped either Douglas Hurd's or John Major's relations with No. 10, nor will an exceedingly unhelpful minute from Robin Butler (revealed to us in strict confidence by Charles Powell) saying that the internal evidence suggests an FCO leak. I rang Robin the next day to say that I had heard that the journalist concerned (Peter Stephens) had told someone in the Treasury that it was a 'political source' in the Treasury itself.

21 JUNE 1990

The Foreign Secretary's diplomatic banquet this evening in the Durbar Court. An excellent, and fairly audible, speech by Douglas Hurd. Virginia and I had the David Harrises at our table. Diana Harris had been at school, as Virginia was, at St Margaret's, Exeter. David is Geoffrey Howe's PPS, and such a popular MP for St Ives that I was offered a free pint of beer in a pub in North Cornwall when I admitted that I knew him.

The *Sunday Express* this weekend produced a story that Geoffrey Howe is to be sacked, and sent to Pretoria. The latter part is most unlikely to be true, though Robin Butler told me this week that he would not be surprised if Geoffrey was dropped at the next reshuffle; the Prime Minister is probably starting to leak hints to the press.

29 JUNE 1990

Len Appleyard reported this evening that the Prime Minister has agreed to hold a pre-NATO summit teach-in next week, at which she herself suggested that two or three officials from the MOD and FCO should attend. Charles Powell has rapidly reversed this, and is now resisting everyone. As Len put it, the meeting is now to be an 'expert-free zone'. I am very keen that at least John Goulden should attend, since the PM hardly knows him.

Knowledge of FCO senior officials makes it all the more outrageous that she virtually offers jobs to those few individuals she knows. John Coles told me today that she had asked him what he was going to do next. When he said that the office was thinking of bringing him back to be a Deputy Under-Secretary, she replied that this would be 'very dull' – as if she has the faintest idea what a DUS does! She then asked him if he would like South Africa. John was a bit thrown by this, saying that he had never given that any thought. The PM had asked him to 'let her know'. I told John that this would considerably throw out our game plan, and pointed out gently that ambassadorial postings (though not, I suspect, high commissioners) are for the Foreign Secretary to recommend to the Queen, and not for the Prime Minister to decide.

There was apparently a discussion about overseas accommodation on the aircraft returning from Dublin this week, with the PM stating firmly that ambassadors and high commissioners should have the grandest and best houses possible 'so long as they are fighters'. Douglas Hurd replied that it looks as though they will all have to live in bungalows – not apparently implying (as I first feared) that they are not all fighters, but a helpful comment on our lack of resources.

3 JULY 1990

I gave lunch to Bethuel Kiplagat, whose visit here has coincided with a lot of ministerial concern about Kenya. At Douglas Hurd's office meeting this afternoon, William Waldegrave made the fair point that we should not allow our very close relations with Moi to lead us to criticise him more than other, much less satisfactory, African governments. It is ironic that Kenya should be the first candidate for our new aid policy, as announced in Douglas Hurd's speech to the Overseas Development Institute in June, i.e. making aid conditional on political pluralism and economic reform.

In one of the best Freudian misprints of the year, Charles Powell circulated a speaking note for the Prime Minister to use at the NATO summit, referring to the success of the NATO Alliance in resisting 'a hostile and destructive *Community* ideology'.

4 JULY 1990

A meeting this evening to discuss the BBC's renewed proposal for a film of the FCO. I was amused to discover from the file that in 1988 I had advised in favour of accepting the proposal, and Geoffrey Howe had turned it down; the situation this year is reversed.

5 JULY 1990

I had an early meeting to prepare for Douglas Hurd's meeting later this month on FCO resources. It is not clear what Douglas wants; he is probably aiming for a fairly radical look at what the service does, and whether our levels of manpower and resources are right. There is always a danger that ministers will discount the value of any work they don't see themselves (cf. the PM's comments on DUSs, above). But I would welcome quite a radical review at this moment, when resources are so heavily stretched.

6 JULY 1990

A late bilateral with Douglas Hurd, at which he gossiped about ministerial changes. He does not think the Prime Minister will ditch Geoffrey Howe; but he had had some difficulty persuading Geoffrey not to throw in the towel. The Chief Whip had asked Douglas if he could do with one less minister; Douglas has firmly said no. When Douglas commented approvingly on Brabazon's latest account of his visits to Brunei and other places, Stephen Wall and I told him it had virtually all been written by his private secretary, Robert Court.

Douglas complained about his programme, which he described as out of control; but he surprisingly denied that he was getting too much paper. I think the office really has succeeded in reducing both paper and long hours in the past two years; but there are still some notable exceptions.

11 JULY 1990

Virginia and I went to the US ballet, as guests of Trevor and Susan Chinn. Jim Prior was there, and talked to me about the Prime Minister's treatment of Geoffrey Howe, and indeed all her original Cabinet colleagues, including himself.

I recall an occasion when I was ambassador in Damascus and called on Peter Carrington while I was home on leave. After a twenty-minute talk, Peter accompanied me to the corridor (with his usual, impeccable manners), and there was Jim Prior, Secretary of State for Northern Ireland, waiting to see him. Peter introduced me as 'our man in Damascus', to which Jim replied: 'God, that must be a bloody awful job.' I said: 'Actually, it's a perfect job. Everyone assumes it must be bloody awful; but I enjoy it very much.' Jim replied: 'I wish I could say the same about my job.'

12 JULY 1990

An astonishing article in this week's *Spectator*: an interview by Dominic Lawson with Nicholas Ridley, containing very insulting comments on the Germans and the European Commission, comparing the latter with Hitler. Ridley himself is in Budapest today, but issued a statement expressing regret, and withdrawing his remarks unreservedly (rather than the usual excuse that he had been quoted out of context). Tim Yeo said at my morning meeting that the party was outraged, and thought Ridley would have to go. Happily, the Prime Minister dissociated herself from his remarks at Question Time, and is said to be 'livid' after TV produced earlier shots of her claiming to be 'a great Nicholas Ridley fan'.

13 JULY 1990

I held a meeting to discuss Tom King's 'Options for Change', and to prepare advice for Douglas Hurd before ministers meet next Wednesday to consider the proposed cuts in the armed forces. I mentioned this briefly to Douglas yesterday, who seemed very reluctant to press for a delay in an announcement until the autumn (as we would much prefer, both to give MOD time to work out the implications, but also to allow for proper consultations with our allies). Since it is in fact a major Defence Review, ministers ought really to have a proper discussion on the major strategic and foreign policy implications, preferably in a Cabinet committee, before going any further.

The Ridley affair rumbled on today, with Ridley issuing a brief retraction, allegedly before No. 10 had pressed him to do so.

14 JULY 1990

Nicholas Ridley finally resigned this afternoon, after a long dither, and statements by his friends saying that he would only leave if the Prime Minister thought it would be helpful. It remains to be seen how damaging it will be, but it has certainly left the impression (in spite of her statement on Thursday) that the PM half shares Ridley's views on Germany and the Commission. [This impression will have been strengthened by the full publication of Charles Powell's record of her recent Chequers seminar on Germany, at which German national characteristics were explicitly and insultingly listed in the next day's *Independent on Sunday* – though Douglas Hurd did very well with a long and penetrating interview by David Dimbleby on 15 July.]

16 JULY 1990

Television tonight used the *Independent* leak to do a twenty-minute feature on Charles Powell (addressed in a message today from Scowcroft as Sir Charles Powell).

Douglas Hurd has been at a Foreign Affairs Council in Brussels today, and is widely assumed to have been picking up the pieces. The past few days must have been a great boost to him politically, with *The Guardian* (no doubt trying to stir up trouble) describing him as real prime ministerial material.

I received a message last week from Fatie Darwish in Damascus (initially conveyed in a virtually illegible postcard and later confirmed in a telephone call to Virginia) conveying a message from Mustafa Tlass, the Syrian Defence Minister, to me about Terry Waite, claiming that Princess Diana (with whom Tlass claims a mutual interest in roses, and to whom Tlass told me, during my farewell call in 1981, that he wished to dedicate his book of poetry) was the only person who could free him (though without explaining how).

The Iraqis today freed Mrs Parish (the nurse arrested with Bazoft), apparently at the request of Kenneth Kaunda. Sad for Ian Richter, who remains in jail.

17 JULY 1990

The Prime Minister sent congratulatory messages this morning to Kohl and Gorbachev, following their agreement in Moscow that a United Germany should be allowed to choose their own alliances. Charles Powell, who called this afternoon, told me that the atmosphere between Margaret Thatcher and Kohl at the European Council in Dublin had been very bad, and that it was a lost cause to try to get her to telephone him about the Ridley affair. It has been left to Douglas Hurd to try to pick up the pieces at the Foreign Affairs Council and the '2+4' talks later this week. Kohl made some excellent remarks about 'this silly affair', which the PM was able to use at Questions today.

Charles Powell thinks that Neil Kinnock made a serious error in going abroad this week, since he could have caused the government real problems in Parliament – e.g. by putting down a PNQ on the Ridley affair yesterday.

18 JULY 1990

Joe Haines published an article in the *Daily Mirror* today, claiming that Charles Powell had been seen clapping enthusiastically at the PM's speech to Conservatives Abroad in Houston last week, contrasting it with my apolitical approach during my time in No. 10. The article ended with a suggestion that I should speak to Charles about it. I rang Robin Butler, who agreed that if anyone said anything, he should, and he undertook to speak to Andrew Turnbull. I later received a complaining letter from Charles, asking whether I would speak to Joe Haines. I replied that I doubted whether that would be wise.

I held a meeting this afternoon to discuss how to reply to a letter from the law officers, asking for a damage assessment on the leak of Charles Powell's record of the Chequers seminar on Germany. This poses an awkward dilemma; it undoubtedly has caused some damage (and Charles Powell's letter covering the original record explicitly said that a leak would 'damage the interests of the United Kingdom'); whereas Douglas Hurd has said publicly in Brussels that it has not – and even (rather oddly) that it is not a government document! I discussed it with Douglas, who agreed that the compromise wording which we had worked out at my meeting was probably the best we could do.

I think it is inconceivable, given what ministers have said publicly, that the *Independent on Sunday* could be prosecuted. There is also the intriguing possibility that *Der Spiegel* actually published it first; could it have been Nicholas Ridley himself who leaked it? He (or one of his allies) is about the only person who could possibly have thought he might benefit from it.

20 JULY 1990

Stephen Wall called this morning, having been asked by Douglas Hurd to tell me in confidence that there is likely to be a reshuffle on 23 July. William Waldegrave stays, as does Lynda Chalker at the ODA. Poor William will probably be back in deep gloom, realising that, disasters apart, he has no hope of a Cabinet post this side of the election. Frances Maude (just off to Hong Kong and China for the first European Community ministerial visit since Tiananmen Square) is to go to the Treasury to take the place of Peter Lilley, who succeeded Nicholas Ridley at the DTI last week. All Mrs Thatcher's original Cabinet colleagues in 1979, other than Geoffrey Howe, have now left.

Ivon Brabazon and Tim Sainsbury go, but apparently – in Tim's case – on promotion (which he well deserves, having been an effective and imaginative minister). In their place, we get Mark Lennox-Boyd (ex-PPS to the Prime Minister); Tristan Garel-Jones (ex-whip) and Malcolm Caithness, an ex-Home Office minister, who is said to be quite an effective minister. We shall see. It is a bit awkward to have six ministers coming and going while Douglas Hurd is in Czechoslovakia. Although he has worked out with Stephen Wall a distribution of portfolios, he may decide to wait until he has discussed it with them before finalising the distribution. He has, I think, already discussed it with Waldegrave.

21 JULY 1990

After two days entertaining my Japanese opposite number, Takakazu Kuriyama, at Merton, I took him to see St John's, which the young Prince Aya has just left. As we passed the Martyrs' Memorial, I commented that, in those days, we burnt Ridleys at the stake!

23 JULY 1990

The reshuffle was completed today. There were pictures on television this weekend of Gerald Kaufman leaving for Damascus, which reminded me of how little I would have relished working for him (though this unfairly underestimates his extraordinary courage, as a Jewish MP, in constant criticism of successive Israeli governments).

I was asked to call at 11 a.m. on Ivon Brabazon, who is indeed leaving, but returning to Transport. He is miserable about it, though the PM apparently reminded him of the need to look cheerful. I thanked him for the interest (excessive, in some people's views) he had taken in administration and the service.

Lord Caithness telephoned later to ask for my advice on when he should start; I advised him to wait until the announcements had been made this evening. Tristan Garel-Jones, the new Francis Maude (though he will also take Latin America – being a fluent Spanish speaker – instead of Hong Kong), similarly rang me later.

I called on Tim Sainsbury, who leaves to take Lord Trefgarne's place as Minister for Trade – a good promotion, and helpful for the FCO. He is due to leave for Colombia, Bolivia and Peru on Thursday. Douglas Hurd has asked that Tim and Garel-Jones sort out between them which of them should do it.

24 JULY 1990

I called successively this morning on Lord Caithness, Tristan Garel-Jones and Mark Lennox-Boyd. I think it is a pity we did not get Gloria Hooper – but that might have overdone the pro-European wets. As it is, the press are making a great deal of the change in European balance, with Francis Maude's departure.

I told Lord Caithness that his top priority should be Hong Kong/China, with Cambodia second priority. David Wilson later telephoned me from Hong Kong, a bit worried that Hong Kong will be dealt with in the Lords, though I pointed out that this would mean that Douglas Hurd would deal personally with much of the Commons work instead.

On my way to call on Tristan Garel-Jones, I met him coming down the staircase to call on me – astonished to discover that nowadays PUSs call on junior ministers, not vice-versa. He is full of enthusiasm for his new job. Apparently, he and his wife speak nothing but Spanish at home, and is all for ringing all his Spanish and Latin American friends today. I discovered that, by a happy coincidence, he had inherited a Hispanophone private secretary in Nicola Brewer.

Garel-Jones suggested, rather sensibly, that he should telephone Bossano in Gibraltar (in English), in view of his own, pro-Spanish reputation. He did so later, and it was clearly appreciated. He also told me that he had invited both Julian Amery and Denis Healey round for a chat.

Mark Lennox-Boyd is tall and languid, speaks Arabic and Persian (I decided not to greet him with *Ahlan wa Sahlan*), and apparently accompanied Freya Stark as a boy on one of her expeditions.

25 JULY 1990

Douglas Hurd held a long meeting on resources, which turned out to be more of a briefing for the three new ministers. Tristan Garel-Jones had a word with me afterwards, obviously astonished by the pressure on FCO resources; I gave him my favourite comparison between the relative size and cost of the service and Wandsworth Borough Council). [By 2015, I think an even more telling comparison is that, even before further cuts in public expenditure, the total FCO budget is only double what we give Ethiopia in aid each year. He has asked if he can 'come and see' me about once a week; not surprisingly, he is feeling a bit new and uncertain.]

Douglas Hurd held his party this evening for ex-foreign secretaries and their private secretaries in his refurbished office. Sadly, the Howes turned up too late for what should be quite an amusing group photograph in the main staircase, But there were the Carringtons; the Owens; the Pyms; the Callaghans; John Major and Susan Crosland; plus a host of private secretaries. Virginia and I were in fact the only unqualified guests, apart from a few recent and new junior ministers.

Peter Carrington drew me aside to say that he had met the Prime Minister at lunch with the Colnbrooks, and that she had talked quite dottily about the Ridley affair – describing Douglas Hurd's remarks at Ditchley as 'quite disgraceful' in the light of Ridley's withdrawal of his interview, though she went on to talk in a way that showed that she agreed with it. She had talked about being surrounded by Euro-wimps, and talked very dismissively and rudely about Kohl as a second-rate provincial politician. I advised Peter to tell all this to Douglas.

Douglas Hurd held his first ministerial meeting this morning with his new team. I had a chance to put in a word about the recent meeting that had virtually relaxed all export controls to Iraq, pointing out that export controls for Israel would now be more severe. Douglas later discussed this with the Prime Minister, and agreed to suspend any further action, at least while Iraq continues its bullying of Kuwait.

This evening, Virginia and I entertained a good turn-out of ex-PUSs and PS/PUSs with their wives and widows – rather a copy of Douglas Hurd's party last night, though Antony Acland said he thought ours was better! The Gladwyns, at ninety and ninety-two respectively, were the Doyens, but the Caccias ran them fairly close.

27 JULY 1990

The recess starts today, with a general feeling of winding down, though Douglas Hurd is using next week as an opportunity to have a series of meetings on subjects he has not yet been able to focus on, such as the Antarctic. Lynda Chalker will be in charge for much of August – her moment of glory! Roger Tomkys and John Boyd will be around for most of the month to hold her hand.

The list of ministerial portfolios was promulgated today; public attention is likely to focus on which minister is taking Hong Kong.

I lunched with Peter Unwin at the club, to respond to his personal letter about the FCO's attitude to the Commonwealth. The FCO has a difficult balance to strike between being too tough, and nagging on house-keeping and budgetary questions in the Secretariat, while making sure that our interests, as major contributors, are protected.

30 JULY 1990

Ian Gow's assassination this morning by a car bomb will have been a horrendous shock for Margaret Thatcher – almost as bad for her as Airey Neave's murder. The car pool are worried (rather touchingly) about my security, and have urged Virginia to get me to vary my walking route in the morning (since I regularly get out of the office car at Buckingham Palace, and walk to the ambassadors' entrance through St James's Park).

1 AUGUST–2 SEPTEMBER 1990: SUMMER HOLIDAYS IN ITALY

In spite of a major international crisis blowing up with Iraq's invasion, and later annexation, of Kuwait, and the launching of a major international force to Saudi Arabia to protect it against the Iraqi invasion, I left Roger Tomkys in charge of the office (having obtained Douglas Hurd's agreement); and very effective he was. In fact, at one point he was called over to brief Margaret Thatcher, and to discuss a draft speech for her to make in the House of Commons. When she commented that Charles Powell had produced an excellent draft, Roger was able to tell her firmly that it had been produced, word for word, by planning staff in the FCO. She later commented appreciatively on the help she had received.

12 AUGUST 1990

Simon telephoned very early this morning from Bonn to say that Felix Dominic (our first grandchild) had arrived at 11.50 p.m. last night. Mother and son (and father, who was present throughout) are said to be flourishing.

3 SEPTEMBER 1990

I returned to the office today, after a full month's leave, feeling a bit guilty at having missed a near-war situation, while ministers and officials were being recalled from leave. The office and Roger Tomkys in particular seem to have won good reports from the Prime Minister. Roger told me that this was entirely a matter of good luck, as far as he was concerned, since Charles Powell had warned him that the PM was mainly interested in the International Red Cross (on the one day that Roger had gone to No. 10 for a meeting with her), and was able to answer her questions in detail. But he is very pessimistic about the way the crisis is likely to develop, and thinks it will probably come to a head in October.

[I learned later that when the PM had commented on the excellence of the draft speech, thinking it was the work of Charles Powell, Roger told her that it was in fact the work of Simon Fraser in planning staff (later to be PUS, retiring in 2015). The PM immediately suggested that she should write to him, which Roger said would be unnecessary, but undertook to pass on her appreciation. When Douglas Hurd later mentioned to the PM that Roger himself was destined to go to Nairobi as planned, in October, Margaret Thatcher said (as she had of John Coles in relation to his DUS-ship) that he was 'far too good for Nairobi'.]

4 SEPTEMBER 1990

I called on William Waldegrave this afternoon, who is feeling understandably bruised by his press treatment, though I think he has been rather unwise, e.g. in carrying children off the aircraft (from Amman) for publicity purposes. He spoke very warmly of the support he had had from the office. Francis Maude also sent David Gillmore a very warm letter from the Treasury, saying how impressed he had been by the Rolls-Royce service he had received.

Douglas Hurd is still on his Gulf travels, having called today on the ruler of Kuwait in Taif. The behaviour of the Kuwaiti 'exiles' in Taif during the Gulf War did nothing to enhance their reputation in Saudi Arabia. There are many stories – no doubt some of them exaggerated – of their lack of appreciation for Saudi hospitality and generosity, and the familiar stories of hotels being virtually trashed by careless behaviour.

7 SEPTEMBER 1990

Charles Powell called for the first time since the holiday. I introduced a slightly sour tone at the start by saying that I was glad that Roger Tomkys and Frank Berman had been able to 'break into the fortress', to which he replied sharply (but defensively) that they had been invited in through the front door. A good illustration of the extent to which he is now political was his comment that 'we would have liked a much bigger vote against the government today' – i.e. because it would have discomfited Neil Kinnock. When I mentioned this later to Christopher Everett at an Everett wedding, Christopher (who had worked with Charles Powell in planning staff) commented that Charles seemed to have outdone de Zulueta and Oliver Wright in identifying themselves with their boss.

10 SEPTEMBER 1990

Simon McDonald's first day in planning staff today, working alongside Simon Fraser (whom he was to succeed as PUS in 2015).

11 SEPTEMBER 1990

I called today on Tristan Garel-Jones, who is keen to get himself involved in the PESC round, commenting that in all his time in the Whips' Office, he had been engaged in backstairs negotiation between No. 10 and the Treasury, but had never done anything for the FCO. He clearly thinks that we are much too naïve and upright to get our way. I suggested that it was too late for this year, but that he might put some ideas to Douglas Hurd at the end of this round.

Tristan also has ambitious ideas for British schools, à la Madrid (which is in fact unique in having a subsidised British school abroad), all round the world. A splendid idea in principle; but both the British

Council and the DES will be highly resistant; and money would be a major problem.

I went to the Guildhall for Roger Brooke's celebration dinner to mark Candover's tenth anniversary, at which I sat next to Nicholas Scott, now Minister of State in the DSS (Department of Social Security), an amusing, and wildly indiscreet, dinner companion. He talked about his political reputation as an 'Arch-Wet', and quoted someone as saying that his retention in Margaret Thatcher's government was the only known evidence that she has a sense of humour. He claimed co-membership with Douglas Hurd of the Geriatric Dads' Club, having also produced small children from his second marriage.

Roger Brooke told quite a good story of how one of his first acts as private secretary to the ambassador in Bonn had been to serve a guest sherry and tonic, in place of whisky and soda – adding that it was perhaps just as well that he had not stayed long in the service.

12 SEPTEMBER 1990

I lunched at British Airways today, where Peter Jay was talking sensibly about the economic effects of the Gulf crisis. He seems like a lost man; it is difficult to believe that he was once ambassador to Washington (although it is now clear to me that the responsibility for putting his name forward, in my view putting his father-in-law, Jim Callaghan, in an impossible position, was entirely David Owen's).

The new Hungarian ambassador, Antalpéter, called today. He was interesting about changes in the Hungarian Foreign Service, with practically every ambassador being changed, and in some cases the entire embassy staff. He is unusual in having been promoted from within the embassy here, so he is (or presumably was) a party member, though he has been mainly concerned with commercial work.

14 SEPTEMBER 1990

One of the first papers to reach me this morning was an astonishing record by Charles Powell (hastily withdrawn) of a meeting which the Prime Minister held yesterday to cross-question the military and Vickers on the reliability of the Challenger Tank, revealing shocking shortcomings, but ending with a demand from the Prime Minister that all of them should sign a document guaranteeing its reliability in the desert [which they all later did]. I entirely share the PM's doubts (from my own experience in Jedda), and indeed had minuted to William Waldegrave earlier this week, expressing the hope that Tom King would be pressed very hard on the question.

[David Plastow and Colin Chandler called on me ten days later to lobby for the Vickers Tank. I pointed out, rather unkindly, that the government's decision would be heavily influenced by Challenger's performance at its trials in Saudi Arabia.]

17 SEPTEMBER 1990

The Finnish ambassador called, to hand me an oral note about the post-war treaty between Finland and the Allies, notifying us that they no longer regard the clause relating to Germany as valid. I have asked for urgent legal advice on it, and how we need to respond.

18 SEPTEMBER 1990

In a short bilateral, Douglas Hurd talked to me about some of the heads of mission he has met. On one, he claimed to be a bit disappointed by the ambassador's low-key manner, and failure to weigh in during his meetings. I later pointed out to Stephen Wall that complaints about heads of mission were divided almost equally between those who didn't weigh in, and those who did. The Prime Minister tends either to complain that heads of mission interrupt her; or that they are silent, and therefore need not be there.

20 SEPTEMBER 1990

Today's PESC bilateral was predictably tough, with Norman Lamont (who had a private word with Douglas Hurd beforehand) reading us a lecture on the economic squeeze, and describing this as the most difficult round since 1981. There was a long discussion on running costs, with the Treasury side arguing that the FCO were in no worse position that any other department, and suggesting on each item that we could surely absorb these small sums in our '£900,000,000 budget' – ignoring the fact that half of this is for the BBC World Service and the British Council. Douglas did well, pointing out that his Cabinet colleagues wanted Britain to maintain her position as a world power, and that he must have the resources to do it.

25 SEPTEMBER 1990

Alan Pover called on me before his last posting, to Gambia. I told him that one of his predecessors, who had been posted to Aden, had told me that the contrast between the hostility and suspicion of the South Yemenis, compared with the friendliness and trust of the Gambians, had been staggering. On one occasion, the Gambian Prime Minister had undertaken to give an economic report to his Cabinet colleagues, and had come round to the residence in a panic one evening to ask the High Commissioner to write it for him.

28 SEPTEMBER 1990

William Waldegrave talked to me today about his own security, following an incident at an anti-terrorism conference William was supposed to address yesterday at the Royal Over-Seas League. Like Virginia and myself, William and Caroline have been thoroughly scared by the briefing they have had from their local police, with no follow-up except, as William put it, the occasional visit with torches to scare the rabbits away. He has more reason to worry since the press are presenting him as the Minister for Counter-Terrorism; he has also played quite a prominent role over the Gulf crisis.

I minuted today on the tricky question of Iranian refusal to shake hands with women. I have pointed out that the procedure for credentials is not immutable – the Fijian, for instance, dropped to one knee and clapped his hands (see p. 103); and also that Buckingham Palace would not dream of serving pork to a Muslim or Jewish guest. The essential thing is that it should not become an issue – there are already far too many hurdles in our bilateral relations with Tehran as it is – still less should it become a publicly aired issue in the press. *The Sun* or the *Daily Star* would certainly make a meal of it.

1 OCTOBER 1990

Douglas Hurd has received a letter from Michael Latham (an Old Marlburian MP with strong Zionist connections) proposing himself as ambassador to Israel, which Douglas wants to discuss with me – the second case in a week of an MP seeking an embassy. Coincidentally, I saw Bill Squire today, who had once told me that the essential quality for an ambassador in Tel Aviv was a cynical detachment towards both Jews and Arabs.

Robin Butler held an official meeting this morning to discuss a change in the rules on homosexuality and positive vetting. Luckily, both the Security Service and Michael Quinlan (for the MOD) have independently come to the conclusion that the present rules need changing (and could expose the government to legal action on the grounds of sex discrimination). But since Diplock singled out the diplomatic service for an automatic bar on recruitment, the Security Commission will certainly have to be told about, if not authorise, any change for the service.

The celebrations in New York tomorrow for German reunification have been slightly marred by some sour comments from the Prime Minister on German domination of the European Community, and German aspirations for permanent membership of the Security Council. She watered down a draft statement produced by the FCO, omitting any reference to 'rejoicing' (cf. her famous statement on the recovery of the Falklands!).

3 OCTOBER 1990

Douglas Hurd commented this morning that he saw real signs of dissolution in the Soviet Union. He thinks that the Prime Minister, for the first time, believes that Gorbachev may have had it. There are some scary forecasts of 3 million refugees from the Soviet Union seeking work in the West.

There was a brilliant photograph in *The Times* this week of David Hannay, Bernard Ingham and the Prime Minister, with David apparently saying his prayers. I have offered a prize for the best caption; but I told Geoffrey Adams privately that it might be: 'Please, God, make me more like Crispin Tickell' (i.e. Margaret Thatcher's favourite diplomat).

The new Bulgarian Foreign Minister, Gotsev, who had been my host in Sofia last year as Deputy Minister, called on me today, in the absence of both Douglas Hurd and William Waldegrave – though William would have refused to see him after their last meeting in Sofia, when Gotsev was Deputy Minister of the Interior, and William had brought the conversation round to the murdered Georgi Markov (of the BBC, and killed by a poisoned umbrella in London); Gotsev had immediately brought the meeting to a close, saying that the discussion was pointless.

Gotsev spent much of my meeting with him today bewailing Bulgaria's economic situation, and asking for British help. I asked pointedly how many of the present government are former members of the Communist Party, and made it clear that help would depend on political and economic reform. He apparently told the press later that I had spoken very offensively about the extent to which the Bulgarian Socialist Party still rules Bulgaria!

We finally joined the ERM today, with an announcement at 4 p.m. Charles Powell, who called on me at 3.30 p.m., later rang me to apologise for not having mentioned it. Douglas had apparently told Stephen Wall yesterday, but under oath to mention it to no one.

On another subject, Charles told me that although the inquiry into the leak of the Chequers record had, as usual, produced a lemon, he is convinced that the culprit was Steve Norris, Nicholas Ridley's PPS, and the Tory choice, in January 2000, for London Mayor, following the disgrace of Jeffrey Archer.

I gave lunch to Simon Jenkins of *The Times* – a lively and interesting man, but rather over-pleased with his own 'radicalism'. At least we no longer have a Foreign Secretary who thinks, as Geoffrey Howe did, that Simon Jenkins could give useful advice on how to run the diplomatic service. He argued hard today against a fixed retirement age and a career structure, claiming that the diplomatic service would do much better simply to take people on with five-year contracts – no doubt on the familiar assumption that any old fool can be a diplomat.

I pointed out that diplomacy only half consisted of reporting on events; the more important and interesting part was developing contacts and influencing other governments, for which a career-long training was desirable.

8 OCTOBER 1990

The new Dutch ambassador, Hoekman, called and offered his congratulations on our entry into the ERM. As Simon Broadbent said at my morning meeting, all the experts who have been pushing for our membership for years are now discovering reasons why we should not be in.

9 OCTOBER 1990

The United Nations has been thrown into confusion by an appalling massacre of Palestinians on the Temple Mount, following the annual attempt by extreme Orthodox Jews to plant a foundation stone for a synagogue. William Waldegrave is convinced that it was almost certainly provoked by pro-Iraqis wanting to muddy the waters in New York – provocation to which the Israelis overreacted disgracefully. Douglas Hurd thinks that the Prime Minister will be very reluctant to vote differently from the Americans at a time when our troops are alongside each other in Saudi Arabia, even though Research Department has produced some helpful figures showing the fourteen-odd times when the Americans have vetoed in isolation in recent years.

10 OCTOBER 1990

Len Appleyard called this afternoon, discussing the lack of any proper ministerial discussion about our real objectives over Kuwait. The Prime Minister tends to use OD(G) to discuss irrelevant details; no one has yet grappled with the real question, or discussed with the Americans, how to deal with Iraq's nuclear, chemical and biological facilities. As for talks with the Americans, Percy Cradock plans to visit Washington for talks with the National Security Council on 22/23 October. I later argued that it was high time ministers tried to establish what our objectives are, reminding them that the Franks Committee had criticised ministers in 1983 for failing to meet before the Falklands War, and that one of the reasons had been that the Foreign Secretary, Peter Carrington, was away in Israel. Douglas Hurd goes there next week.

15 OCTOBER 1990

Douglas is in Israel today, with the Israelis in a very sour mood, after the

United States had joined the vote in the Security Council for a resolution which any previous administration would have vetoed. The Israelis showed their displeasure (having already complained about Douglas Hurd's speech last week), by refusing to welcome him properly on arrival; by searching all his party's luggage; and by arresting one of the Palestinians he was due to meet the next day.

Tom King told me privately at dinner this evening that US Defense Secretary Cheney had told him that absolutely no decisions have yet been taken in Washington on whether to launch military action, or if so when.

16 OCTOBER 1990

The Russians have just signalled that we can probably keep our residence in Moscow. When Charles Powell put a note to the Prime Minister telling her this, but saying that the FCO had no money for it, she minuted: 'Rubbish.' When the Chief Secretary spoke to the PM about our PESC round, she is quoted as saying: 'They have too many meetings' – whatever that means?

17 OCTOBER 1990

An Emergency Unit meeting this morning, to discuss the total apparent confusion between Washington and New York on what resolution to go for next. Antony Acland has meanwhile asked for assurances that people here are both thinking about strategic and long-term policies towards Iraq, and are discussing these with the White House. It is not easy to keep Antony informed, when the Prime Minister has ruled that her talk with Cheney this week is not to be recorded at all; and when the mere fact of a meeting of ministers (now scheduled for next week) is classified as Top Secret.

18 OCTOBER 1990

More confusion today over UN resolutions, with the US apparently pressing for something which will give them a pretext to attack Saddam Hussein.

I wrote three personal letters this morning: one to Lynda Chalker, to thank her for her staunch defence of David Colvin against opposition attacks during Questions on Cambodia this week. Second to Brian Mower, to express my outrage at a silly article in the *Times* diary today, claiming that FCO officials were smirking with satisfaction at the trouble Douglas Hurd had got into in Jerusalem, over his remarks about a Palestinian State, and claiming that this proved that Brian was 'not one of us'. And thirdly to Harold Caccia, who has developed cancer, and is reported by Philip Adams to be sinking fast (though still mentally alert).

19 OCTOBER 1990

Percy Cradock called, before leaving for Washington, having received firm instructions from the Prime Minister that he is not to discuss military matters at all. I aired my continuing worries about the failure of ministers to clarify their aims and objectives towards Iraq. Percy replied that the Prime Minister was very clear in her objectives, and that he agreed with them! I pointed out that none of the rest of us (including, most importantly, the military) had been told what they were.

The Prime Minister has sent two messages to Bush this week, and has had one long telephone conversation – all of which have been recorded for the eyes of the Foreign and Defence Secretaries, and no one else. I told Percy that I was adult enough not to mind not seeing them myself; but that there was a serious risk that if war broke out, and there were heavy casualties or some disaster, a later version of the Franks Committee would be severely critical of the failure of ministers to discuss these things in a proper committee.

Patrick Fairweather called, on his return with Douglas Hurd from Cairo, Israel and Jerusalem. He revealed that, unknown to me, Douglas had received a message in Luxor from the Prime Minister telling him to go easy on his criticisms of Israel, which had no doubt inclined him to be rather more resistant on the question of a Palestinian State than he would have been otherwise. He has had an appalling press this week (not helped by today's disaster for the Tories at Eastbourne), though he has personally come top of the poll as the best Conservative politician. He himself seems typically to have been unmoved by it all. As I told Stephen Wall, if it had been Geoffrey Howe, I would have written him a personal letter of encouragement and sympathy; but if I were to do that for Douglas, I suspect that his first reaction would be: 'What on earth has he written this for?'

22 OCTOBER 1990

Nigel Broomfield and I attended the first of Robin Butler's twice-weekly meetings with Michael Quinlan and David Craig to discuss the Gulf crisis, and how to brief ministers for their first real discussion of objectives tomorrow. Robin revealed that he has been given sight of the Prime Minister's exchange with the President (though unknown to the PM herself, who is being formidably sensitive about secrecy). There seems to have been quite a sharp difference of view at one of last week's exchanges, in particular over whether the United States should use the Security Council Resolution on their embassy in Kuwait as a means of provoking Iraqi military action. David Craig seems very unenthusiastic and uncertain about the military balance, even though the Americans now have more than 100,000 men in Saudi Arabia.

Ted Heath, meanwhile, seems to have succeeded in extracting some of the sick and elderly hostages from Iraq, though the Iraqis were still haggling over numbers this evening.

23 OCTOBER 1990

Douglas Hurd held a meeting to prepare for his talk with Tom King, and their later meeting with the Prime Minister – their first real attempt to tackle the basic question of what we want to achieve. Douglas told David Craig this evening that the meeting with the Prime Minister had gone well.

Curious stories today of Saddam Hussein having had a vision, with the Prophet calling on him to leave Kuwait – either a very clever ploy to save face, or Kuwaiti black propaganda. We are having some difficulties with William Waldegrave, who takes an extremely hawkish view, and finds it difficult to grasp the problems involved in military action involving only the United States and ourselves.

24 OCTOBER 1990

Persistent reports today that the Iraqis may be about to do a partial withdrawal from Kuwait. One way to react might be to put Arab forces in at once, though Charles Powell told me today that virtually no Syrians or Egyptians have yet arrived at the front.

Douglas Hurd attended a meeting at No. 10 on the Soviet Union, at which the Prime Minister made the memorable remark that she had been 'a bit hard on the Foreign Office'!

25 OCTOBER 1990

Robin Butler chaired another of his Gulf meetings today, at which it emerged that Michael Quinlan and I are the only two who are not privy to the Prime Minister's meetings and exchanges. No. 10 has ruled that only one extra official in each department can be brought in, and Nigel Broomfield and Richard Mottram have been nominated for the privilege.

29 OCTOBER 1990

The press is full of splits and rows at the European Council in Rome, where the Prime Minister was arguing (quite rightly) for an agreement on agriculture for CAP negotiation, while the Italian presidency was pressing for a discussion of Political and Economic Union. A *Times* editorial included an outrageous reference to 'inefficient and fiercely disloyal diplomats'.

Both the Prime Minister and Douglas Hurd want me to find an embassy for Richard Luce. But as there can be no question of a by-election, David Gillmore will have to tackle that one.

30 OCTOBER 1990

I attended a meeting in Douglas Hurd's office with David Waddington and others to discuss political asylum and frontiers, on both of which Waddington is in something of a panic, given the very high rise in numbers (though nothing like the French or German figures). Unfortunately, on frontiers, our island status has yet again isolated us from the other eleven, including (ironically, but typically) the Irish, with whom we have a free travel area.

1 NOVEMBER 1990

A very highly classified telegram from Antony Acland, addressed to four named officials, reporting on American plans to rescue their hostages in Kuwait – allegedly known only to six officials in Washington. This was followed about four hours later by a front-page report in the *Evening Standard*, attributed to 'White House officials'!

The Princess of Wales visited the office this afternoon. On very good form, and very chatty with both the Emergency Unit and with East European Department. William Waldegrave flatly denied that he had ever sent me a message saying that he wanted to accompany her throughout, and insisted that I came as well – just as well, since I was able to jolly the staff into behaving naturally. Everyone was charmed by her, and the crowds were literally five deep on both sides of King Charles Street when she left.

I went to a dinner at which Geoffrey Howe was to have been the speaker. The news that he had scratched, having resigned from the government today, reached us after I had arrived. Richard Ryder, the Paymaster General (and a former PPS of Geoffrey's), stood in, and gave a very witty speech. He explained that he had looked at Geoffrey's text, but was unable to use the jokes, which consisted of headings only, such as 'Patrick Wright = the Singing Detective'.

Sad news about Geoffrey's resignation, but perhaps it will lance the boil. Richard Ryder's private reaction was that it would be very damaging for the Conservative Party. Tim Yeo had already reported to my meeting this morning that the party was badly split on Europe. I am not sure whether this brings the election nearer or not – the Prime Minister may be tempted to make Europe an election issue.

2 NOVEMBER 1990

Robin Butler described Geoffrey Howe's resignation last night, saying that the Prime Minister is in a fiercely resentful mood and had already dealt very brutally with the consequential ministerial changes. Someone has described her as 'a woman incapable of love'.

At lunchtime, I saw a rather flushed William Waldegrave going into No. 10. It later emerged that he has taken Kenneth Clarke's place as Secretary of State for Health, with Douglas Hogg (from the Home Office) taking his place at the FCO.

Douglas Hurd is thinking over the weekend whether to change ministerial portfolios; but Hogg is likely to keep the Middle East. The general view is that Geoffrey's resignation pushes back the election date;

but there must now be a real possibility that Douglas Hurd will be pushed forward in a leadership contest.

Yesterday's *Sun* carried the headline 'Up Yours Delors'. As Christopher France commented to me: 'If their diplomatic correspondent can write that, what do you think their non-diplomatic correspondent would write?'

5 NOVEMBER 1990

A weekend of press speculation on whether Michael Heseltine will make a leadership challenge to the Prime Minister this year or next, following Geoffrey Howe's resignation.

I called on William Waldegrave this morning to say goodbye. He is obviously thrilled to have reached the Cabinet at last (and, at forty-four, the youngest member of it). He seemed to be genuinely grateful for what he called 'the Rolls-Royce treatment' he had received from the FCO. He thought there would be a leadership struggle this autumn, and referred to his own appointment as 'joining a sinking ship'.

I called on William's successor, Douglas Hogg, this afternoon – a very bright politician, described as a 'chip off the old Hailsham'. He assured me that he was a hard and quick worker, though he is a bit daunted by the size of his portfolio. (William Waldegrave had told me that he would have recommended passing responsibility for Eastern Europe to Tristan Garel-Jones.) I told Douglas Hogg that I remembered his father's strong interest in Israel from my time in Middle East Department, and hoped that he would not find the FCO the biased den of Arabists, as portrayed by the press. I told him about my own efforts to cultivate the Jewish community (and vice versa!). I also warned David Gore-Booth this morning that he would have to tread carefully.

Douglas Hurd made a major speech today on Europe, and did brilliantly on the Brian Walden show. He is having to play his hand very carefully to avoid accusations of disloyalty or policy differences from Margaret

Thatcher. He has hardly put a foot wrong so far. The PM has meanwhile referred (in my view, unwisely) to her contempt for Michael Heseltine.

I gave lunch today for the chiefs of staff and Michael Quinlan. Not much talk of the Gulf, since most of those present have a very restricted knowledge of what is going on (including myself, who – unlike the Chief of Defence Staff – has had no account of the Prime Minister's telephone call to the President this weekend).

6 NOVEMBER 1990

Lynda Chalker made a bid today to take over ministerial responsibility for Africa. I later advised Stephen Wall against the idea, on the grounds that Africa provides more policy differences with the ODA than any other part of the world. I also argued that the Africa departments are already fairly demoralised by the low priority given to Africa; to be supervised by a minister a mile away would not help. Douglas Hurd is nevertheless likely to give her what she wants. He must realise that she is in a low state, having again missed Cabinet rank to William Waldegrave.

7 NOVEMBER 1990

Robin Butler today gave perm secs a fairly frank account of Geoffrey Howe's resignation, and the PM's 'insensitive' behaviour towards reshuffles. John MacGregor in particular was clearly very dismayed to be transferred from Education to be Lord President. There is still some mystery about last night's news that a challenger to the party leadership has emerged; Robin reported that the party managers still didn't know this morning who it was (if anyone). Martyn Lewis of the BBC told me after the speakers' reception that there had been a row last night, since he, as newsreader, had queried the inclusion of the news if no one knew who it was.

I attended a one-and-a-half-hour meeting with Douglas Hurd to prepare for Baker's visit on 9 November, in preparation for decisions to be taken in Washington next week. I am still alarmed at the prospect of decisions being taken without adequate military advice; we have still not agreed our objectives with the Americans, and it looks as though Bush, and the Prime Minister, may be about to take decisions on reinforcement which will in fact commit them to war.

The handling of the Gulf crisis is still worrying; so few people (not including either Michael Quinlan or myself) are allowed to know everything that it is impossible for most of us to give ministers sensible advice. I can see all the makings of a very critical Franks-type inquiry at a later stage.

8 NOVEMBER 1990

Geoffrey Howe was waiting as I emerged from credentials this morning, and commented: 'Here comes the Stalking Horse.' I reminded Geoffrey that, if anything, I was a 'Stalking Puss' (a reference to what he called me as his PUS).

At the Buckingham Palace diplomatic reception this evening, I nobbled Hermann von Richthofen, at Douglas Hurd's request, about Genscher's behaviour at the recent European Council meeting, where Genscher himself had pressed colleagues to 'discourage further missions to Baghdad', immediately before appearing to sponsor Willi Brandt's visit. There are other signs that German behaviour in Rome ruffled Community feathers; one member (probably Portugal) commented: 'This is what a unified Germany is going to be like.'

9 NOVEMBER 1990

An early meeting with Douglas Hurd to divide our responsibilities vis-à-vis Baker and Kimmitt. When I suggested a similar division of responsibilities between himself and the Prime Minister, he commented: 'There is no point; she would pay no attention to it anyway.'

Bob Kimmitt called for one and a half hours, mainly reporting on Baker's other visits, while Baker himself was upstairs with Douglas Hurd. Bob was suitably apologetic on being told that the State Department had not (although instructed by Baker) forewarned our embassy about US plans for reinforcement in the Gulf. An impressive man. As usual, he spoke at length, and in great detail, without a single note.

12 NOVEMBER 1990

Mark Lennox-Boyd took the early meeting in Kuwait – horrified to discover that no one present had seen the record of the Prime Minister's talks with Baker on Friday. As the talks had a direct relevance to whether we should now instruct David Hannay to discuss a further Security Council Resolution on the use of force, Mark said he would take it up with No. 10. I later had a quiet word with him, and advised him not to pursue this, as Douglas has already taken it up on several occasions. But it is quite revealing to see how shocked the PM's former PPS is to discover the extent of No. 10's paranoia over secrecy.

Nevertheless, the PM made an astonishing tribute to 'the best traditions of the diplomatic service' in her Guildhall speech tonight.

Douglas Hurd looked in to tell me today that he had more or less decided to give responsibility for Africa, including South Africa, to Lynda Chalker. I later discussed this with Patrick Fairweather and agreed that she should have an office and private secretary in Downing Street. Not an easy arrangement, though I think it has been done before, and was done again, rather unsatisfactorily, when David Simon had offices in both the DTI and the FCO.

Both Michael Heseltine and John MacGregor (respectively the Stalking Horse and the new Lord President) called on Douglas Hurd today. I was unable to extract any comment from Douglas about the current political turmoil beyond a remark that the more he stayed out of the tearoom, the better. He is certainly in high spirits.

13 NOVEMBER 1990

Geoffrey Howe made his devastating resignation speech today ('cricket bats and all that'). It will almost certainly lead to Michael Heseltine declaring his candidacy tomorrow; he claims to have at least 100 supporters. We shall see.

Virginia and I went to the Hurds' farewell lunch for the de Nanteuils at Carlton Gardens. He will not be much missed (at least by the FCO), though reports of his successor, Bernard Dorin, are awful. The Swiss ambassador in Brasilia has described Dorin's appointment as a sign that Mitterrand must want to make life difficult for Mrs Thatcher. He sounds intolerable, and enjoys dressing up in uniforms.

14 NOVEMBER 1990

Douglas Hogg took the 8.30 a.m. meeting on Kuwait. There is a problem over discussions in New York between David Hannay and Tom Pickering; as Douglas Hurd put it later, our systems (and David Hannay) have moved too fast for the Americans, who have still not sent Pickering instructions following Baker's talks here.

Douglas Hurd told me of a talk he has had with the Prime Minister on personnel questions. Three points came up which shed some light on Margaret Thatcher's personal views and prejudices. On Charles Powell, she is (again) adamant that Charles should not leave No. 10, but that when he does, he should get either Paris or Bonn. Secondly, her description of another member of the service as 'twee' apparently relates to a suit she once saw him wearing with crocodile-skin shoes. She also reverted to her well-known prejudice for tall men by saying she did not think another member of the service was 'big enough' for a certain post.

A row is brewing over Christianity in Saudi Arabia, both on the question of Christmas trees and on army chaplains. David Gore-Booth and I tried to explain the need to take Saudi sensitivities into account, however illogical and outrageous they are. But everyone else at the meeting, including Douglas Hogg and David Lidington, clearly thought the Camel Corps had gone too far. There has already been quite a dispute about women driving in the armed forces. I later pointed out that almost anything can be done in Saudi Arabia, if it is done discreetly. But the press will no doubt continue to cause trouble.

Douglas Hurd has asked for some research to be done on how ministers produced public support at the time of the Falklands War, e.g. what statements were made and what consultations took place. This has produced some fascinating papers from my safe, including a draft minute from Antony Acland to Francis Pym on exactly the same lines as my current worries: i.e. pressing for proper military briefing and a clear statement of objectives.

16 NOVEMBER 1990

Robin Butler came to see me this afternoon, having discussed the 'unthinkable' with Andrew Turnbull, i.e. what to do if Margaret Thatcher is either defeated, or decides to resign, next Tuesday 20 November. Robin clearly has some hint that Denis is inclined to advise her to go if the result is at all humiliating. Douglas Hurd made it clear for the first time today that he would stand, but not against Margaret Thatcher.

Stephen Wall tells me that there are rumours that Peter Carrington is about to come out against Mrs Thatcher. This would certainly have a very powerful, and probably decisive, effect on the party. Meanwhile, Robin told me that the Thatcher camp, including Peter Morrison, claim to be totally confident of victory and of her remaining at No. 10; Morrison told Robin that they had a 'certain' 230 votes. As Robin pointed out to me, if you are asked whether you are going to support the Prime Minister, there is only one answer any career-minded MP is likely to give.

19 NOVEMBER 1990

I had a brief meeting with Lord Caithness about the Indian residence, in preparation for his meeting with Lord Mansfield, the Crown Estates Commissioner. General agreement that we must at least try to retain our New Delhi residence. If Mrs Thatcher remains Prime Minister, she would be furious if we allowed it to go. But the commissioners are demanding vast sums from the Indians, and we don't yet know who the new Indian High Commissioner will be.

20 NOVEMBER 1990

The leadership contest results in 152 votes for Heseltine and 204 for Margaret Thatcher. (Jonathan Powell of Planning Staff won the office sweepstake with an exact forecast – insider intelligence from his brother?)

21 NOVEMBER 1990

An extraordinary day in British politics. On return from Paris at lunchtime, Stephen Wall told me that Douglas Hurd had telephoned him on 7 November to say, rather coyly, that Judy wanted to speak to him. She then said that Douglas did not think it right to ask his private secretary this question; but did Stephen think he should run for the leadership? Stephen had replied that there seemed to be considerable support for him in the party, and he thought that he should. Douglas later thought he had reached agreement with Margaret Thatcher that he would not commit himself to back her on the second round, until she had returned from Paris and consulted the party managers.

Douglas was therefore considerably put out by her hurried announcement last night, on the steps of the Paris embassy, that she would fight the second round. Robin Butler reported to perm secs this morning that the party managers were calling on the Prime Minister at lunchtime, and that everyone thought that Michael Heseltine would do much better on the second round than he had on the first. Conservative MPs, including several Cabinet ministers, were said to be switching their support, and the Chief Whip is believed to have advised the Prime Minister that she should stand down. As it was, she emerged from No. 10 after lunch, saying: 'I fight; and I fight to win.'

Andrew Turnbull then asked me to call, saying he had been researching Harold Wilson's resignation, and had come across a sheaf of messages to heads of government (apparently not having checked who P. R. H. Wright was!). He asked me to give some thought to what messages the PM should send if she resigned. I pointed out that Charles Powell was much better placed to draft messages in the way the Prime Minister would want, and was well aware of the circumstances surrounding any possible resignation. Andrew showed me a draft statement, saying that she had decided to tender her resignation. [I wonder if Margaret Thatcher herself was aware of the existence of that draft?]

I saw Elspeth Howe at a party this evening, and told her that I had been much moved by Geoffrey's resignation speech. She confirmed that he had decided not to run for the leadership and thinks (as did virtually everyone I talked to) that Heseltine is home and dry.

22 NOVEMBER 1990

Douglas Hogg put on a strange performance at the Kuwait meeting this morning, getting cross with the Saudis about the recent misbehaviour of the Mutawa (the religious police), who have broken into two private parties this week, and beaten people up. Hogg was even crosser with the Americans for not, as he saw it, consulting us properly over a draft Security Council Resolution on the use of force.

When Alan Munro called on me later, I urged him to try to get Hogg to see Saudi fundamentalism in perspective. Hogg proposes to summon the Saudi ambassador to tell him that the Mutawa are 'dotty'. On the Security Council Resolution, I have tried to explain to Hogg the amount of consultation that has already gone on at higher levels.

By the time I left for Dutch credentials this morning, I had heard that Norman Tebbit was also standing for the leadership.

It is not clear what job Douglas Hurd would offer Heseltine, if he wins the leadership election; I assume it would be Foreign Secretary. I rather doubt whether he would bring back Geoffrey Howe.

I discussed the election with Peter Carrington, who is supporting Heseltine. He had been invited to call on Margaret Thatcher yesterday, but had declined. He clearly thinks she should have gone months ago. He commented that Douglas Hurd had looked very much like Anthony Eden when declaring his candidacy, and wondered if he was not just a little too smooth to win.

23 NOVEMBER 1990

Douglas Hurd and John Major went into full gear in their campaigns today, with each of them obtaining open support from about five Cabinet colleagues each. Stories that Mrs Thatcher had 'declared' for John Major were later denied from No. 10.

Robin Butler had seen Mrs Thatcher, and discussed her change of residence, during which she made the throwaway remark: 'Unless of course

I was to become ambassador to Washington' – reflecting a half-serious ambition?

25 NOVEMBER 1990

In a letter to the service, dated today, I wrote:

> The Thatcher years have been remarkable for all sorts of reasons, perhaps for none more so than the radical changes which they have brought about in domestic and economic policies. But none of us would, I think, deny the substantial impact which she has made on Foreign Policy and on Britain's reputation overseas. Like her or hate her, no foreign statesman could ignore her; and some of the tributes reaching her (often through your telegrams) this week are an eloquent testimony to that. From this side of Downing Street, it has not always been easy, if only because Mrs Thatcher, like so many of her predecessors, has often suspected the service of an excessive readiness to compromise, and a failure to fight to the last ditch for British interests. In her attitudes to the office as an Institution, she sometimes reflected the comment of Churchill, quoted by Sir John Colville in his diaries:
>
> 'What is wanted in that department is a substantial application of the boot.'
>
> Her attitude to individual members of the service, on the other hand, was almost invariably appreciative and complimentary, and she believed passionately in the role which diplomacy and representation could and should be playing in the promotion of Britain's image and interests abroad. It is sad that her style of government, and her treatment of ministerial colleagues, occasionally meant that she did not make full use of the ministerial and official advice which the service and the department could provide…

26 NOVEMBER 1990

Both Heseltine and Major were today claiming about 160 supporters each, with Heseltine commenting wittily that the number of Conservative MPs seemed to have risen to over 500!

A letter from No. 10 today reporting that Zamyatin had handed over a farewell message from Gorbachev, describing the PM as 'Margaret' for the first time, and describing the consternation in Moscow when the news reached him – 'how can such a thing happen?' Zamyatin himself commented that times had changed since the East had party coups, and the West had elections!

27 NOVEMBER 1990

John Major wins the leadership election today. I wrote a note to Douglas Hurd in commiseration, saying that we had all much admired the way he had conducted his campaign, and expressing relief that he would remain at the helm of the FCO. I was not enthralled by the idea of a fourth Foreign Secretary in two years.

I called on Douglas Hogg this afternoon to try to avert a row with the Saudi ambassador about the Mutawa, and indications that the Saudis would not allow our war dead to be buried there. I pointed out that the main message should be to reassure the Saudis that government policy on the Gulf would not change with a new Prime Minister.

28 NOVEMBER 1990

Douglas Hurd held a ministerial meeting this morning, at which he told his junior ministers that he had been asked by John Major to stay on as Foreign Secretary, and didn't expect any of them to change jobs either (with interesting reactions, varying from Garel-Jones, who seems to have been half expecting promotion to the Cabinet, to Douglas Hogg, who expressed relief at not being sacked!). There were rumours at lunchtime that Lynda Chalker would get a Cabinet post; she will have been all the more dismayed this evening to discover that she is not.

Robin Butler telephoned me this evening to 'offer' me another parliamentary under-secretary. I pointed out that there was a 'snobbery' problem in the FCO, in that foreigners did not take kindly to being dealt with by a mere parliamentary under-secretary. David Goodall had told me that the Indians had already commented on having their affairs dealt with by Lennox-Boyd. But I did think that Lynda Chalker, if staying on at the ODA, could possibly use one to help her with her African responsibilities.

I had a few minutes alone with Douglas Hurd to debrief him on his first talk with John Major last night. I asked him if he had yet discussed visits to Washington (he hadn't), and told him that I thought John Major ought to make the European Council his first trip.

Predictably, I was tackled by Mrs Thatcher at Robin Butler's farewell drinks for her this evening. I opened by thanking her for what she had done for Britain's image abroad over the past eleven years, and for enhancing the role of diplomacy. Typically, she at once went on the attack, telling me sternly that diplomacy was not just about compromise and negotiation; one needed to work to firm objectives. I said that I saw diplomacy as the promotion and projection of one's national interests.

After some discussion about Charles Powell's future, she said that she was hearing a great deal of *on dit* (repeating this in her speech later) and claiming that the 'FCO' had spread a great deal of hostile comment about John Major's time as Foreign Secretary. When I said this was absolutely untrue, she corrected herself. When I went to say goodbye to her, she again told me firmly (and frankly rather rudely) that I must remember what she had said. I responded by saying that I hoped she would also remember what I had said. I thought that Robin Butler, who was listening, looked a bit alarmed!

30 NOVEMBER 1990

The record of Douglas Hurd's talk with Shevardnadze in the margins of the Security Council's foreign ministers' meeting in New York quotes Shevardnadze as saying he was delighted that Douglas had lost the leadership election (as, incidentally, was Douglas himself, whom I saw beaming from ear to ear just after he had heard the result), because they had established such a good relationship as foreign ministers. Douglas replied that he had suspected all along that there were secret forces undermining his campaign; and now he knew!

The Use of Force Resolution went through last night with a ten-to-two vote, almost entirely achieved by a remarkable piece of diplomatic bullying by Baker – an extraordinary bout of activity involving personal visits to about eight different capitals.

3 DECEMBER 1990

The FCO have let the Royal College of Defence Studies down badly, with Douglas Hogg (who in any case was standing in for Douglas Hurd) falling out at the last minute on the grounds that he had lost his voice. (Geoffrey Adams told me that when this had been mentioned to Hogg's office, they had expressed surprise!) Hogg has told Patrick Fairweather that he doesn't want any Friday engagements, as he always shoots that day.

5–6 DECEMBER 1990: VISIT TO PARIS

A busy programme, as the guest of Ewen and Sara Fergusson, including two and a half hours of plenary talks with François Scheer, at which the French record-taker was Mariot Leslie (on a two-year secondment to the Quai as British desk officer). Scheer was impressive, speaking with great authority and hardly glancing at his briefs; and prepared to commit heresies, e.g. by forecasting that France would have to change her attitude towards NATO's military structure.

7 DECEMBER 1990

Robin Butler has not only got himself included in John Major's Camp David talks with Bush; it is now apparently and explicitly acknowledged that Robin (not Charles Powell) is regarded as Scowcroft's opposite number. I shall have to ensure that Robin now keeps Antony Acland and the FCO properly informed.

10 DECEMBER 1990

Stephen Wall told Geoffrey Adams from Paris that Douglas Hurd had said he was really very angry with David Gore-Booth for misleading him on the handling of the Hindawi case during his negotiations with the Syrians on the resumption of relations, thereby committing the worst error an official could commit – namely advising a minister to give an assurance in the House without justification. I later spoke to David, telling him that I was speaking both as PUS and as a longstanding friend and admirer of the Gore-Booth family. I advised him to make a quick and unvarnished apology to Douglas Hurd.

11 DECEMBER 1990

When Charles Powell called today, he talked about John Major's working methods as Prime Minister. According to Charles, he spends a lot of time on the telephone to colleagues, and is not very thorough on paper. He hardly ever comments on papers, and Charles therefore has little idea whether he has read them or not. Apparently Mrs Thatcher underlined and side-lined a great deal, and one could even tell (as we could when Alec Douglas-Home was Foreign Secretary) at which point she had gone to sleep over her box! Charles also commented on John Major's fear of being caught out underprepared. He sticks firmly to his own brief at OPD or Cabinet.

12 DECEMBER 1990

Douglas Hurd held a ministerial meeting this morning, with his new parliamentary private secretary, David Martin, attending for the first time. Tim Yeo has now been promoted to the Department of Environment.

Paul Zuckerman brought his mother to the office today to see the Goetze murals in the main corridor (which George Brown had wanted to be painted over, since he thought their imperialist message was bad for young diplomats entering the modern service). Goetze was Lady Zuckerman's great uncle, and she remembers visiting his studio in St John's Wood as a girl. He was a vastly rich artist, who spent seven years painting the Foreign Office murals, without a penny in payment. She told me that the Cabinet were so alarmed by reports of nudes in the murals that they insisted on crossing Downing Street to view them!

Unfortunately, Lord Caithness's office was locked, so I could not show her the ministerial room occupied by her father, Lord Reading. And Douglas Hogg was holding a meeting, so I could not show her the room occupied by her grandfather, as Secretary of State for India.

13 DECEMBER 1990

I discussed with Douglas Hurd today Alan Clark's gaffe over NATO, having made speeches in Oman, and now an interview in *The Guardian*, saying that NATO is no longer necessary, and that the United Kingdom should leave Europe – an outrageous and simultaneous contradiction of Douglas's speech on security policy in Berlin this week. Tom King has told Michael Quinlan that he will speak sternly to Clark; but both Michael and Douglas Hurd doubt whether he will.

I later heard from Michael Quinlan, in strict confidence, that Alan Clark is due to get a privy counsellorship in the New Year honours, which will merely confuse everyone even further as to what our security policy really is. Douglas Hurd has agreed to talk to the PM about it.

I discussed with John Boyd and others today whether we are not now paying too much attention to people's wishes. Diplomatic service regulation no. 4 does, after all, require members of the service to go where they are sent; but there is a marked difference between the way junior and senior members of the service are treated. This was, of course, before the later rule that all members of the service are required to apply for their next posting.

15 DECEMBER 1990

Prospects of war in the Gulf look rather worse, with the Iraqis and the Americans having failed to fix a time for respective visits of Baker and Tariq Aziz.

The European Council in Rome seems to have gone well, with the other eleven obviously trying to make John Major's first council a success. He took quite a striking line that the young of Britain (i.e. the under-47s) are keen to make a success of our Community membership. His performance has, if anything, been enhanced by an extraordinary outburst from Delors, threatening to create a 'political crisis' in Britain.

16 DECEMBER 1990

Robin Butler showed me today an extraordinary letter from Mrs Thatcher, complaining in strident terms about a letter 'declassifying' her under the Official Secrets Act, and claiming that she has never had any consideration from the Cabinet Secretary. As Robin and Gill have gone out of their way to welcome the Thatchers to their home in Dulwich, Robin is really very hurt. As he said, presumably a case of 'kicking the cat'. He warned me to be careful in the FCO's dealings with her (of which there have been none yet, thank God).

Tim Simmons theoretically started today as my private secretary, but spent most of it with the department preparing papers for the Foreign Affairs Council this week.

18 DECEMBER 1990

I discussed with Douglas Hurd today whether we should close the embassy in Baghdad in mid-January. Both Hurd and Hogg think we should, though I am in favour of keeping a small core staff, if we can find volunteers.

20 DECEMBER 1990

News broke this morning of Shevardnadze's rather Geoffrey Howe-like resignation speech to the Congress of People's Deputies, with rather sinister implications for the stability of the Soviet Union, which seems to be slipping fast into political and economic disintegration. Shevardnadze's departure will be sad for Douglas Hurd; and if Primakov succeeds him, this could have very unfortunate effects on Soviet policy towards Saddam Hussein.

21 DECEMBER 1990

Still no news of Baker/Aziz exchange of visits. Prospects for war look distinctly worse, though the US General has made an astonishing public statement that American troops won't be ready to fight until mid-February, and that a war could last three to six months.

1991

23 DECEMBER 1990–6 JANUARY 1991:
CHRISTMAS AND NEW YEAR HOLIDAYS
7 JANUARY 1991

Jim Baker was in town today, and I joined Douglas Hurd, Patrick Fairweather and Richard Gozney at a working lunch, with Bob Kimmitt, Henry Catto and Ray Seitz. Bob Kimmitt raised with me privately the awkwardness caused for him with his colleagues, both in the embassy here and in Washington, by the very restrictive handling of Gulf matters, and seeking guidance as to who should be the first point of contact in London (on which I tried to steer him towards Antony Acland in the first instance).

A good discussion over lunch, with Baker preparing an astonishing itinerary of about ten capitals in four days, ending in London again on Sunday for a meeting with John Major.

8 JANUARY 1991

Douglas Hogg's private secretary drew my attention last night to a piece in the *Mail on Sunday* quoting two Foreign Office officials and foreign ambassadors making very derogatory remarks about Douglas Hogg's performance and behaviour. I used Patrick Fairweather's early morning meeting to read the riot act.

At my bilateral with Douglas Hurd this afternoon, he asked me what people really thought of Douglas Hogg. I said that he certainly had his faults, and tended to pay more attention to a brisk, business-like approach than to mastering his briefs. Douglas (who knew Hogg from the Home Office) clearly understands the problem.

A massive exercise was set in hand today to assess the likely terrorist threat to Middle East posts if war breaks out in the Gulf, with the possibility of closing our posts in Khartoum and Sanaa altogether. Douglas Hurd is very reluctant to see any posts other than Baghdad closed, and I assured him that no decisions had yet been taken. But we shall probably have to scale down several posts on a temporary basis.

Henry Catto asked to call on me privately this morning, to air his resentment at being excluded from Gulf meetings, including particularly Mrs Thatcher's meeting with Cheney, and Douglas Hurd's tête-à-tête with Baker yesterday (and my talk with Kimmitt). I pointed out that several of these cases were at American request, though Bob Kimmitt seems (as Douglas Hurd commented to me this morning) to have given Henry the opposite impression. Richard Gozney has confirmed that it was at Baker's insistence that his meeting with Douglas was kept private.

The situation in the Soviet Union looks pretty ugly, with reports today of Mrs Prunskienė's resignation in Lithuania, and of Soviet paratroopers being sent to enforce conscription in the Baltic Republics.

10 JANUARY 1991

Pérez de Cuéllar decided today to visit Baghdad in a last attempt to get Saddam Hussein to withdraw, and will see Community foreign ministers in Geneva en route.

11 JANUARY 1991

Horrific pictures from Vilnius tonight; it may be coincidental, but there are extraordinary echoes of 1956, with the Russians using a Middle East crisis to suppress dissent in Hungary.

14 JANUARY 1991

Douglas Hurd cut short his visit to Ankara to join Douglas Hogg at the Foreign Affairs Council in Brussels to discuss Iraq and Lithuania (which turned very nasty over the weekend, with Gorbachev claiming grotesquely that Soviet troops had acted without orders from Moscow).

John Major flew to Paris for lunch with Mitterrand after his talks with Baker in Alconbury yesterday, a meeting originally designed to deal with European issues, but which turned out to be largely on the Gulf. The French have launched a new initiative in the Security Council this afternoon, without any prior warning to colleagues in Brussels – to the fury of the Saudis and others. Why do the French need to issue bilateral statements with the Germans on Lithuania, while the twelve are actually meeting in political cooperation?

15 JANUARY 1991

The Prime Minister reacted angrily today to a French plan, produced last night with very little warning (though in retrospect Mitterrand dropped some heavy hints at lunch yesterday), and given no warning at all in political cooperation. The Saudis and the Gulf rulers seem to be as fed up with the French as the Prime Minister is. The United States ambassador in Abu Dhabi is reported to have told the UAE authorities that he hoped they would remember French behaviour when it came to future defence contracts.

Today is the deadline for Iraqi withdrawal from Kuwait. But there are no signs of Iraqi movement, and even the French now seem to have given up the idea of sending a mission to Baghdad.

I went to Francis Maude's New Year party this evening, at which John Major appeared, fresh from the Gulf debate in the House of Commons, where Andrew Faulds made a very eccentric speech, accusing all and sundry of corruption and undemocratic behaviour.

16 JANUARY 1991

The Gulf War broke out just before midnight tonight. Richard Gozney had told me this morning that the Secretary of State would be told in advance, but that others would be given only a few minutes' warning of the outbreak of fighting.

Douglas Hurd asked to see me in the House of Commons at 1 p.m., primarily to tell me that the PM had decided not to include senior officials in the War Cabinet. He was obviously slightly embarrassed at passing on this message, and said he assumed it was John Major's preference for small meetings. Robin Butler told me later that he was cross about the decision, which he attributed (almost certainly correctly) to Charles Powell. I pointed out to Douglas that I was not at all put out, but that I might have been able to save him the bother of having to debrief to all of us after the meetings.

17 JANUARY 1991

The first day of fighting in the Gulf, with an extraordinary lack of public reaction round the Middle East, and a rather dangerously euphoric impression given by the media that all Allied air raids had been effective, with very few losses. The office has a curious air of calm, with Douglas Hurd in Brussels and Douglas Hogg in Paris.

We are still facing some difficulty in reconciling the department's inclination to advise caution to airlines and communities, and to slim down posts, with Douglas Hurd's strong tendency to bluff it out – perhaps because, as a former Home Secretary and Northern Ireland Secretary, he realises that terrorism can strike anywhere.

18 JANUARY 1991

News came through early this morning of Iraqi missile attacks against Tel Aviv, initially thought to be carrying chemical weapons, but this was later denied. I pointed out, at Douglas Hurd's ministerial meeting this morning, the urgent need for ministers to make it clear that religious and cultural sites in Iraq are not targeted. An FCO amendment to include this point in the Prime Minister's statement yesterday was cut out by Charles Powell, who telephoned the Israeli minister in the embassy here, without telling us he was doing so.

21 JANUARY 1991

Another weekend of war, with reports last night [later found to be false] of scud missiles landing on Bahrain.

The Prime Minister has received an astonishingly starchy message from Mitterrand expressing 'strong resentment' at what the PM and the British press have said about last-minute French moves in the Security Council last week. Peter Carrington telephoned me to say that he is on *Newsnight* tonight to discuss European responses to the Gulf War, and what on earth can he say that will not be regarded as totally offensive? I got the department to give him some facts and figures, but he remained totally unconvinced that any of our allies had done anything!

22 JANUARY 1991

I gave lunch to my Finnish opposite number, Åke Wihtol. We discussed the

Baltics, where further trouble in Latvia has resulted in several deaths, with Gorbachev still trying to shuffle off responsibility. I also put up a slightly embarrassing marker that we would be asking the Finns, among others, for financial contributions to our Gulf expenditure; our costs for ammunition alone in the past four days total £10 million. Michael Quinlan is seriously worried as to how HMG is going to foot the bill.

24 JANUARY 1991

Douglas Hurd to Paris this afternoon to see Dumas, from whom an extraordinarily offensive letter was delivered this morning, complaining about British comments on the last-minute French attempt to stop the war.

29 JANUARY 1991

As usual, news of the change of US ambassador here broke in the press before we had received any official notification from Washington. The embassy called at noon to request *agrement* for Ray Seitz – an excellent appointment, and probably the first career appointment in London ever?

A long and fierce manuscript letter from Antony Acland today, complaining at his exclusion from correspondence between Charles Powell and the White House. To my surprise, Richard Gozney got Charles to agree to telegraph all but the most sensitive accounts to Antony.

30 JANUARY 1991

I went at lunchtime to Chatham House to hear Tristan Garel-Jones talk about his first six months in the FCO. Michael Franklin, in the chair, hissed at me afterwards: 'I don't think six months was long enough.'

Saddam Hussein now seems to be trying to provoke a land battle by incursions into Saudi Arabia. More of his aircraft have flown to Iran, though the Americans managed to shoot one of them down en route yesterday.

31 JANUARY 1991

I am still pressing for the release of photographs of Najaf and Karbala to disprove Iraqi allegations of Allied bombing of the shrines. The military are still resisting (with some logic). With such large Shia populations in the Gulf area, this is one subject which could really inflame passions.

Douglas Hurd had a successful visit to Bonn yesterday, with Kohl in an ebullient and expansive mood towards Britain, agreeing to £275 million financial contribution for us. David Martin tells me he has had some difficulty persuading people that the FCO have not been slow in pressing for burden-sharing, but has pointed out (as have I) that both Mrs Thatcher and John Major have been very reluctant to be seen passing round the begging bowl. Our drafts to No. 10 on the subject have all been watered down personally by the Prime Minister.

3 FEBRUARY 1991

Denis Greenhill tackled me at the Swiss Red Cross concert this evening about an extraordinary message he had received from Lord Selkirk to say that his dotty brother, the Duke of Hamilton, was on his way to Israel (*sic*) to assassinate Saddam Hussein. It is not clear what our ambassador in Tel Aviv, Mark Elliott, is supposed to do about it.

4 FEBRUARY 1991

I tried unsuccessfully to telephone Bob Kimmitt to pursue our attempts to pick up part of the Japanese $9 billion for burden-sharing. Jim Baker told

Douglas Hurd at the weekend very firmly that it was all for the Americans, and that Congress would not understand anything less.

The Saudis took exception to Douglas Hurd's speech at Blaby over the weekend, and threatened to block his planned visit. Fahd was said to be outraged by his suggestion that the oil producers should share their wealth more equitably, and by the implication that Western troops would remain after the war. Happily, Douglas dealt very skilfully with both points in his lunchtime interview yesterday, and pacified Prince Saud with a telephone call from Brussels last night.

Christopher MacRae called before departing for Lagos. Not an easy job, with the Nigerian Foreign Ministry operating (or not, as the case may be) out of Abuja, and bitterly resenting anyone who bypasses them, e.g. by going direct to the presidency. This led to a row during Lynda Chalker's recent visit, and the cancellation of her call on Babangida (for which he later apologised by telephone).

5 FEBRUARY 1991

I succeeded in contacting Bob Kimmitt today. It looks as though some compromise can be worked out: we get 8 per cent of the $9 billion this financial year, if the Japanese can be persuaded to top up the extra for the United States next year.

John Major is showing welcome signs of a readiness to telephone his opposite numbers – something that successive private secretaries at No. 10 have tried to achieve. In one call to the Australian Prime Minister, Bob Hawke opened by saying that he had sworn not to discuss cricket – Britain are being lacerated in the Test – to which John Major replied that all our best cricketers have been taken away to fight in the Gulf!

In a telephone call to Mitterrand, John Major referred to his meeting with Bernard Dorin, to which Mitterrand had replied that he was a very 'unusual' man. Mitterrand had found that diplomats were either conformist or, more rarely, lively; Dorin was in the second category. Dorin himself had told Patrick Fairweather that he found the French embassy a 'nest of Anglophilia', and he intended to do something about it.

At my bilateral with Douglas Hurd today, I discussed the anomaly of a Minister of State having responsibility for Ireland, and got his agreement that we should ask Tristan Garel-Jones to take it on. When I saw Tristan later, he made it clear that he would only do it with the greatest reluctance and distaste. I later discovered that he had been a very close friend of Ian Gow.

Press stories broke yesterday on the NAO (National Audit Office) report on the FCO accounts, on which I have to appear before the PAC in early March. Douglas Hurd is put out not to have been forewarned. I had in fact mentioned it briefly to him at one of his ministerial meetings, but had fully briefed Caithness instead.

7 FEBRUARY 1991

I was about to invite Geoffrey Adams in for a farewell chat and coffee when a violent explosion shook the building, caused by two mortars landing on the green outside my office, and a major explosion in the Downing Street garden, smashing three of my office windows, with one frame badly damaged. The police prevented me from leaving the building, thereby causing me to miss my first credentials of the year (for Malta).

8 FEBRUARY 1991

Douglas Hurd seems to have obtained an impressively quick commitment from Kuwait for £650 million – only a little less than the entire FCO budget!

12 FEBRUARY 1991

I lunched with Tony Fanshawe at the House of Lords. He was lyrical about

Douglas Hurd, whom he described as the best Foreign Secretary since Curzon. He also referred to an interview which Mark Lennox-Boyd had given in the *House Magazine*, describing it as a disgraceful attack on the service. When I later told Mark that I had been sad to read it, since I thought he had missed an opportunity to destroy some of the myths surrounding the service, he told me he thought he had defended the office!

I later saw a piece by Ian Aitken in *The Guardian*, referring to it as a very unusual ministerial attack on his own department, and saying that Mrs Thatcher, who is widely known to hate the Foreign Office, could hardly have done better.

13 FEBRUARY 1991

I have discussed with Malcolm Caithness whether he would take on responsibility for Northern Ireland, having frankly explained Garel-Jones's reluctance. He agreed to think about it, but pointed out that his wife is related to the O'Neills, and that he had promised her that if he was ever offered the job of Secretary of State for Northern Ireland, he would turn it down.

I asked Douglas Hurd if there is any background to press stories that Margaret Thatcher might go to Washington as ambassador. He totally rejected it, but said that John Major is worried about her, and thinks that someone should think of a role for her, e.g. chairing a second Brandt Commission.

14 FEBRUARY 1991

I discussed with Lord Caithness proposals from Amman and Riyadh that they should have rest and recreation facilities, either to Cyprus or to the UK, for the duration of the Gulf crisis. He has reservations about the idea (on the grounds that unfavourable comparisons might be drawn with the troops).

18 FEBRUARY 1991

David Hannay called, having just called on John Major, whom he found very reasonable and sensible on the need to persuade the Americans to involve the United Nations in post-war settlements; but he had been horrified by the line taken by Charles Powell, who was thoroughly obstructive and Thatcherite. Unfortunately, Baker has twice succeeded in blocking third-world activity at the UN by sheer bull-headedness. Not an easy situation to cope with.

Robin Butler had a private word with me about a proposal that Mrs Thatcher might become chairman of the British Council. I discouraged Robin from raising this with the Prime Minister until I had run it past Douglas Hurd; but I warned him that Dick Francis had thought that both Richard Luce and Tim Raison were 'too political' for the chairmanship, and that Mrs Thatcher would surely be a case of '*a fortiori*'. I wouldn't envy the accounting officer if she got it; she would spend all her time trying, and probably succeeding, to get more money for the Council, and less for the FCO.

Lunch at No. 10 for President Zhelev of Bulgaria, who is making a spectacular gesture of reconciliation by visiting Georgi Markov's grave in Dorset later this week (see p. 254, above). At a lunch for President Zhelev the next day, I sat next to Ludzhov, the Deputy Minister responsible for Bulgaria's Security and Intelligence Services, who virtually admitted Bulgarian guilt over Markov's death, and was sure that an inquest would produce conclusive evidence.

19 FEBRUARY 1991

A flurry of work today on Gorbachev's proposals presented to Tariq Aziz in Moscow yesterday, and delivered to the Americans, the French and ourselves late last night. Douglas Hogg, standing in for Douglas Hurd, held a briefing meeting before OPD(G), where ministers got down to a detailed drafting session to produce a message for the Prime Minister to send to Bush. Ministers quickly decided to call for Patrick Fairweather – a ludicrous illustration of the folly of omitting officials from the ministerial committee.

20 FEBRUARY 1991

There are now real signs of the Iraqis crumbling, and some fascinating reports of Saddam's colleagues advising him to call it a day. Tariq Aziz has arrived back in Moscow apparently bearing a positive message, though there was a very belligerent and negative speech from Saddam Hussein this afternoon.

I used Robin Butler's meeting this afternoon to air my unhappiness at our failure to use the embassy in Washington properly. Robin seemed astonished that there was still a problem, and thought the Prime Minister was unaware of this. I told the meeting that Antony was still only allowed to be told the details of Charles Powell's exchanges with Scowcroft on condition that he does not reveal his knowledge of them to the Americans, or to Andrew Wood.

A splendid row is raging over the Pergau Dam project in Malaysia (see p. 95, above), for which both the ODA and the DTI want to withhold the financial assistance which was earlier promised to Mahathir by Mrs Thatcher after long discussions (and an accounting officer's minute from Tim Lankester). Douglas Hurd has decided to write to No. 10 pointing out that it would cause severe problems if we went back on Mrs Thatcher's promises. No. 10 has replied that they agree, and the Treasury are livid – feeling, with some justification, that they have been bounced. Douglas is quite unapologetic, and has instructed that any complaints about non-consultation should be directed at No. 10. I now have an extremely grumpy letter from Peter Middleton to answer.

21 FEBRUARY 1991

Douglas Hurd's ministerial meeting today was attended, for the first time, by Edward Bickham, his newish special adviser, who also attended my morning meeting today.

22 FEBRUARY 1991

A short statement from President Bush today, announcing a 24-hour deadline for the Iraqis to start withdrawing.

24 FEBRUARY 1991

The deadline having expired yesterday afternoon, the ground war against Iraq started early this morning. There has been very little resistance so far, though the main operation has been a wide sweep northwards by the French and US forces, to encircle Kuwait. British forces moved this afternoon, but no reports yet of how they have fared.

Large numbers of Iraqi prisoners are giving themselves up, filmed singing and rejoicing on TV this evening. I telephoned the emergency unit to suggest that ITN should be reminded that frontal photographs of POWs are a breach of the Vienna Convention.

Virginia and I lunched at Chevening – the Hurds' farewell for Henry Catto. Also there were two of the Hurd children, Jessica and Philip; when they were told we were coming, they apparently asked about Virginia: 'Does she have no hair too?' (a reference to my alopecia, acquired in Damascus in 1981).

25 FEBRUARY 1991

Another day of apparent success in the land campaign, with thousands of prisoners being taken, and no British casualties (though the first Iraqi scud to hit a military target in Saudi Arabia has killed twenty US soldiers).

I suggested to Douglas Hurd that he should send a message to David Hannay to tell him that President Bush had spoken very warmly of him – a welcome contrast to Baker's criticism of the Pickering/Hannay axis in New York.

26 FEBRUARY 1991

Radio Baghdad this morning announced Iraq's acceptance of UN Security Council Resolution (SCR) 660, and that the Iraqi Army are starting to withdraw from Kuwait. This was followed by an extraordinary speech from Saddam Hussein, which my friend, the Kuwaiti ambassador, described as 'meaningless'. Since Allied forces are now deep inside Iraqi territory, I have suggested that ministers should reiterate that we have no territorial claims on Iraq, and that we do not want to see any border changes. Tom King included a good passage in his statement this afternoon.

27 FEBRUARY 1991

The Gulf War drew to its close today, with successive Iraqi statements accepting all twelve SCRs.

28 FEBRUARY 1991

President Bush announced this morning that all offensive action in the Gulf had ceased. Sadly, there was a horrific mishap today when nine British soldiers were killed by a misguided US air attack. Otherwise, there have been an astonishing number of dogs that did not bark: no chemical weapons attacks; virtually no attacks, or even demonstrations, against British official premises; hardly any sign of the threatened Iraqi terrorist activity; the total collapse of the famed Iraqi Republican Guard Forces; and remarkable cohesion between the military and the politicians among the coalition forces. The only negative surprises so far are that a) the Syrian forces eventually did nothing; and b) Saddam Hussein is still there.

At lunchtime, I attended Mark Lennox-Boyd's meeting for minority MPs, though only Northern Ireland and Liberal Democrats turned up. Mark put on an unimpressive performance, repeating some of his *canards* about the FCO's failure to understand domestic politics.

I told Douglas Hurd this evening that the Trade Union Side had written a letter of protest to Mark about his interview in the *House Magazine*. Douglas virtually said that it served him right and would teach him that 'not everyone appreciates his sense of humour'.

At our bilateral this evening, Douglas Hurd confirmed that he would like junior ministers involved in the tactics of the PESC round (both Tristan Garel-Jones and Malcolm Caithness are itching to be involved). He also agreed that I should drop the idea of any junior minister supervising Irish affairs, Caithness having decided that he could not do it, and I having persuaded Tristan Garel-Jones that he should do it after all. I agreed with Douglas that it would not be satisfactory to have anyone doing it as reluctantly as Tristan would.

1 MARCH 1991

At the DUSs' lunch, there was some talk about the Treasury's insensitivity towards burden-sharing, on which David Mellor is running into trouble. No. 10 has already issued one implied rebuke, recording the PM's views that the Yamamah project should continue to be dealt with sensitively.

4 MARCH 1991

The Russians have been extraordinarily cooperative in the past few days, with Vorontsov working helpfully with the other permanent four; the Cubans must feel thoroughly let down, with no support for any of their spoiling amendments to SCRs.

First day back to normal hours. In contrast to the congratulations we have received on the FCO's role during the Gulf War, I received no congratulations during a gruelling and bruising two-hour session with the Public Accounts Committee this afternoon. I had a very difficult case to defend, as the NAO report had not only turned up two major computer failures, but also a host of clerical inefficiencies and inexperience. All the committee members were extremely rough, with one even asking if I had considered resignation. My only potential ally, Michael Latham (who had telephoned me yesterday to give me covert insight into the committee's brief), was not there.

5 MARCH 1991

Only *The Times* carried any account of my PAC hearing, though David Martin told me that my confrontation with Campbell-Savours had been on breakfast TV. John Bourne telephoned me to say he thought I had been entirely right to admit the FCO's errors. Michael Morris (a member of the committee) also telephoned me and sympathised, advising me to pursue Price Waterhouse for a reduction of fees.

I later telephoned the managing partner of Price Waterhouse, Howard Hughes, who made no commitment, but was politely appreciative of the extent to which I had tried to deflect criticism from them.

6 MARCH 1991

Ministers are beginning to focus on subjects other than Iraq; both Douglas Hurd and I sent messages to the service to thank them for their work.

I attended the last meeting of Robin Butler's group, during which we drank champagne, and I recited a limerick to celebrate the event, to which Percy Cradock produced a brilliant rejoinder. Both are reproduced, with a slight inaccuracy, in Peter Hennessy's *The Prime Minister*. The original versions are as follows:

> *Robin Butler, preparing for doom,*
> *Gathered mandarins round to his room;*
> *As he switched on the light,*
> *He said, 'Let's get this right,*
> *Who says what, and on what, and to whom?'*

To which Sir Percy replied:

> *'Dear Robin,' the mandarins said,*
> *'There are records that cannot be read;*
> *There are letters as well*
> *Of which no man can tell,*
> *And which all must be kept in the head.'*

> *'And from this the conclusion is stark,*
> *That we all must remain in the dark,*
> *While our masters decide*
> *Without pilot or guide,*
> *Who does what, and to whom, in Iraq.'*

A bilateral with Douglas Hurd this afternoon. When I started to talk about public expenditure, he nearly went to sleep – a clear indication of how he is basically uninterested in the financial procedures of Whitehall.

8 MARCH 1991

I went to farewell drinks in the emergency unit, which closes this evening. Quiet Dunkirk spirit all round, with people obviously going to miss the camaraderie of the unit. One or two who had also served in the Falklands Unit pointed out the odd coincidence that both crises had broken out on the second day of a month beginning with A.

A disastrous dinner last night between the Prime Minister and Jacques Delors, who launched into an attack on British policies towards the Community, with what Charles Powell described in the record as 'staggering ineptitude' towards a Prime Minister who is trying to pull our attitudes towards the Community in a positive direction. Delors seem to have got hold of some idea that we are engaged in a murky plot with the Germans and the French to undermine him; I should think he will now have achieved it!

11 MARCH 1991

I called on Tristan Garel-Jones this morning. He takes a childish pleasure in thinking up ideas that will shock his fellow ministers or civil servants; but he is quite fun. I tried to talk him out of the idea he is peddling of swapping the residences in Brussels. I also told him that Douglas Hurd would almost certainly want to involve him in the tactics of the PESC round before the bidding letter goes in to the Treasury in May.

12 MARCH 1991

Yesterday's Anglo-German summit seems to have confirmed the extraordinary improvement in relations between Helmut Kohl and 10 Downing Street. Mrs Thatcher's noises over the weekend have merely highlighted the change in tone towards both Germany and the European Community. Douglas Hurd tells me that Major and Kohl appeared genuinely to get on very well together, though the relationship is still slightly lacking in substance.

We dined with the Canadians to say goodbye to the South Africans. John Wakeham was there, having just announced his decision not to stand again at the next election (though he told me privately that the Prime Minister might well decide to make him Leader in the Lords). He admitted that the government is in a mess over the poll tax, but thinks that by throwing enough money at it, they can get it straight before the election. I conclude from that that they will have to choose a later, rather than an earlier, date for the election.

13 MARCH 1991

Robin Butler told perm secs this morning that the government has got itself in a real twist over the poll tax. Even when they have produced a new rating system, it will apparently take at least two years to introduce, and is likely to cause upheavals in the Conservative Party whatever happens.

Peter Gregson gave an account of the new joint management unit to be announced tomorrow, in a way which could have come straight out of *Yes, Minister* – giving the impression that both the FCO and the DTI had managed to outwit ministers and the British Overseas Trade Board.

I called on Mark Lennox-Boyd, who referred rather guiltily to his exchange with the Trade Union Side. He seems to be under-employed, but didn't rise to my suggestion that we might consider some redistribution of ministerial portfolios (though, as an Arabist, he would love to supervise Middle East work).

Credentials for Bulgaria this morning, for which Johnny Stancioff wore his grandfather's diplomatic uniform (remodelled for him by a London tailor), and carried a sword with the Bulgarian crown on it from the 1920s, when his grandfather was Bulgarian minister here.

He told me that his staff were finding it very difficult to adjust, and had complained to him that there were too many people coming into the embassy. He commented that, having kept away from Bulgarian embassies for forty years, he was not now going to allow himself to be incarcerated inside one.

15 MARCH 1991

I called on Malcolm Caithness for a general talk. He thinks it is almost certain that there will be a June election, though he admits that he feels more out of touch with politics in his present job than ever before; this no doubt reflects Mark Lennox-Boyd's criticism of diplomats for being 'unpolitical'. I told Malcolm that I hoped he would use his experience as an ex-Treasury Paymaster General to advise us on tactics for the PESC round, adding the comment that I rather doubted whether it was top of Douglas Hurd's interests.

Percy Cradock told me today that he thought John Major's reaction to Rodric Braithwaite during his recent visit to Moscow had been 'a bit tepid'. It is possible that the Prime Minister was a bit put off by Rodric's cleverness; but he can hardly have failed to be impressed by his Russian contacts. Rodric has told Rod Lyne privately that he had given Chernyaev, Gorbachev's private secretary, an apposite piece of Pushkin about the difficulties of reform, and that Gorbachev now quotes it in every speech.

18 MARCH 1991

Charles Powell called on me for the last time today. He told me that the Prime Minister is exhausted after Bermuda, and is finding the going pretty tough – unlike Margaret Thatcher, he needs at least seven hours of sleep, and Norma is obviously restless about him accepting engagements at the weekend.

Eric Hetherington, a partner at Price Waterhouse, called this afternoon to seal their agreement to reduce their contract by £40,000 in light of the PAC's criticism. I think this should do the trick, though the office's performance over the whole accounts saga has been most unimpressive.

20 MARCH 1991

A two-hour session this afternoon with the Foreign Affairs Committee. As I told the chairman, David Howell, after the meeting, it was an astonishing contrast in atmosphere with the Public Accounts Committee two weeks ago. Luckily, the clerk, Robert Wilson, had given me a very precise indication of the questioning, and a rehearsal had certainly paid off. David Howell made a nice little speech at the end, wishing me well in my retirement.

21 MARCH 1991: VISIT TO BONN

The visit included two hours of talks with German Permanent Under-Secretary Dieter Kastrup, mainly on the Gulf and the Soviet Union. Kastrup seemed much more at ease than Sudhoff had, though he tended to rely on his briefs rather more than his predecessor had done. He congratulated me on running 'the best diplomatic service in the world' – no doubt in part a tribute to the qualities of his previous opposite numbers, John Fretwell and John Weston.

26 MARCH 1991

I met Margaret Thatcher today at David Craig's farewell party in the MOD – almost a parody of herself, attacking me with starry eyes, and accusing the Foreign Office of being 'wobbly' about everything, including EMU and the Gulf War. She said she had heard that the FCO were trying to stop the fighting 'because people were getting killed'. She claimed that the SAS should be going in to finish off Saddam Hussein, and was appalled that we had 'allowed' the Republican Guard to survive. I fought back hard, and she obviously enjoyed the exchange.

8 APRIL 1991

I returned to the office from an Easter break, with the plight of the Kurds uppermost in the news. John Weston has put forward some ideas for an initiative on the Kurds by the Prime Minister at the European Council this afternoon, and I attended a meeting chaired by Douglas Hogg to put flesh on these ideas, which include a plan to create a safe haven in Iraq for the thousands of Kurdish refugees shivering on the Turkish and Iranian borders.

John Coles told me today of his call last week on Margaret Thatcher, hoping for a friendly, nostalgic chat. But he found her sitting angrily at her desk, exactly as if she were still Prime Minister, and flicking through the latest Security Council Resolution on Iraq. She spoke very bitterly about John Major, saying he had betrayed nearly all her principles, and had been so angry about Norman Lamont's Budget she had walked out. She had tried to talk to John Major, to complain about the absence of any reference to Saddam Hussein's war crimes in the Security Council Resolution, but after eight hours had still only managed to talk to Stephen Wall. She tried again, in John Coles's presence, but having failed, slammed down the telephone. She said she had deliberately refrained from criticising John Major to the press, but she had now had enough.

9 APRIL 1991

Stephen Wall called this afternoon, his first call since succeeding Charles Powell as John Major's private secretary. I congratulated him on the significant improvement in tone and substance of his correspondence. FCO officials are now again being invited to attend the Prime Minister's meetings; and Tim Simmons tells me that Stephen is actually prepared to talk to him, and telephones him.

Stephen told me that John Major sadly does not have totally happy memories of his time at the FCO, and is clearly suspicious that some of the stories about him have emerged from FCO officials.

I told Stephen that Mrs Thatcher is obviously steamed up about the governorship of Hong Kong. I wondered whether she had stimulated a letter in the *Telegraph* today, proposing her as governor? There is also a suggestion running that she might head a consortium to get contracts in Kuwait. John Coles thinks that her energy is going to cause us major problems.

10 APRIL 1991

Douglas Hurd gave a brief account to his ministerial meeting this morning of his visit to Hong Kong. He claims that he does not regret going there, even though he has failed to bring off an agreement on the airport, or on other problems. He is deeply worried about the ability of the Hong Kong government to cope with the problems of the next six years. On the other hand, he is much impressed by Guangdong (formerly Canton), which is virtually a free-market economy run from Hong Kong, and an encouraging example of what a Hong Kong special administrative region could be like.

11–13 APRIL 1991

An interesting Sunningdale, at which we went over the conclusions of the last spring Sunningdale. They held up quite well, though the situation in the Soviet Union is much worse than we forecast then. Rodric Braithwaite has described the crisis this week as 'deepening, widening and accelerating'.

The first afternoon included an extraordinary paper and presentation by David Plastow on relations between government and business. He seems to have been slightly unhinged by the Vickers Tank affair – full of uncomplimentary remarks about civil servants and the supposed 'lack of respect' between business and government. Very odd.

16 APRIL 1991

I gave lunch today to Dick Woolcott, the Australian PUS. He has more problems than I with political appointments, though he says that there are fewer than usual at present. Most unusually, there is a career High Commissioner, Dick Smith, at present in London, who apparently has been given a written assurance by Gareth Evans, the Australian Foreign Minister, that he will not be ousted by a politician during the time of the present government, and that if he does have to move out at any point, he will be given a 'comparable' post. But there is still a tendency in Australia to use the Foreign Service as a dumping ground for failed politicians. Woolcott has succeeded, with the help of Gareth Evans, in resisting a political appointment to Washington. When he had suggested moving a political incumbent from San Francisco to Los Angeles, Hawke had protested that the man was incompetent!

I met John Drew, the European Commission's representative in London, at a reception this evening, who told me a good story about a meeting between Jacques Delors, John Major and Mrs Thatcher. At one point, Thatcher had fixed Delors with her basilisk stare, and said: 'Mr Delors, I am watching you very carefully,' to which Delors had replied: 'Don't watch me, Mrs Thatcher; it's this young Prime Minister of yours you need to watch!'

Percy Cradock told me this afternoon that Mrs Thatcher still rings him up and summons him to Eaton Square exactly as if she was still Prime Minister. When I asked Douglas Hurd last week if we should consider running her for New York, he gave me an emphatic 'No!'

18 APRIL 1991

Peter Middleton's appointment as deputy chairman of Barclays, and Terry Burns's appointment to succeed him, were announced today. In writing to congratulate Terry, I said (rather ambiguously) that I hoped that David

Gillmore would enjoy as good a relationship with him as I had with Peter. I remember, though I did not say this to Terry, that when I had replied to a letter from Peter Middleton about the Pergau Dam project, saying: 'I am sorry you felt it necessary to write as you did,' Peter had replied: 'I am sorry you felt sorry!'

Following on from David Plastow's behaviour at Sunningdale (see above), I dined at the Whitehall Dining Club this evening, where David Plastow chaired a discussion on 'Reasoning with the Unreasonable' – a further Plastow swipe at Whitehall. I intervened briefly to say that I was paid to deal almost exclusively with that most unreasonable category of people, namely foreigners, and that I just wanted to remind the industrialists present that, although David Plastow included government in his list of the unreasonable, they had, in the diplomatic service, an organisation geared to reason, on their behalf, with the unreasonable. This drew some amused applause.

19 APRIL 1991

Stephen Wall told me today that John Major is very upset by a silly mistake he made in the House yesterday when he challenged Neil Kinnock to say why he had been absent from a debate the night before, and Kinnock had floored him by saying, rather modestly and wittily, that he had been staying with the Queen at Windsor Castle, but hadn't wanted to drop names! The PM had commented to Stephen that he hadn't made a mistake like that for twelve years.

Patrick Fairweather gave me an amusing account of Lynda Chalker's briefing methods before the Foreign Affairs Committee hearing on the Kurds this week. She writes everything out in long hand and, as Patrick describes it, snatches any piece of paper when asked a question, irrespective of its relevance to the answer. When Patrick slipped her notes, she simply read them out in full. The FAC were very kind to her, though Bowen Wells did, at one point, say: 'Some committees might not have regarded the last reply as totally adequate.'

Len Appleyard gave a pen picture today of John Major's handling of Cabinet. A very different style from Margaret Thatcher, though Tom King hasn't changed his tendency to mirror the Prime Minister's views. Douglas Hurd towers above his colleagues, and obviously enjoys an excellent relationship with John Major. When I was asked whether Douglas had really not minded losing the leadership election, I said I was absolutely confident that he hadn't – comparing him, anonymously, with those ambassadors who genuinely prefer not to be PUSs.

23 APRIL 1991

Our last attendance at a state banquet this evening in St George's Hall at Windsor, for Lech Wałęsa. After dinner, I had quite a long talk with John Major, who asked if it would be 'a terrible bore' for us to go to lunch at Chequers on Sunday! He claimed to be feeling guilty for not having adequately thanked me for my letter on his appointment as Prime Minister, or for my help during his time as Foreign Secretary. He denied that he had loathed his time at the FCO, saying that this was a silly rumour spread by 'one politician'. He talked quite angrily about Margaret Thatcher, saying that most of the press attacks on his 'dithering' came directly, or indirectly, from her; he really thought she had become unbalanced. Her most recent accusation (over the council tax) was that he had treated Cabinet like a tyrant – as he said, a pretty ripe accusation from her! He admitted to me that Cabinet discussion had been pretty tough, and that he had nearly lost five members of it. I asked him if he was doing too much on foreign affairs, and he said he probably was: 'Foreign affairs don't win elections.' He admitted that he was far too sensitive to criticism; I urged him to follow the example of Clement Attlee, who famously ignored the media (see p. 101, above). The Majors are clearly finding domestic life difficult, and their son is obviously thrown by their official duties. Both were very friendly towards both of us – John describing Virginia as 'the wife of my favourite mandarin'.

I also had a brief word with the Kinnocks, whose son is still keen on joining the diplomatic service, and doing a year off in Madrid.

24 APRIL 1991

Douglas Hogg had a word with me this morning about Dominic Asquith, who was provoked last week into being very rude to Robin Maxwell-Hyslop over a visa case. Douglas told me that (as I knew) Maxwell-Hyslop is quite the rudest and most intolerant Member in the House, and urged that it should not be held against Dominic. I assured Douglas that I had had experience of Maxwell-Hyslop myself.

25 APRIL 1991

Lord Caithness's private secretary sent me a draft minute which Caithness wants to send to the Foreign Secretary, virtually proposing a new Central Policy Review Staff-type review of FCO functions. When I called on Caithness this afternoon, I argued that a review of this sort would cause considerable alarm and dismay in the office, who have not only just completed a top management round, and preparations for the PESC round, but have also been heavily scrutinised in the past few years into most aspects of our work. I have at least persuaded him not to copy his minute to under-secretaries other than myself. I have also warned Richard Gozney what is afoot.

At my bilateral with Douglas Hurd today, he gave me an account of his call on Margaret Thatcher yesterday, taking her (as he put it) telegrams like flowers. No complaints against the FCO, but she is obviously unhappy and angry.

26 APRIL 1991

I got a nice letter this morning from former British ambassador to Poland Kenneth James, thanking me for getting him invited to the Polish lunch at No. 10. When he greeted John Major, Kenneth said: 'Do you know that the only person I ever saw kissing your predecessor's hand was a Communist Polish Foreign Minister?' To which John Major replied: 'More than I ever did.'

29 APRIL 1991

Tristan Garel-Jones told me today that it was one of our strengths that officials could block things ministers wanted to do, whereas in Spain even a Prime Minister could not be told by his officials how to behave.

I attended an aid strategy meeting this afternoon, with a familiar argument about aid to India, on which several ministers think we give the Indians far too much for no thanks.

30 APRIL 1991

Douglas Hurd held a meeting this afternoon to look at the hostage situation, and the chances of getting the Iranians (who we increasingly think are the only people with the real levers to get them released) to move. There are at last some signs of hope; but there have been too many false dawns before. On the other hand, the Iranians seem to be anxious to exchange ambassadors, and to improve their image in the European Community, so we should have some leverage over them.

I lunched with the Government Hospitality Fund Wine Committee at Lancaster House, chaired by Bill Harding and with two vintners present, to choose wines for future Foreign Office entertainments. We tasted some superb wines, including a 1970 Beychevelle and a 1955 Latour, both described by the experts as 'spectacular'. I staggered back to the office, after a lunch of four different wines, port and brandy (a 1906 Hine), for a meeting of the top management board.

1 MAY 1991

Robin Butler showed me the invitation list for Charles Powell's farewell dinner at No. 10 – an astonishing catalogue of senior Conservatives, including the McAlpines, the Keswicks, Carol Thatcher (but not Mark or Margaret), and so on. The only public servant included is Andrew Turnbull.

2 MAY 1991

There was a semi-humorous editorial in *The Times* today called 'Why, Minister?', pointing out that Douglas Hurd has been abroad for one day in four this year, and asking whether this is worthwhile – attributing the Foreign Secretary's travels to anachronistic FCO delusions of grandeur. I think he probably is travelling too much, and recall that the ministerial visits committee had queried whether a further visit to the Middle East at this stage was necessary.

3 MAY 1991

Percy Cradock is worried about signs of divergence between John Major and Douglas Hurd over resuming talks with the Chinese on Hong Kong airport. The PM's approach is much more forthcoming, presumably reflecting Percy's advice.

4 MAY 1991

I caught an RAF flight to Glasgow to attend the remembrance and thanksgiving service for the Gulf War in Glasgow Cathedral. I travelled on a bus from Chelsea with Michael Howard (Employment), John Gummer (Agriculture) and Patrick Mayhew (Attorney General). The last of these gave us a hilarious account of a meeting at which he had sat next to a Turk, whose intervention was greeted by total silence, and who started to walk out in protest. Mayhew had tried to explain to him by gestures that the silence was due to interpretation, which was still going on; but the Turk misunderstood his gestures and thought Mayhew had deliberately insulted him. As the Turk reached the door, the interpretation finished, and the whole room burst into applause, which the Turk also interpreted as an insult!

The Cathedral service was superb and very moving.

7 MAY 1991

David Owen talked to me about his autobiography, which Susan Watt is publishing. I told him that he ought to send the manuscript to Robin Butler for clearance. He said, rather nervously, that there wasn't much that should worry us 'except possibly a few references to MI6'. He also told me that there had indeed been discussions with the government about giving jobs to himself and his two SDP colleagues; but that his own conditions (that they would remain in the SDP, and that the Tories would not contest their seats) were likely to be too much for the government to swallow. He thinks he will probably leave Parliament at the next election, and look for a job.

At a No. 10 dinner this evening, I talked to Neil Kinnock, and asked him if the rumours were true that the Labour Party planned to bring in a number of political ambassadors. He denied it firmly, though he acknowledged that he was tempted to send Bernie Grant, a Labour MP, to Pretoria. He also mentioned Egypt as a possibility, but did not reveal for whom. He claimed to believe that professionals were nearly always the best candidates, though he would want to have a selection to choose from, including younger officials. I said that David Gillmore or myself would be happy to explain to him how the selection process worked sometime. Moderately reassuring.

8 MAY 1991

Douglas Hurd told me today, at our bilateral, that he had had a blast from Margaret Thatcher, at the party he had held for Charles Powell, about our policy towards Yugoslavia. She seems to have got the idea that Croatia is the heartland of Thatcherite democracy! Douglas now finds himself as virtually a runner between Mrs Thatcher and No. 10. She is presumably responsible for the press stories that Gorbachev is to be invited here for the London economic summit, since she certainly feels she has committed us to this in her Aspen speech last August. The Prime Minister is himself very cautious about the idea, and thinks that a decision will need to be taken by all seven participants.

8-10 MAY 1991: VISIT TO TORONTO AND OTTAWA

A busy day each in Toronto and Ottawa. Brian and Delmar Fall's dinner for me in Ottawa included the Delvoies (whose wedding we had attended in Cairo) and Gary Harman (recently retired from Damascus).

13 MAY 1991

An early meeting in Robin Butler's office with Clive Whitmore, Percy Cradock and the heads of the intelligence agencies to discuss avowal and parliamentary oversight. The SIS staff are strongly in favour of the former, and accept that this will probably lead to some form of the latter, perhaps by a group of privy councillors. Percy Cradock is fiercely opposed, arguing that there is no need to change the present arrangements. (Mrs Thatcher would certainly have resisted any change strongly, and would have seen today's discussion as another attempt at a U-turn.) We concluded that a Working Party should draw up the terms under which we could move to both avowal and oversight by the time of the general election, if only because the Labour Manifesto makes it clear that the Labour Party will press for some sort of oversight, at least for the Security Service.

I had a quiet word with Robin after the meeting, to tell him that Douglas Hurd is unimpressed by my arguments in favour of a 'blanket' suppression of intelligence records, and is likely to instruct me to press for a reduction in the closure period to, say, eighty-five years. Robin looked pretty glum about this, since he has just completed a major exercise on the subject.

Stephen Wall gave me a hilarious, but very sensitive, account of why the press had suddenly carried reports of John Major's violent attack against the United Nations Secretary General two weeks ago for his apathy and inactivity over the Kurds. I had been mystified by this (as was the Secretary General himself), since both of us know that the Prime Minister's letter to de Cuéllar was in fact warm and supportive. Stephen told me that he had himself drafted the letter after OPD(G) had decided that the PM should write to urge the UN to be more active. John Major had himself signed off the letter without reading it, and had told the No. 10 spokesman, Gus O'Donnell, that he had sent a blast to de Cuéllar.

O'Donnell had then briefed the press that a scorching message had been sent (again without himself reading it).

14 MAY 1991

John Coles had a word with me about Lord Caithness, whose judgment he finds very shaky, and who is inclined to intervene excessively in the detail of both policy and administration. His office issued a minute today which enraged me, detailing the grading of staff who ought to be left in Rangoon [now Yangon]. I will have to find a way of stopping him from taking over the service.

15 MAY 1991

At a DUSs' lunch, held unusually in John Boyd's home, John Coles gave us a vivid description of a fundraising dinner for the Thatcher Foundation in Texas, at which Mark Thatcher behaved so boorishly that no money was given at all. He outraged all the guests by asking if there would be wine, and then calling the waiter to bring some larger and correctly sized glasses.

This evening, I attended a RUSI (Royal United Services Insitute) dinner, and tackled Labour MP George Robertson on the question of political ambassadors. He claimed that the stories originated from an article written by Labour MP George Foulkes on April Fool's Day. He thought that the only possible political appointment which a Labour government might make could be a Minister for Disarmament (à la Lord Chalfont).

16 MAY 1991

A row has burst out in Sri Lanka, following David Gladstone's written protest at irregularities during their general election last week. The Sri Lankan PUS is flying to London next week to see me about it – presumably to ask for David Gladstone's withdrawal. A tiresome problem which, if mishandled, could lead to the expulsion of the Sri Lankan High Commissioner, and a virtual break in relations just before the Commonwealth Review and CHOGM. It emerged later that the PUS is bringing a written message; I decided that the High Commissioner here should be urgently advised against any written messages, which will make it much more difficult for the Sri Lankans to back down.

I gave lunch today to Pierre Schori, the Swedish PUS, and discussed the recently departed Swedish ambassador, Leif Leifland, who had virtually gone to ground (or the Public Record Office) for the past four years. Schori said he was mystified by Leif's performance, or non-performance. Apparently, Leif had issued some last-minute statement (i.e. before leaving London?) that was very critical of his government, and has joined something called the Free Sweden Group. I commented that I had assumed that Sweden was already free!

17 MAY 1991

I gave lunch to Robin Butler at the Club. He told me, in strict confidence, that the Prime Minister is 'hell-bent' on an October election, and is thus causing serious strains within the Cabinet, and particularly with Norman Lamont, who no doubt wants to wait longer for the economy to pick up. The party must be feeling pretty bruised after losing Monmouth, the second safest Tory seat in Wales.

Today was largely taken up with two current problems: Sri Lanka and David Gore-Booth. On the second, David has come under fierce attack after someone leaked what he said four weeks ago about Israel at a CAABU (Council for Arab–British Understanding) meeting. There have been calls for his resignation, and predictable comments about FCO Arabists, including one reference to my attempts (by implication, unsuccessful!) to persuade people that we are balanced and fair. I am wondering whether, for Douglas Hurd's sake, I ought quickly to extract myself from Bilderberg; if the press hear that the FCO's 'Arch Arabist' is speaking there on the Middle East, it seems doubtful that even Bilderberg's 100 per cent record of discretion will stop something leaking out; either that, or it will require me to say nothing of interest whatsoever.

On Sri Lanka, the Foreign Secretary (i.e. PUS), Bernard Tilakaratne, delivered a message to Stephen Wall at No. 10 calling for David Gladstone's early withdrawal, and then came to call on me half an hour later. I defended David Gladstone (who appears to be quite a close friend of Tilakaratne), pointing out that he would soon have completed longer in Sri Lanka than most of his predecessors. I tried to get him to accept a package whereby David would express regret at the 'misunderstanding', and come naturally to the end of his posting in about three months' time. Tilakaratne tried to sell this to Premadasa overnight, but returned on 21 May (see below).

21 MAY 1991

Tilakaratne told me he had spoken to Premadasa, who was said to be displeased with my response, and insisting on David Gladstone's immediate withdrawal. Tilakaratne had persuaded him to wait for the Prime Minister's reply to his message, and urged me to get a swift reply back. I later discussed the problem with Mark Lennox-Boyd, who disagreed with the official advice, saying that we should recall David Gladstone for 'consultations', aiming to finish his posting in about three months' time. He was in favour of calling Premadasa's bluff, and staring him down. I think Lennox-Boyd may be nervous of parliamentary reactions, though Michael Morris MP, who is chairman of the UK/Sri Lankan Parliamentary Association, telephoned this morning, in my absence, to say that he thought Gladstone should be withdrawn.

I went to the CBI dinner, where John Major was speaking. Formidable security arrangements – no doubt tightened by the horrific news this afternoon of Rajiv Gandhi's assassination. I sat next to Campbell Fraser, who welcomed me on the assumption that I had already accepted Bob Horton's invitation to join the BP board. He said it was a super job – even comparing it to an orgasm!

22 MAY 1991

Colin Chandler called, to complain about Michael Alexander (UKDEL NATO), who is said to have made several semi-public comments about the choice of the new main battle tank, arguing on NATO grounds for the German Leopard. Vickers is getting very impatient, having waited for the government's decision for over a year, and claim that it will have to lay off staff at any moment.

Richard Gozney had a quiet word with me this morning after Douglas Hurd's ministerial meeting, to warn me that Douglas was toying with the idea of using Richard Luce as some sort of commissioner or special representative in the Gulf. I reminded Richard that Luce's father, Sir William Luce, had done precisely that for Alec Home (during my year as deputy political representative in Bahrain), but pointed out that the terms of reference would have to be worked out very carefully if our ambassadors' noses were not to be put severely out of joint. Although Richard claimed that the main idea was to reduce Douglas Hurd's need to visit the Gulf, I suspect that the main motive is to find Richard Luce something to do.

More to-ing and fro-ing today on Sri Lanka after the High Commissioner told us that Ghandi's assassination had taken the heat off, and that neither Premadasa nor the Sri Lankan press were any longer pressing for David Gladstone's immediate withdrawal. I have still recommended that David should be brought back in slow time, if only to explain his own version of events.

23 MAY 1991

I had a bilateral with Tristan Garel-Jones – a minister who tends to fly off at all tangents, producing sparky ideas without much discipline or consultation. He is still determined to swap John Kerr's residence in Brussels, arguing (with some justification) that it is ludicrous for the holder of one of the most important jobs in the service to live in the sticks, while the ambassador 'to a non-country like Belgium' lives in that magnificent house in the Place Royale.

Patrick Fairweather called to discuss the Gore-Booth/CAABU affair. He is worried that David Gore-Booth himself is cock-a-hoop at all the encouragement he has been given, including the very firm and decent support which Douglas Hurd gave him in the House of Commons yesterday (with a remarkable slap-down of Greville Janner by Douglas Hogg, who commented on the 'strong smell of humbug'). Today's *Evening Standard* carries banner headlines of the outgoing Chief Rabbi's criticism of Israel. I telephoned David Gore-Booth and advised him to make no comment at all on it; the *Standard* has already linked him with Abramowitz. When I gave my advice to David, he replied: 'Can I not even discuss it with the PUS?' – a pretty cheeky response, but typical of his curious mixture of thick and thin skin.

25–26 MAY 1991

The only interruption of our weekend celebrations for the eightieth birthday of Virginia's mother was a telephone call from David Gore-Booth to say that the *Evening Standard* had rung him to ask if he knew that the Israeli authorities were bringing pressure to bear on British newspapers to run a smear campaign against him. I advised him to talk to the legal advisers, and later agreed to talk to the Israeli ambassador, Yoav Biran, on a personal basis. Biran predictably assured me that neither the Israeli authorities nor, to his knowledge, the Jewish community would want to make David Gore-Booth a martyr in this way. In fact, the *Mail on Sunday* ran another editorial (no doubt written by Stewart Steven, who had launched the attack against me after the Mellor affair (see p. 86, above)), saying that Britain and Israel would never have a normal relationship so long as David Gore-Booth remained in the FCO.

28 MAY 1991

Talks this morning with François Scheer. Bernard Dorin sat doodling maps, which he does with remarkable accuracy, including the very complicated relationship between the various Yugoslav provinces and the outlying states of the Soviet Union. Scheer is an excellent interlocutor, and speaks with apparent frankness about the shortcomings of French presidential policy. He had also told me of the pressures on his service from the French Treasury, telling me that if he had to take these pressures seriously, he would have to close half the posts in the French Foreign Service.

A DUSs' meeting this afternoon to look at a planning paper, and a despatch from Ewen Fergusson on 'How do we beat the French?' – i.e. how perfidious can Albion be?

This evening, I had a word with Denis Greenhill about his draft memoirs, which I had read over the weekend. He is not yet certain that he will publish, since he thinks his publisher will insist on sharing the cost, which could be as much as £8,000. They reveal two remarkable differences between our times as PUS: first, that Denis never attended a single Select Committee, not even the Public Accounts Committee; and secondly, that he and Angela claim to have attended every national day reception, which he describes as 'useful'. What a horrendous thought!

29 MAY 1991

Robin Butler told PUSs this morning about the increasingly political way in which the Prime Minister handles Cabinet meetings. He has dismissed officials from about half his meetings, to allow Cabinet to have a totally political discussion. At a Cabinet meeting last week, ministers decided to launch a series of major policy speeches – a discussion which most ministers were later revealed not to have informed their officials about. It looks increasingly like preparation for an October election. Labour are still well ahead in the polls.

The Commonwealth took a blow today when the Sri Lanka High Commissioner called to say that David Gladstone is now *persona non grata*. In retrospect, it is a pity that my recommendation (rejected by Lennox-Boyd) to call David home quickly for consultations just might have defused the row. We shall certainly have to cancel Lennox-Boyd's visit, and ministers may press for Attygalle's expulsion, which would be sad, as he is an effective and helpful High Commissioner. Attygalle himself doubts whether he could stay here in these circumstances – with the clear implication that he would want to leave in protest at his own government's behaviour.

30 MAY 1991

I spent much of today writing one of my last letters to the service. There is so much going on that it is increasingly difficult to know which subjects to select. Events like the last Cuban troops to leave Angola this week, which would have been sensational news three years ago, now hardly get a mention in the press.

Stephen Wall tells me that Mrs Thatcher has apparently told Percy Cradock that she has decided to go to the Lords 'so that she can speak her mind about Europe'. When Percy gently queried whether this would not damage the party, she compared herself to Churchill in the 1930s, and said that there were moments in history when one had to speak out. Stephen added that John Major has now twice called on her, but is increasingly irritated by her erratic behaviour, including her unhelpful remarks in Moscow about Gorbachev being invited to the economic summit in London in July.

A brief note from Denis Greenhill today, thanking me for my comments on his manuscript, but pointing out that his publishers had commented that his memoirs were insufficiently indiscreet.

31 MAY 1991

Ewen Fergusson called for a brief farewell talk before my retirement.

1 JUNE 1991

Virginia and I were driven to Chequers for John Major's large buffet lunch, at which Virginia had some post-lunch conversation with John Gielgud, sitting at his feet. Geoffrey Howe was also at the lunch, and I reminded him that five years had now passed since he had queried the forecast in my valedictory despatch from Riyadh that the Saudi regime was good for at least five years.

3 JUNE 1991

I lunch with Trevor Chinn at the Connaught – a further opportunity for me (made more difficult by the David Gore-Booth affair) to counter the Jewish view that the FCO is totally sold on the Arabs. When I told him about the *Evening Standard* warning to David Gore-Booth, he totally denied that either the Israeli authorities or responsible members of the Jewish community would do any such thing; but he volunteered that there were certainly people in London who were capable of it. He agreed that Stewart Steven of the *Mail on Sunday* was blindly prejudiced against the FCO.

Trevor Chinn asked me (half-jokingly?) if the FCO or ODA would provide money for the Jewish Agency to help settle the Falashas in Israel. I described the pressures on our budget (saying that I had even wondered whether to ask the Jewish Agency for some of their money!), but said seriously that it was inconceivable that ministers would agree to help any settlement so long as the Israeli government maintained their present illegal policy of settlements in the occupied territories. He also asked if the FCO could provide some modest funds towards the new Auschwitz museum. I recalled that Sigmund Sternberg had sent me a book about the longstanding controversy over the Carmelite Monastery at Auschwitz, and asked if this had now been resolved: Trevor seemed a bit doubtful about this. He is very keen to keep up a similar contact in future with David Gillmore, and I will try to encourage that.

4 JUNE 1991

My last meeting of the British Council board, preceded by a discussion about David Orr's successor as chairman, on which David Orr has happily plumped for Douglas Hurd's preference, namely Martin Jacomb, though he reported Douglas's view that politicians should not be excluded from the field. Most board members agreed with David that this was inappropriate – a slightly awkward discussion, since Tim Renton was present.

A bilateral with Douglas Hurd, at which he told me of a recent talk he had had with Margaret Thatcher, at which 'shafts' had been sent in all directions, including me – the last, because she claimed that we were wasting money on refurbishing the office which would be better put towards a consulate in Leningrad. I told Douglas that I was determined not to slow down, or interfere with, the refurbishment (a point in which Douglas has some personal interest, having served, as a third secretary, in the cardboard offices, put up in one of the Locarno rooms). When he said that Margaret Thatcher had referred to Leningrad as 'one of the great cities of Europe', I pointed out that the FCO was one of the great buildings in another great European city!

5 JUNE 1991

An early meeting with Robin Butler to follow up yesterday's ministerial discussion on community frontiers. Recent legal opinion (allegedly written personally by the Solicitor General, Nicholas Lyell, and described, at our meeting, by Brian Unwin as 'seriously flawed') claims that community law will actually make it illegal to retain any customs or immigration checks at our internal frontiers – i.e. at any of our main ports. This has thrown ministers into confusion, and Kenneth Baker has been calling wildly for Britain's departure from the Community. Clive Whitmore asked if Douglas Hurd could not exercise more control over Kenneth Baker; I pointed out that Douglas was reluctant to intervene too much with either of his old departments, i.e. the Home Office and the Northern Ireland Office.

7– 9 JUNE 1991:
BILDERBERG CONFERENCE AT BADEN-BADEN

A three-day conference, at which I had been invited to be one of the panellists on the Middle East. My fellow panellists, under the chairmanship of Peter Carrington, were Richard Haass and Bill Quandt of the National Security Agency, Laurie Freedman of King's College London. Among the familiar faces at the conference were Roz Ridgway, who told me that she had only been able to cure her insomnia by reading the social column of Friday's *Times*, in which my attendance at credentials had provided the final morphine; Bob Blackwill, now at Harvard, with whom I had an interesting exchange on our respective Foreign Services, during which I discovered that senior State Department officials earn just about half the salary of equivalent FCO officials; Henry Kissinger, who made broad and elder-statesman interventions in his deep, gravelly growl; and George Ball, looking old in his early eighties, and reading a lengthy diatribe on the Arab–Israel problem – extremely critical of Israel, and countered by a strong, pro-Zionist intervention from Conrad Black and Bob Bartley of the *Wall Street Journal*.

Bearing in mind the Gore-Booth affair, I opened my intervention by quoting Norman Hogg's contribution in the House of Commons, who said that no public servant had the right to make private comments on a question as serious as Palestine – noting with relief that the Bilderberg rules seemed not to accept this.

On Friday evening, I had a late drink in the bar with John Smith, the Labour spokesman for Trade and Industry, and Gordon Brown; also with Christopher Hogg, an Old Marlburian from Courtaulds, and John Polanyi, a Canadian writer on nuclear questions.

[One conference colleague I do not record having met was an obscure, and rather shy, Governor of Arkansas, called Bill Clinton. Someone (I've forgotten who) told me years later that he had felt so sorry for this shy man that he had sought him out for a conversation, and had a one-hour, fascinating talk about American politics in the south.]

12 JUNE 1991

Today's press is full of stories of attempts to muzzle Margaret Thatcher (some hope!); today's *Evening Standard* carries an unhelpful interview with Nicholas Ridley, supporting her right to speak out. His memoirs (bits of which I have now seen) will be quite controversial, and could come out at an awkward time for John Major. Ridley has some fairly damning comments on Mrs Thatcher's attitude to the FCO, claiming that she deliberately kept on Charles Powell in order to exclude FCO officials.

13 JUNE 1991

An embarrassing mistake was revealed today when a retired colleague returned the farewell letter I had sent him which referred to a post in which he had never served. I wrote back to say I was appalled, and that it was obviously high time I retired myself.

Douglas Hurd had his annual session with Angus Fraser, from the Prime Minister's Efficiency Unit, this afternoon. I tried to get Douglas to show genuine interest in our management plan (in which he is clearly totally uninterested); but he did it quite well, and I think we have passed with flying colours this year. But it does involve a horrific amount of work and paper.

A bilateral with Douglas Hurd, at which it emerged that the Prime Minister has definitely decided to appoint a politician to Hong Kong after the election. I asked Douglas if he had considered talking to the opposition, and he agreed that this might be sensible. It is always a bit delicate for officials to suggest to ministers that there is any need to prepare for a change of government; Labour is today leading the polls by ten points.

I told Douglas that the Cabinet Office study on the change to the homo-sexuality/positive vetting rules is under way, and that the Prime Minister has expressed support for the idea of a statement during the recess.

14 JUNE 1991

Malcolm Caithness told me, in very conspiratorial terms, that he had something very private to divulge. It emerged that an elderly peer called Lord Fortescue had contacted him, in total bemusement, to say that he had been telephoned by Mark Englefield of the *Evening Standard*, to ask if he knew David Gore-Booth. When he replied that he didn't, he was asked whether he knew that David was trying to mount a smear campaign against Mossad. We concluded that this was a classic case of journalistic incompetence and nastiness.

17 JUNE 1991

Marcus and Rebecca came up to my office over the weekend, for Rebecca to take some photographs for the wall of my private office. We have decided (no doubt to the embarrassment of my successors) to break with precedent, and have a joint photograph of Virginia and me – the first accompanied photograph since one of my Victorian predecessors decided to include his dog in his!

19 JUNE 1991

I attended my last meeting of perm secs this morning, at which Robin

Butler made a brief valedictory speech about Alan Bailey and myself (Alan, who reaches sixty the day before me, is one of four Mertonian PUSs in Whitehall – the other two being Michael Quinlan and Robert Andrew). I responded with a short account of some of the extraordinary things that are happening in foreign affairs this month alone: a report today from Cape Town on the last pillar of apartheid coming down (adding that the South African ambassador in London had invited Oliver Tambo to use his embassy whenever he wanted – 'After all, it is your embassy'); a report from Budapest that the last Soviet troops have left Hungary; and a report that James Baker is about to visit Albania 'to celebrate the return of democracy'.

Tim Simmons rang Denis Greenhill, at my request, to find out if he had attended perm secs when he was PUS. Interestingly, Denis revealed that perm secs had been suspended under Wilson's first administration, since ministers (or was it Joe Haines?) disliked the idea of 'Tory mandarins' getting together. When Denis had paid his last call on Ted Heath, Heath had asked him what could be done to improve the standard of government in Whitehall; Denis had suggested the resumption of perm sec meetings. He was delighted to hear from me that this had happened.

Denis Greenhill also told Tim Simmons that he hoped my farewell speech would be better than Tom Brimelow's, which had been so rude about the civil service that several of his guests had walked out. At tonight's farewell dinner, Robin Butler gave a good speech about the three leavers (Peter Middleton, Alan Bailey and myself), referring back to our time together in No. 10, when Robert Armstrong had warned Ken Stowe about the loudness of my telephone conversations – in contrast to Tom Bridges, who had always spoken on the telephone as if his civil service colleagues were not old enough to hear these things.

In reply, I referred to the British Public Service as the best in the world, though I quoted Lord Kennet's remark in the House of Lords in January

1989, when he said that we might have the best diplomatic service in the world, but that 'one or two absolute fools had risen to the top in recent years' – adding that they had not done much harm in the end, and that by and large the standard had been extremely high.

Papoulias, the Cyprus High Commissioner, held a farewell lunch for us today, at which he was much impressed by my quotation of William Lithgow's seventeenth-century description of Cypriots, which I repeated in my thank-you letter – asking my PA to be careful not to include the subsequent passage from the quotation in the reference book, which is extremely rude about the Cypriots and their dishonesty!

Calls today from two colleagues departing for their first ambassadorial postings, to whom I gave three pieces of advice: the first (given to me by John Wilton before my posting to Saudi Arabia), 'If it moves, call on it'; the second, remember that when abroad your profile should be as high as it should be low at home; and thirdly, that by far the most effective tool for a diplomat (and, in my experience, extraordinarily rare) is to show that you love the country you are serving in. As I told my callers, several of my foreign colleagues in Luxembourg and Saudi Arabia made it all too obvious (for different reasons) that they thought their posting was either beneath them or thoroughly unpleasant. The last was particularly true of some of my Dutch and German colleagues, one of whom was described as having 'the sensitivity of a tank'.

21 JUNE 1991

Tony Reeve called before leaving for South Africa, understandably daunted by the prospect of succeeding Robin Renwick, whose performance has been quite spectacular. Someone recently commented, in reply to a remark that the United States suffered from having no policy on South Africa, that they soon would, when Robin Renwick arrived in Washington as British ambassador.

24 JUNE 1991

John Boyd told me today that one (unnamed) head of mission had replied to Mike Shingler's invitation to my farewell party with a frosty response: 'I see that you addressed your letter to my Head of Chancery. My Head of Chancery was abolished by Patrick Wright.' I told DUSs at my lunch for them today that this decision to abolish Heads of Chancery was one of my main regrets as PUS, having enormously valued my own experience as Head of Chancery in Cairo. But everyone else seems to be convinced it was right. At least I have stopped them abolishing the Chief Clerk and Deputy Chief Clerk (though some have tried hard to do this, on the grounds that the terms are 'not understood' elsewhere in Whitehall).

25 JUNE 1991

I attended my last of Douglas Hurd's ministerial meetings, at which he gave an account of the Prime Minister's meeting with Mitterrand in Dunkirk yesterday. It had not been a bad session, though the French are clearly put out by the formation of NATO's Rapid Reaction Corps, and have been quite grumpy with both the Germans and ourselves on the subject.

My last credentials this morning, for Ray and Caroline Seitz, of which a photograph later appeared in Ray's excellent book *Over Here*, with a description of myself apparently holding a 'pet ostrich' (see p. 5, above). The proceedings were filmed throughout for next year's BBC Jubilee film (as were the French credentials earlier this year).

26 JUNE 1991

I paid a farewell call on the Prime Minister this morning. I talked about FCO resources (particularly for information technology and the estate), pointing out that our permanent membership of the Security Council and global diplomacy needed adequate funds to sustain our foreign policy and our aid. I thanked him for making good use of the FCO machine; he replied that his own relationship with Douglas Hurd was excellent: 'Few people probably know that we talked to each other every day during the leadership campaign.' I said that I hadn't known that, but that the look on Douglas's face when John Major won suggested to me that they had hardly been in fierce competition.

On relations with the FCO, John Major pointed out that the main problem 'under previous dispensations' had been the appalling relationship between the Prime Minister and the Foreign Secretary. He asked me about my future, commenting quite crossly that it was ridiculous that I should have to wait three months before taking up any directorships. He commented that, in contrast to Peter Middleton (for whom he had fought personally to reduce his period of purdah from one year to six months), Nigel Lawson could go straight to Barclays from the Treasury – 'where he presumably knew something of what the Treasury were doing'.

This evening, a mammoth party, organised by John Boyd and Mike Shingler, to say goodbye to us in the Durbar Court. The irrepressible Shingler appeared dressed in a sort of Moroccan magician's outfit. A fantastic collection of old friends and colleagues, including two of my ambassadors, Harold Beeley and George Middleton. There were songs and recitations (not helped by the appalling acoustics of the Durbar Court), and some amazing belly-dancing by Doreen Fishwick (my PA in Jedda) and Sarah Rowland-Jones. We were presented, at the end, by a vast volume of farewell messages from nearly every post in the world.

27 JUNE 1991

I had a meeting with Malcolm Caithness and others to discuss post closures. I reported briefly on my remarks to the Prime Minister about

FCO resources, and also told Malcolm (as I later told Douglas Hurd) that ministers should not always strive to put 'the best people' into every job; they need to remember that the service relies on a large core of middle-ranking stalwarts who can hold down (and not be frustrated by) rather unexacting and routine jobs around the world. It would be disastrous to staff the service only with Fellows of All Souls!

I had my last bilateral with Douglas Hurd this afternoon, when I reported to him in more detail on my farewell call on the Prime Minister. On the question of a Minister for Europe, Douglas told me (but has not yet told the Prime Minister) that he is rather in favour of the idea, though he accepted some of my arguments against it. Richard Gozney told me last night that even Douglas Hurd, with his amazing stamina, is beginning to be worried about the sheer burden of all the meetings he has to attend. But I still think that a Minister for Europe will detract from the Secretary of State's status and credibility, and that even if such a minister had full Cabinet status, his attendance at meetings with other foreign ministers would inevitably look as though we were fielding a B team.

I also talked to Douglas about Tim Sainsbury's resistance to charging increases for commercial work abroad; but I advised him against intervening in the argument, since it could be quite a powerful weapon for him in the next PESC round, when the Treasury could be quite surprised that the FCO were arguing for more revenue against other departments.

Our official farewell in the Durbar Court this evening, with some disappointing absences, but a good turn-out, including masses of MPs. Two Cabinet ministers came (John Wakeham and Chris Patten), as did a good handful of senior businessmen and retired diplomats – including three past PUSs and Pat Gore-Booth, who told me that she gathered that David had been a 'naughty boy'. I reassured her, and made some nice remarks about Paul, which nearly reduced her to tears.

Happily, there were no speeches; Douglas Hurd had to leave for the European Council in Luxembourg, and had, in any case, very nicely looked in briefly last night. The poor man has already had to make two farewell speeches about me. Then our last car-pool drive home with Martin Madden.

I ended my last letter to the service, dated 22 June, as follows:

> I would like to close this last letter with a genuine word of thanks and appreciation for what all of you have done, in various ways, over the past five years to smooth my path as Head of the Service. I have loved every moment (well, almost every moment) of it, and have been proud to head what I (and others) seriously believe to be the best Diplomatic Service in the world. Journalists and commentators were fond of describing the alleged contempt and dislike with which Mrs Thatcher was said to regard the Foreign Office. It is worth remembering that the past five years has seen no single political appointment to any post in the Service; and that throughout her Prime Ministerial involvement in Foreign Affairs, even Mrs Thatcher relied most heavily on past and present members of the Service for advice. I am personally encouraged by the extent to which Ministers on both sides of Downing Street increasingly appreciate the Rolls Royce machine available to them for the conduct of the Government's Foreign Policy; and that there is now, I believe, a much better appreciation within the Service that our job is, and must be seen to be, the vigorous and skilful promotion and protection of British interests, rather than some woolly objective called 'good relations'. In thanking you all for your support, may I wish you all and every one of you all the best in what will continue to be a fast-moving and challenging period ahead for the Service.

INDEX

Abbott, Diane 80

Abdullah, Crown Prince 103–104

Abramowitz, Chief Rabbi 317

Abu Sharif, Bassam 135, 152, 154

Acland, Sir Antony 1, 3, 44, 59, 62, 105, 124, 142, 177, 197, 207, 209, 221–2, 246, 257, 261, 268, 276, 281, 286

Acland, General John 75

Adams, Christian 170

Adams, Sir Geoffrey 156, 168, 169, 175, 184, 230, 232, 254, 275, 276, 289

Adams, Sir Philip 258

Aitken, Ian 290

Akers-Jones, Sir David 42

bin Alawi, Yousuf 92

Alexander, Sir Michael 86, 170, 171, 196–7, 315

Alston, Robert 18–19, 92, 149

Amery of Lustleigh, Lord (Julian) 82, 107, 186, 207, 244

Anderson, Bruce 113

Anderson of Swansea, Lord (Donald) 89

Andrew, Sir Robert 35, 51, 68, 91, 325

Anson, Sir John 161

Aoun, General Michel 194

Appleyard, Sir Leonard 92, 211, 236, 256, 306

Arafat, Yasser 122, 152

Arbuthnott, Hugh 202

Archer of Weston-super-Mare, Lord (Jeffrey) 255

Arens, Moshe (former Israeli Foreign minister) 129

Armstrong, of Ilminster, Lord (Robert) 3 and passim

Arthur, Sir Geoffrey 93

Ashburton, Lord (John) 13

Ashdown of Norton-sub-Hamdon, Lord (Paddy) 95

Asquith, The Hon. Sir Dominic 307

al-Assad, Hafez 139

Atkinson, Michael and Veronica 200, 203

Attlee, Earl (Clement) 101, 306

Aziz, Tariq 278–9, 291–2

Babangida, Ibrahim (former President of Nigeria) 86, 136, 288

Bailey, Sir Alan 325

Bailey, Sir John 29

Baker, James 117, 126, 131–2, 137, 139, 165, 167, 197–8, 212, 225, 226, 265–7, 275, 278–9, 281–3, 287, 291, 294, 325

Baker of Dorking, Lord (Kenneth) 321

Ball, George 322

Banham, Sir John 212
Barrington, Sir Nicholas 56, 85
Barrington-Ward, The Rt Revd Simon
   215
Bartley, Bob 322
Bassett, Richard 186
Bates, Judge Stuart 148
Bathurst, Sir Ben 224
Battishill, Sir Anthony 77
Bazoft, Farzad 220–23
Beaumont, Sir Richard (Dick) 109
Beeley, Sir Harold 328
Benn, Tony 6
Berman, Sir Franklin (Frank) 218, 249
Bevin, Ernest 5
Bhutto, Benazir 129
Bickham, Edward 293
Bidwell, Sir Hugh 190, 222
Bidwell, Jim and Valerie 190
Biffen, Lord (John) 100
bin Ali, Hussein 149
Biran, Yoav 317
Black of Crossharbour, Lord (Conrad)
   322
Blackwill, Bob 170, 197, 208, 217, 322
Blair, Tony 24, 89
Blelloch, Sir John 98, 114, 151
Bogdanor, Vernon 233
Botha, P. W. 6–7, 17, 130
Bottomley of Nettlestone, Baroness
   (Virginia) 69, 71, 88, 110
Bourne, Sir John 296
Boyd, Sir John 115, 183, 201, 221, 246,
   278, 313, 327–8
Brabazon of Tara, Lord (Ivon) 158, 164,
   168, 184–5, 218, 221, 238, 242–3
Braithwaite, Sir Rodric 75, 110, 112, 174,
   300, 303
Brewer, Dame Nicola 244
Brimelow, Lord (Thomas) 3, 325
Broadbent, Simon 255
Brooke, Roger 250

Broomfield, Sir Nigel 259–60
Brown, Gill 43
Brown, Lord George-Brown 79, 93, 277
Brown, Gordon 322
Browne, Sir Nick and family 26
Budgen, Nicholas 93
Bullard, Sir Julian 214
Burns, Sir Andrew 181, 190
Burns, Bill 24
Burns, Lord (Terry) 304
Bush, George H. W. (41st US Presi-
   dent) 102, 117, 131–2, 137, 139, 167,
   170, 186, 188–9, 190, 193–6, 198, 200,
   208, 217, 258, 265, 276, 292–4
Butler of Brockwell, Lord (Robin) and
   Lady (Gill) 10 and passim

Caccia, Lord (Harold) and Lady
   (Nancy) 43, 219, 246, 258
Cadogan, Sir Alexander and Lady 22
Caines, Sir John 39, 78, 94
Cairns, Earl (Simon) 151, 155
Caithness, Earl of (Malcolm) and Lady
   (Diana) 150, 243, 269, 290, 295, 300,
   307, 312, 324, 328
Callaghan of Cardiff, Lord (Jim) 23,
   50, 119, 163, 217, 220, 250
Campbell, Duncan 45
Campbell, Jeremy 137
Campbell-Savours, Lord (Dale) 235,
   296
Carol, King 107
Carrington, Lord (Peter) 5, 11, 27, 88, 107,
   227, 232, 238, 245, 268, 271, 285, 321
Casey, Bill 9, 34
Castle of Blackburn, Baroness (Bar-
   bara) 6
Catto, Henry 152, 196–7, 206, 281–2,
   293
Ceauşescu, Nicolae (former Romanian
   President) 201–202
Chalfont, Lord (Alun) 8, 28

Chalker of Wallasey, Baroness (Lynda) 1, 5, 33, 51, 61, 66, 71, 75, 88, 91–2, 96, 102, 115–6, 145, 148, 151, 154, 158, 161, 164, 175 and passim to 288

Chandler, Sir Colin 95, 251, 315

Channon, Paul (Lord Kelvedon) 48

Chaplin, Sir Edward 62–3

Checkland, Sir Michael 64

Cheney, Dick (former US Defense Secretary) 168, 257, 282

Chesterton, G. K. 165

Chetwood, Sir Clifford and Lady (Pamela) 155

Cheysson, Claude 175

Chinese Foreign Minister, Qian Qichen 176

Chinn, Sir Trevor and Lady (Susan) 238, 320

Chirac, Jacques 90

Chissano, Joaquim (former President of Mozambique) 61

Clapham, Sir Michael 62

Clark, The Hon. Alan 13, 36, 59, 62, 155, 205, 277–8

Clarke, Kenneth 110, 262

Clinton, Bill 323

Coles, Sir John 2, 217, 236, 248, 302–303, 312–13

Colnbrook, Lord (Humphrey) 83

Colvin, David 258

Cook, Robin 89, 96, 119

Cooper, Sir Robert 119, 153, 190

Court, Robert 168, 238

Cowper-Coles, Sir Sherard 2, 45, 105

Cradock, Sir Percy 21, 73, 97, 104, 132, 185, 201, 204, 211, 225, 256, 258, 297, 300, 304, 309, 311, 319

Craig of Radley, Lord (David) 259–60, 301

Craig, Sir James 28

Cromer, Earl (Evelyn) 221

Crouch, David 51

Crawford, Charles 29

Cubbon, Sir Brian 41

de Cuellar, Perez 282, 312

Currie, Edwina 120

Dalyell, Tam 147

Darwin, Henry 55

Darwish, Fatie 240

Davey, Timothy 53

Day, Sir Derek 82

Day, Stephen 124

Dell, David 176

Delors, Jacques 113, 137, 278, 298, 304

Denman, Lord (Charles) 32

Diana, Princess of Wales 240, 261

Dimbleby, David 240

Diouf, Abdou (former President of Senegal 117

Donald, Sir Alan and Lady (Janet) 119, 133, 187, 219

Donoughue, Lord (Bernard) 55

Dorin, Bernard 267, 288, 289, 317

Drew, John 214, 304

Dukakis, Michael 105, 109, 117

Dumas, Roland 163, 196, 286

Eagleburger, Lawrence 208

Eden, Sir Anthony (Earl of Avon) 271

Eggar, Tim 8, 32, 36, 51, 53, 63, 66, 81, 91, 103, 111, 113, 116, 130, 156, 159

Egerton, Sir Stephen 185, 232

Elles, Baroness (Diana) 150

Elliott, Mark 287

Englefield, Mark 324

English, Sir David 100

Ennals, Lord (David) 199

Evans, Gareth 304

Evans, Sir Geraint and Lady 6

Everett, Christopher 249

Ewart-Biggs, Sir Christopher 33

Fahd, King 121, 288

Fairweather, Sir Patrick 174, 259, 266, 275, 281, 283, 289, 292, 305, 316

Fall, Sir Brian and Lady (Delmar) 42, 53, 90, 311

Fanshawe of Richmond, Lord (Tony) 70, 146, 289

Faulds, Andrew 284

Favell, Tony 162–3

Fawcett, John 15

Fayed, Mohammed al 130

Fenn, Sir Nicholas 35

Fergusson, Adam 49, 144

Fergusson, Sir Ewen and Lady (Sara) 16, 76, 209, 275, 318–9

Fieldhouse, Lord (John) 10

Fishwick, Doreen 328

Forsyth of Drumlean, Lord (Michael) 59

Foulkes of Cumnock, Lord (George) 313

Fowler, Lord (Norman) 50

France, Sir Christopher 263

Francis, Sir Richard 291

Franklin, Sir Michael 64, 286

Fraser, Sir Angus 323

Fraser, Sir Campbell 315

Fraser, Sir Keir 67

Fraser, Sir Simon 55, 248–9

Freedman, Sir Lawrence 322

Fretwell, Sir John 124, 139, 185, 202, 301

Galsworthy, Sir Anthony 2, 42, 57, 61, 79, 100, 108

Gandhi, Rajiv (former Prime Minister of India) 153, 315

Garel-Jones, Lord (Tristan) 152, 243, 244–5, 249, 273, 285, 288, 295, 298, 308, 316

Gates, Robert 34, 97, 132, 208

Genscher, Hans-Dietrich 25, 169, 175, 205, 213, 265

Gielgud, Sir John 320

Gilchrist, Sir Andrew 118

Gillmore of Thamesfield, Lord (David) 10, 42, 52, 94, 139, 158, 173, 230, 305, 311, 320

Gladstone, David 313–6, 318

Gladwyn, Lord and Lady 246

Glenarthur, Lord (Simon) 66, 72, 85, 93, 116, 123, 125, 150–51, 156, 159

Goodall, Sir David 12, 22, 35, 51, 124–6, 274

Gorbachev, Mikhail 122, 126, 131, 175, 178, 190, 202, 207, 225, 233, 254, 273, 283, 285, 291, 319

Gordievsky, Oleg and wife 26, 42, 226

Gordon Lennox, Lord (Nicholas) 4, 36, 143, 203

Gore-Booth, Sir David 88, 122, 128, 149, 173, 200, 204, 222, 263, 268, 276, 314, 317, 324, 329

Gore-Booth, Lord (Paul) and Lady (Pat) 10, 329–30

Gorman, Theresa 234

Goronwy-Roberts, Lord 8

Goulden, Sir John 139, 236

Gow, Ian 235, 246, 288

Gozney, Sir Richard 210, 281, 284–5, 307, 315

Grant, Bernie 310

Greenhill of Harrow, Lord (Denis) and Lady (Angela) 105, 107, 123, 125, 150, 287, 318–9, 325

Greening, Sir Paul 117

Gregson, Sir Peter 119, 133, 183, 224, 233, 299

Gummer, John (Lord Deben) 310

Haass, Richard 322

Haines, Jo 141, 241

Hamilton of Epson, Lord (Archie) 117

Hamilton, Duke of 287

Hammond, Philip 102

Hannay of Chiswick, Lord (David)
124, 137, 164, 190, 195, 204, 209, 254,
266–7, 291, 294
Hanson, John 191
Harding, Sir William 21, 308
Hardinge of Penshurst, Lord (George)
22
Harman, Gary 311
Harris, David and wife 116, 235
Hassan II, King 129
Hastings, Sir Max 165
Hattersley, Lord (Roy) 64
Haughey, Charles 97, 106
Havel, Václav (former President of the
Czech Republic) 223, 227
Havers, Lord (Michael) 29, 39, 76, 80
Hawke, Bob 288
Hayes, Sir Brian 13, 36, 130
Healey, Lord (Denis) 6, 64, 244
Heath, Sir Edward 54, 71, 88, 99, 136–7,
213, 259
van Heerden, Neil 98
al-Helaissi, Abdulrahman 27
Henderson, Sir Denys 24
Henderson, Sir Nicholas 150, 160, 174
Hennessy of Nympsfield, Lord (Peter)
297
Heren, Louis 118
Hervey, Sir Roger 45
Heseltine, Lord (Michael) 32, 137, 147,
226, 263–4, 266–7
Heseltine, Sir William 45
Hetherington, Eric 300
Hills, Denis 220
Hindawi trial 30, 276
Hirohito, Emperor 113
Hogg, Sir Christopher 322
Hogg, Douglas (Viscount Hailsham)
262–3, 268, 270, 273–5, 277, 282–3,
291, 307, 316
Hogg of Cumbernauld, Lord (Norman)
322

Holdsworth, Sir Trevor 131
Holland, Sir Geoffrey 230
Holmes, Sir Peter 139
Home, Lord (Alec) 50
Hooper, Baroness (Gloria) 150, 244
Houston, John 49, 71, 79
Howard of Lympne, Lord (Michael) 310
Howe of Aberavon, Lord (Geoffrey)
and Lady (Elspeth) 156, 158, 262, 267
South Africa 2
visa regimes 22
FCO budget 25
Hong Kong 28, 163
valedictory despatches 28
Syria 30
AIDS 34
Spycatcher 39
Falklands 45
FCO accommodation 49
relations with PM 79, 139
Star Chamber 87
Europe 134
Charles Powell 145
hawk trainers 147
women in the service 154
Jewish boycott 210
Pretoria 236
Howell of Guildford, Lord (David) 133,
301
Hoyer Millar, Derek (Lord Inchyra) 43
Hughes, Howard 296
Hungarian Ambassador, Tibor Antal-
péter 250
Hunt, Sir Rex 173
Hurd of Westwell, Lord (Douglas) and
Lady (Judy) (and children) 4, 72,
91, 134, 150, 170, 183–4, 187, 194–5,
196–7, 201, 211, 218–9, 222, 228–9,
231, 246, 254–5, 257, 259, 263, 269,
271, 273, 304
Foreign Secretary 181
Hong Kong and EMU 182, 187

Hussein, King and Queen Noor 16, 27, 82, 90

Hussein, Saddam 221–2, 258, 260, 282, 286, 292, 301

Ingham, Sir Bernard 15, 100, 254

Inchyra, Lord (Derek) 43, 194

Inchyra, Lord (Robin) 194

Israeli Ambassador, Yehuda Avner (1983–88), Yoav Biran (1988–93) 94, 152, 317

Italian Foreign Minister, Gianni De Michelis 232

Jacobovitz, Chief Rabbi 97

Jacomb, Sir Martin 321

James, Sir Kenneth 308

Janner of Braunstone, Lord (Greville) 32, 108, 123, 316

Jay, Peter 250

Jenkin of Roding, Lord (Patrick) 227

Jenkins, Sir Michael 36

Jenkins, Peter 86, 89–90, 100

Jenkins of Hillhead, Lord (Roy) 123

Jenkins, Simon 67, 110, 223, 255

Johnston, Sir Maurice 9

Jonkman, Hans 48

Joseph, Sir Keith 34

Kamil, Dato 181

Kastrup, Dieter 301

Kaufman, Sir Gerald 243

Kaunda, Kenneth 241

Kealy, Robin 221,

Keays, Sara 181

Kerr of Kinlochard, Lord (John) 89, 112, 136–7, 139, 144–5, 164–5, 220, 316

Kershaw, Anthony 61

Khan, Yaqub 181

Khomeini, Ayatollah 127

Kimmitt, Bob 131, 168, 189, 265–6, 281–2, 287–8

King of Bridgwater, Lord (Tom) 9, 35, 51, 68, 75, 106, 114, 151, 154, 200, 239, 251, 257, 260, 277, 294, 306

Kinnock, Lord (Neil) 57, 72, 140, 213, 241, 249, 305, 307, 310

Kiplagat, Bethuel 237

Kirkham, Norman 71

Kissinger, Henry 322

Klestil, Thomas 128

Kohl, Helmut 25, 170, 188, 226, 227, 287, 298

László, Kovács 193

Krenz, Egon 196

Kuriyama, Takakazu 243

Lambert, Sir Richard 227

Lamont of Lerwick, Lord (Norman) 132, 169, 252, 302, 314

Lankester, Sir Tim 95, 136, 149, 187, 228, 292

Landon, Sir Tim 18, 149

Latham, Sir Michael 253, 296

Lawrence, Sir Ivan 123

Lawson, Dominic 239

Lawson of Blaby, Lord (Nigel) and Lady (Therese) 61, 64, 87, 99, 122, 133, 137, 140, 143, 184–5, 328

Leifland, Leif 313

Leigh-Pemberton of Kingsdown, Lord (Robin) 221

Lennox-Boyd, The Hon. Sir Mark 243–5, 266, 290, 295, 299–300, 315, 318

Leslie, Dame Mariot 275

Lever, Sir Paul 90, 139

Lewis, Sir Martyn 264

Lilley, Peter 242

Limerick, Earl (Patrick) 234

Lloyd-Jones, Sir Richard 67

Loehnis, Anthony 29

Logan, Sir David 86, 224

Lončar, Budimir 132

Luce, Lord (Richard) 261, 291, 316
Luce, Sir William 316
Lyall Grant, Sir Mark 163
Lyell, Sir Nicholas 321
Lyne, Sir Roderic 226–7

McDonald, Felix 55, 247
McDonald, Sir Simon and Olivia 5, 10, 55, 116, 163, 232, 247, 249
McFarlane, Robert 33
MacGregor of Pulham Market, Lord (John) 148, 264, 266
Maclean, Lord (Chips) 230
Maclean, Sir Fitzroy 80
McLaren, Sir Robin 49, 51
Mackay of Clashfern, Lord (James) 76, 80
MacRae, Sir Christopher and Lady (Mette) 63, 69, 288
McNally, Lord (Tom) 135
Madden, Martin 330
Mahathir, Mohamad (former Prime Minister of Malaysia) 94, 292
Maitland, Sir Donald 229
Major, Sir John and Lady (Norma) 25, 67, 132, 156, 158, 160–61, 163, 165, 167, 169, 171–2, 174–5, 178, 180–81, 192, 222, 273, 284, 306, 318 et seqq.
Mallaby, Sir Christopher 13, 22, 58, 92, 184, 194, 204
Mandela, Nelson (President of South Africa) 209
Manzie, Sir Gordon 35, 49–50
Margaret, Princess 45
Markov, Georgi 254, 291
Marshall, Michael 165
Martin, David 277, 287, 296
Maud, Sir Humphrey 109
Maude of Horsham, Lord (Francis) 148, 151, 155–8, 163–5, 172–3, 176, 188, 210–11, 218, 220, 242, 248
Maxwell-Hyslop, Sir Robin 307

Mayhew of Twysden, Lord (Patrick) 310
Melhuish, Sir Ramsay 14, 21
Mellor, David 66, 68–9, 72, 74, 80–81, 85, 88, 92, 94, 96–7, 106, 109, 134, 205, 295
Meyer, Sir Christopher 23, 108, 150, 160
Meyer-Landrut, Nikolaus 82
Middleton, Sir George 328
Middleton, Sir Peter 14, 94, 122, 140, 232, 235, 292, 304, 328
Miers, Sir David 54, 60, 91
De Mita, Ciriaco (former Italian Prime Minister) 133
Mitterrand, François (former French President) 90, 153, 163, 170, 175, 267, 283, 285, 288, 327
Mladenov, Petar (former President of Bulgaria) 193
Modrow, Hans 208
arap Moi, Daniel (former President of Kenya) 35, 86, 237
Montgomery of Alamein, Lord (David) 164
Moore of Lower Marsh, Lord (John) 91
Morris, Michael 296, 315
Morrison, Sir Peter 119, 124–6, 133, 137, 268–9
Morse, Sir Jeremy 116
Mottram, Sir Richard 260
Mower, Brian 234, 258
Mubarak, Hosni (former President of Egypt) 16
Mugabe, Robert (former President of Zimbabwe) 21, 57
Munro, Sir Alan 78, 271
Mure, Geoffrey 215
Murphy, Richard 91
Museveni, Yoweri (President of Uganda) 35

Namibian Cabinet Secretary 216

Nanteuil, le Vicomte 37, 48, 267
Napier, Lord 45
Neave, Airey 106, 247
Neil, Andrew 67
Neville-Jones, Baroness Pauline 23, 33
Newton, John 148
Newhouse, John 73
Nicholas, Sir David 49, 160
Nicolson, Harold 6
Nitze, Paul 52–3
Nixon, Patrick 31, 55
Norris, Steve 255
North, Oliver 37
Norwich, John Julius 232

Oldfield, Sir Maurice 58
O'Donnell, Lord Gus 312
O'Rourke, 106
Orr, Sir David 191, 321
Ortega, Daniel (President of Nicara-
    gua) 89
Owen, Lord David 53, 57, 73, 105, 250,
    310
Owen, Geoffrey 100

Pakenham, Sir Michael 53
Palliser, Sir Michael and Marie 5, 62,
    222, 228
Patten, Lord (Chris) passim to 225,
    229, 329
Patten, Lord (John) 65, 76
Pendleton, Ray 79
Pennant-Rea, Rupert 74
Perol, Gilbert 75
Perle, Richard 52–3
Pestell, Catherine 80, 116
Pick, Hella 110
Pickering, Tom 267
Pincher, Chapman 58
Pinter, Harold 223
Plastow, Sir David 251, 303, 305
Poindexter, Admiral John 34, 37

Polanyi, John 322
Pover, Alan 252
Powell of Bayswater, Lord (Charles) 1
    and passim to page 300, 309
Powell, Jonathan 269
Pravda, Alex 47
Premadasa, Ranasinghe (former Presi-
    dent of Sri Lanka) 314–6
Preston, Peter 225
Price, Charlie 91
Prior, Lord (Jim) 238
Pym, Lord (Francis) 268

Qaboos, bin Said al Said (Sultan of
    Oman) 18, 82, 149–50
Quandt, Bill 322
Quayle, Dan (former Vice-President of
    the US) 131, 167
Quinlan, Sir Michael 154, 200, 253,
    259–60, 264–5, 277–8, 285, 325

Rafsanjani, Iranian Speaker 135, 150
Raison, Sir Timothy 15, 199, 229, 291
Ramphal, Sonny 8, 117, 234
Ratford, Sir David 185
Reagan, Ronald (former President of
    the US) 30, 102, 138, 228
Reddaway, Sir Norman 12
Reading, Marquess (Rufus Isaacs) 186,
    277
Reese, Mitch and Mary-Ellen 34
Reeve, Sir Anthony 78, 326
Reid, Sir William 10
Renton of Mount Harry, Lord (Tim)
    16, 30, 41, 49, 66, 228, 321
Renwick of Clifton, Lord (Robin) 33,
    98, 121–4, 141, 326
Rhodes, Sir Peregrine 134
Rhodes James, Robert 61, 69, 107, 226
Richter, Ian 241
von Richthofen, Hermann 23, 205, 213,
    216, 265

Ridgway, Rozanne 132, 322
Ridley of Liddesdale, Lord (Nicholas)
    and Lady (Judy) 49, 96, 110, 117, 170,
    181, 183, 212, 224, 233, 239–40, 242,
    255, 323
Rifkind, Sir Malcolm 66, 217, 225
Robertson of Port Ellen, Lord
    (George) 313
Rowland, Tiny 125
Rowland-Jones, Revd Canon Dr Sarah
    328
Rowlands, Lord (Ted) 37
Runcie, Robert 54
Rushdie, Salman 126, 129, 223, 229
Russell, Sir Mark 87, 154, 158
Rutherford, Malcolm 228
Ryder of Wensum, Lord (Richard) 110,
    262

Sadovsky, Pavel 193
Sainsbury, Sir Tim 158–9, 162, 173, 191,
    201, 206, 228, 242, 244, 329
St John of Fawsley, Lord (Norman St
    John-Stevas) 186
Savimbi, Jonas 86, 207
Scheer, Francois 165, 209, 275, 317
Schmidt, Helmut 24, 227
Schori, Pierre 313
Scott, Sir Kenneth 117
Scott, Sir Nicholas 250
Scowcroft, Brent 132, 240
Seitz, Raymond 5, 24, 97, 135, 281, 327
Selkirk of Douglas, Lord (James
    Douglas-Hamilton)287
Sergeant, John 141
Shamir, Yitzhak (former Prime Minis-
    ter of Israel) 9, 123, 128
Sheldon, Lord (Robert) 235
Shevardnadze, Eduard 11, 197, 225–6,
    275, 279
Shingler, Michael 201, 327–8
Shultz, Foreign Minister 82, 91

Simeon, King 71
Simmons, Tim 10, 279, 302, 325
Simon of Highbury, Lord (David) 266
Singh, Daulat 19
Slater, Duncan 98, 188
Smith, Dick 304
Smith, John 322
Soros, George 122
Squire, Bill 253
Stancioff, Johnny 299
Stanley, Sir John 68, 91, 98, 114
Stark, Freya 245
Sternberg, Sir Sigmund 320
Steven, Stewart 105, 317
Stevens, Peter 235
Stewart of Ardshiel, Appin and Lorn,
    Sir Dugald and Lady (Cibi) 132
Stewart of Fulham, Lord (Michael) 105
Stowe, Sir Kenneth 34, 50, 231, 325
Strachan, Dame Valerie 119
Sudhoff, Jürgen 82, 211–2
Sultan, Prince 138–9
Suzman, Helen 183
Sykes, Sir Richard 33

Tambo, Oliver 1, 79, 325
Tapsell, Sir Peter 155
Tebbit, Lord (Norman) 16, 50, 199, 228,
    271
Teltschik, Horst 194
Temple-Morris, Lord (Peter) 51
Thatcher, Baroness (Margaret) and Sir
    Denis 170, 184–5, 196, 198, 201, 204,
    222, 242, 270, 274, 278, 301, 319
South Africa 1
FCO and ODA accommodation 9,
    16, 24, 30, 48
Falklands and Argentina 10, 164–5
intelligence service 14
Commonwealth 20, 22
Germany 25, 128, 174, 182, 188, 196,
    209, 212, 214, 217

diplomatic service 35, 60, 64, 73, 95, 127, 142, 205, 214
    aid to Africa 35
    Peter Wright 38
    security 42, 58, 111
    SDI 52
    Israel and Palestine 58, 122
    Maurice Oldfield 58
    women in the Cabinet 65
    Syria 68, 139
    Europe (including Bruges and Delors Report) 90, 132–3, 137, 186
    Ireland 97, 119
    Iran 102, 127
    Japan 104, 203
    SNF 133
    Charles Powell 141–2
    France 153
    resignation and promotion 155
Thatcher, The Hon. Sir Mark 313
Thomas, David and Baroness (Sue) Thomas of Walliswood 17
Thomson of Monifieth, Lord (George) 65
Thomson, Sir John 59
Tickell, Sir Crispin 39, 49, 56, 59, 173–4, 205, 254
Tilakaratne, Bernard 314–5
Tlass, Mustafa 240
Tomkys, Sir Roger 139, 246–7, 249
Townsend, Sir Cyril and Lady 69, 108
Trefgarne, Lord (David) 77, 106, 173, 176, 183, 244
Trelford, Donald 125
Trend, Lord (Burke) 10
Turnbull, Lord (Andrew) 141–3, 146, 241, 268, 270, 309

Uno, Sōsuke (former Japanese Prime Minister) 153

Unwin, Sir Brian 77, 223, 321
Unwin, Peter 246
Urwick, Sir Alan 82

Velayati, Ali Akbar (former Iranian Foreign Minister) 63, 125–6
Venkateswaran, Venkat 19
Viot, Jacques 14

Waddington, Lord (David) 206, 261
Wade-Gery, Sir Robert 20
Waite, Terry 46, 54, 240
Wakeham, Lord (John) and Lady (Alison) 72, 80, 299, 329
Walden, Brian 182, 185, 263
Waldegrave of North Hill, Lord (William) and Lady (Caroline) 37 onwards passim to 262
Waldheim, Kurt (former President of Austria) 92
Wałęsa, Lech 195, 306
Walker of Worcester, Lord (Peter) 59, 67, 218
Wall, Sir Stephen and Lady (Catherine) 121, 147, 156, 160, 181, 190, 204, 210, 242, 269, 302, 312
Wallis, Sir Peter 58
Walsh, Arthur 64
Walters, Sir Alan 144, 185
Walters, Sir Dennis and Lady (Bridgett) 210
Walters, General Vernon 90, 124
Watkins, Alan 20
Watt, David 35
Watt, Susan 310
Watts, Sir Arthur 55, 200
Waugh, Auberon 187
Weatherill, Lord (Jack) 234
Weidenfeld, Sir George 28
Weir, Sir Michael 43
von Weizsäcker, Richard 6
Wellington, Duke of 62

Wells, Bowen 305
Westbrook, Roger 130
Weston, Sir John 98, 113, 121, 199,
    301–302
Wetton, Philip 59
Whitehead, Sir John 138
Whitelaw, Viscount (William) 79, 83,
    87
Whitmore, Sir Clive 67, 182, 205, 223,
    311, 321
Whitney, Ray 115, 186
Wicks, Sir Nigel 12, 27, 104, 109, 112
Wihtol, Åke 285
Wilson of Tillyorn, Lord (David) 41,
    76, 153, 211, 244
Wilson of Rievaulx, Lord (Harold) 101,
    104, 203
Wilson, Robert 96, 301
Wilton, Sir John 326
Winchester, Ian 74
Winnick, David 147
Wood, Sir Andrew 217, 292
Wolfson of Sunningdale, Lord (David)
    129
Woolcott, Dick 304
Worsthorne, Sir Peregrine 134
Wright, Sir David 93
Wright, Herbert 33
Wright, Marcus and Rebecca 147, 183,
    324
Wright, Sir Oliver 226, 249
Wright, Virginia 80, 99, 116, 136, 146,
    155, 158, 189, 192, 197, 235, 246, 293,
    307, 320

Yamani, Ahmed Zaki 32, 59
Yazov, Dmitry 155
Yeo, Timothy 239, 277
Youde, Sir Edward 44, 50
Young of Graffham, Lord (David) and
    Lady (Lita) 119, 146, 154
Young, Hugo 100

Young, Baroness (Janet) 5, 21, 28, 54,
    62, 66, 123, 125, 150
Young, Sir Rob 127, 172
Younger, Viscount (George) 10, 60, 71,
    95, 97, 149, 154, 157

Zamyatin, Soviet Ambassador 131,
    273–4
Zayed, Sheikh 154, 172
Zhelev, Zhelyu (former Bulgarian
    President) 291
Zhivkov, Todor (former Bulgarian
    President) 189
Zoellick, Bob 208
Zuckerman, Paul 277
de Zulueta, Sir Philip 2, 142, 147, 249